Psycholinguistics

Psycholinguistics
Central topics

Alan Garnham

METHUEN: London and New York

First published in 1985 by
Methuen & Co. Ltd
11 New Fetter Lane, London EC4P 4EE

Published in the USA by
Methuen & Co.
in association with Methuen, Inc.
29 West 35th Street, New York NY 10001

Printed in Great Britain at
the University Press, Cambridge

British Library Cataloguing in Publication Data
Garnham, Alan
    Psycholinguistics: central topics.
    1. Cognition   2. Psycholinguistics
    I. Title
    153.4   BF311

    ISBN 0–416–36610–4
    ISBN 0–416–36620–1 Pbk

Library of Congress Cataloging in Publication Data
Garnham, Alan, 1954-
    Psycholinguistics: central topics.

    Bibliography: p.
    Includes index.
    1. Psycholinguistics.   I. Title.
P37.G34   1985   401'.9   85–7223
ISBN 0–416–36610–4
ISBN 0–416–36620–1 (pbk.)

cjs
5-20-87

To my mother and father

Contents

Acknowledgements

I would like to thank the copyright owners and authors for permission to use the following figures.

Figure 3.1 from 'A functional model for memory' (p. 205) by J. Morton. In D.A. Norman (ed.), *Models of Human Memory*, 1970, New York: Academic Press. Copyright 1970 by Academic Press, Inc. Adapted by permission.

Figure 3.5 from 'Accessing the mental lexicon' (p. 268 and p. 270) by K.I. Forster. In R.J. Wales and E.C.T. Walker (eds), *New Approaches to Language Mechanisms*, 1976, Amsterdam: North Holland. Copyright 1976 by North Holland Publishing Company. Adapted by permission.

Figure 4.1 from 'An ATN approach to comprehension' (p. 135) by E. Wanner and M.P. Maratsos. In M. Halle, J.W. Bresnan, and G.A. Miller (eds), *Linguistic Theory and Psychological Reality*, 1978, Cambridge, MA.: MIT Press. Copyright 1978 by the Massachusetts Institute of Technology. Adapted by permission.

Figure 7.4 from 'Notes on a schema for stories' (p.217) by D.E. Rumelhart. In D.G. Bobrow and A.M. Collins (eds), *Representation and Understanding: Studies in Cognitive Science*, 1975, New York: Academic Press. Copyright 1975 by Academic Press, Inc. Adapted by permission.

Figure 8.3 from 'Levels of processing and the structure of the language processor' (p.34) by K.I. Forster. In W.E. Cooper and E.C.T. Walker (eds), *Sentence Processing: Psycholinguistic Studies Presented to Merrill Garrett*, 1979, Hillsdale, NJ: Lawrence Erlbaum Associates. Copyright 1979 by Lawrence Erlbaum Associates, Inc. Adapted by permission.

Preface

This book reflects my beliefs about how psycholinguistics, and cognitive psychology in general, should be taught. Since psycholinguistics is a scientific discipline, the book discusses *theories* about the central cognitive aspects of language understanding, rather than presenting a morass of unstructured facts on a series of loosely connected topics. It also attempts to reflect the emergence of *cognitive science*, an interdisciplinary approach to the study of language and other cognitive processes. It describes not only psychological studies, but also ideas from linguistics, artificial intelligence, the philosophy of language and formal logic. There is no pretence that the discussion is exhaustive. The studies I have chosen were included to make particular points. No piece of work has been described simply because it is new, nor have I excluded one on account of its age. Some experiments are summarized briefly, others are discussed in more detail. Where an experiment is examined carefully, the intention is to give a flavour of psycholinguistic argument and its difficulties. In particular, an attempt has been made to indicate the problems of using experimental data to draw conclusions about the truth or falsity of theories. However, I have tried to show that this task is not an impossible one.

Something should be said about the contents of the book. My primary goal has been to describe in detail the major *cognitive* processes that contribute to language understanding in normal adults. This goal explains a number of omissions. First, there is no treatment of perceptual processes – no chapter on speech perception, for example. It hardly needs pointing out that speech perception and psycholinguistics are quite distinct research fields. Second, language development and language pathology are not discussed. Again, these are specialist areas, but they are also areas in which much of the work is descriptive. It must, however, be noted that conclusions about normal language processing are increasingly being drawn from studies of patients with language deficits. Nevertheless, the arguments are difficult to make, I did not feel that such evidence crucially affected any of the conclusions I wanted to draw. Neither did I want to present case histories, intriguing though many of them are. Third, topics covered in some psycholinguistic texts, such as sociolinguistics, and the relation between language and thought, have been omitted both because they are peripheral, and because they do not have well-developed theories.

The book can be used in a number of ways. It covers ample ground for a one-term or one-semester course on psycholinguistics, such as is common in psychology departments. I suspect that such courses will soon be taught under the head of cognitive science as well. It has been based – albeit rather loosely – on a course of this kind. Used in this way the book will provide an introduction to the studies that it discusses. The book could also serve as the text for part of a more broadly based course in psycholinguistics, language and thought, or cognitive psychology. In this case the material in the book itself should prove adequate. I hope that what I have to say will also be of interest to those requiring a survey of psycholinguistics – postgraduate students embarking on independent research in the field, and those whose primary interest is in other branches of psychology.

Many people – mainly friends and ex-colleagues from the Laboratory of Experimental Psychology at Sussex University – have helped in the preparation of this book. I should like most of all to thank Jane Oakhill, first for coaxing the idea of writing it out of the back of my mind and persuading me to consider it seriously, second for reading and commenting on two complete drafts, and third for a series of invaluable discussions about the organization of the material in what is now chapter 7. Special thanks are also due to Phil Johnson-Laird, who provided extensive comments on all the chapters, despite many other demands on his time. The influence of his teaching will also be apparent throughout the book. Other people without whom the book would have been a poorer effort include Anne Cutler, who read chapter 9 and gave much valuable advice on its structure and content, Steve Isard, who helped with the artificial intelligence references, and read the chapters on meaning, Dennis Norris, from whom I learned most of what I know about word recognition, and who commented on chapters 3 and 8, Al Parkin, who pointed out some errors in chapter 3, and John Morton, who was kind enough to check my account of the logogen model. For the most part I have followed the advice I was given, and the book is much improved for it. The figures were prepared by Graham Luke and photographed by Yvonne Robinson in the Psychology Department at Reading University.

Finally, thanks to Mary Ann Kernan of Methuen for her commitment to the book from the beginning, and for making the administrative work invisible.

Reading, November 1984

1

Introduction – how to study language understanding

Overview

Psycholinguistics is the study of the mental mechanisms that make it possible for people to use language. It is a scientific discipline whose goal is a coherent theory of the way in which language is produced and understood. This book describes the most important discoveries that have been made in the attempt to construct such a theory. The present chapter begins by explaining certain biases in psycholinguistic research – why, for example, the emphasis is on language understanding rather than language production. It then outlines the overall goal of psycholinguistics – the identification of what information is conveyed by language, and how. This goal is broken down into a number of subgoals, and the subprocessors that contribute to the interpretation of discourse and text are described. The genesis and evaluation of psycholinguistic theories are then considered with reference to some ideas from the philosophy of science, and the use of statistical methods for analysing psycholinguistic data is briefly discussed. Some problems with the experimental approach to psycholinguistic problems are outlined, and the computer modelling approach of artificial intelligence (AI) is introduced as a possible alternative. Its strengths and weaknesses are discussed, and a synthesis of the two approaches – *cognitive science* - is suggested.

In the remaining chapters of the book theoretical and empirical issues in psycholinguistics are discussed in detail. The major subprocessors of the language understanding system are introduced starting with low-level processors, and moving on to higher-level ones. When all the processors have been described, the relation between them is considered, as is the relation between understanding and producing language. Theoretical material from related disciplines is discussed as and when it is appropriate.

The topics covered in the individual chapters are as follows. Chapter 2 is about linguistic theory and its relevance to psycholinguistics. The first half of the chapter shows that a simple description of how language is used is simple-minded, and considers the question of how a description of language might contribute to an account of how language is understood and produced. The second half gives an overview of the branch of linguistics that has had most influence on psycholinguistic research – syntax. Chapters 3 and 4 describe two subprocessors of the language understanding system – the word recognizer and the parser. Chapter 5 provides a general introduction to the concept of meaning, in its broadest sense, drawing on work from a number of disciplines – most importantly philosophy – which have contributed to theories of language processing. Chapter 6 discusses the mental representation of word meanings, and chapter 7 describes the way the language understanding system determines the meaning of discourses and texts. Chapter 8 addresses the question of how the subprocessors of the language understanding system operate together, and chapter 9 discusses language production and its relation to language understanding. The final chapter provides an overview of the book, and considers the likely directions that future research will take.

Biases in psycholinguistic research

The contents of this book reflect certain biases in psycholinguistic research. For purely practical reasons attention has focused on understanding language *understanding* rather than language production. It is easier to study understanding in a systematic way, since the experimenter can select words and sentences with great care. In production the investigator is constrained by what people happen to say, although the situation in which they say it can be controlled. For this reason comprehension has been studied more thoroughly than production. However, it is reasonable to assume that much of our linguistic knowledge is shared by the mechanisms responsible for generation and analysis, and that the study of comprehension sheds light on production. Nevertheless, production needs to be studied in its own right, for two reasons. First, there are a number of questions about production that are independent of questions about comprehension. These questions are briefly considered in chapter 8. Second, it is possible that some mechanisms are not shared between production and comprehension. For example, people might have different lexicons for speaking and listening – we tend to have many more words in our sight vocabularies than in our speaking vocabularies. However, stronger evidence would be required before this unparsimonious view was adopted.

Another bias that recurs throughout the book, though a less marked one, is toward the study of written, as opposed to spoken, language. Again the reasons are largely practical – the problems, both experimental and theoretical, are, or at least can be made, more tractable in the case of written language, so more research has been carried out. This bias is stronger in some areas than others, perhaps being most apparent in the study of word recognition.

Psycholinguistic theory

The primary purpose of language is communication, and hence a psycholinguistic theory must give an account of what information language conveys. Although there may be no single answer to the question of what language expresses, in the most important cases communication is about, in a rather general sense, how the world is, was, will be or might be. Newspapers report recent events. History books describe how things used to be. Textbooks survey current knowledge in the sciences and humanities. This information has been successfully communicated if the reader correctly updates his or her mental representation of the world. However, not all uses of language are about the real world, and not all conversations and texts are descriptive.

Works of fiction describe fictional worlds rather than the real world. Representations of such worlds can be created by analogy with those of the real world. They contain people, things and events, and locations at which events can occur. A mental representation of a fictional world is similar in form to one of the real world. The difference lies in whether the representation corresponds to how things really are.

In the case of spoken language in particular, description is only one use of language among many. Much communication is in the form of commands, questions, requests, promises and so on. In an extended sense these uses of language are also 'about' the world, since in order to understand them it is necessary to have an internal representation of the world, and of how it would be if, for example, the command was obeyed, or the request complied with. In each of these cases, therefore, understanding language requires the construction of, or reference to, internal mental representations of how things are or might be. It also requires that the point of the utterance should be recognized, and an appropriate response formulated. Examples of appropriate responses are that a description should be added to an internal representation of the world, and that a question to which the answer is either 'yes' or 'no' should initiate a search through such a representation to see if the fact that is questioned is true. There are only a very few uses of language – some exclamations, for example – that do not require for their comprehension an internal representation of the real world or a fictional world.

These considerations indicate the outline of a theory of language understanding. The language understanding system extracts the content of incoming sentences, and constructs a representation of the situation to which they refer. It further determines the point of what is being said so that the intended message can be computed, and an appropriate response formulated. The content extracted from a sentence or a set of sentences will be referred to as the *mental model* of the situation that the sentences are about. This term will be used rather than *semantic representation,* which was favoured in earlier writings on psycholinguistics and AI. There are two main reasons for rejecting the earlier term. First, to say that something is a semantic representation suggests that it is closely related to a linguistic structure, but a mental model is structurally similar to a part of the world, rather than to any linguistic representation. Second, in line with recent practice in linguistics, the term *semantics* will be used in this book in a restricted sense to be explained in chapter 5. A mental model contains much more than semantic information in this restricted sense.

Subprocessors of the language understanding system

As in any scientific discipline, it is useful to divide the overall problem that psycholinguists are trying to solve into a number of subproblems. From the point of view of language *understanding*, psycholinguists would like to know: first, how words are recognized, second, how the structure of a sentence is determined, third, how its meaning is computed, fourth, how its meaning is integrated with what has gone before, and fifth, how the intended message is worked out. When tackling these subproblems it is, of course, important that the overall goal of psycholinguistics should be kept in mind.

Low-level perceptual processing

This book is concerned only with cognitive processes, and not the 'low-level' auditory and visual analysis that precedes them. Nevertheless, all language understanding starts with perception, and it will be assumed that the results of perceptual processing are made available to the language understanding system. In the case of written language, low-level processes identify lines and curves, and perhaps the shapes of words. With spoken language there is an additional complication since it has been suggested (for example, Liberman, 1970) that there is a special linguistic mode of perception.

Word recognition

The understanding system receives an input of lines, curves and spaces, or an acoustic waveform, and it must use this input to make contact with a store of information about words – the mental equivalent of a dictionary – in order to decide what words have been presented. The processing of auditory inputs is especially difficult. They almost always occur against a background of noise, which must not be confused with the speech; there are no simple cues to segmentation in the waveform (that is to deciding which parts of the waveform belong to the same word, and which to different words), and no simple cues about how fast words are arriving. Analysing untidy cursive script is almost as difficult, but recognizing typewritten or printed words is comparatively easy. The cues to segmentation – spaces and new lines without hyphenation – are relatively simple to detect, and every occurrence of the same word in a single fount is effectively identical. The question of how we are able to cope with many different founts is another, more difficult, one.

For a number of years word recognition was studied primarily by cognitive psychologists whose main concern was not with language understanding. However, identifying words is an essential stage in comprehension, and psycholinguists (e.g. Forster, 1979; Marslen-Wilson and Tyler, 1980) are becoming increasingly interested in both word recognition itself, and its relation to other parts of the language understanding system.

Parsing

The words in a sentence are not simply strung together, they form natural groups – phrases and clauses. Working out the appropriate grouping is essential for understanding a sentence. For example, in the sentence:

The little old man walked in the park.

the words *the little old man* must be grouped together, because they refer to a single thing – in this case a person. Other similar phrases have slightly different interpretations. For example, *the little old men* refers to a group of people. The words *in the park* form a group describing a location, and, at a higher level, *walked in the park* describes an action. Other potential groupings of words, for example *man walked in,* do not form coherent units. The correct interpretation of the sentence therefore depends on the words being grouped together appropriately. This job is performed by the parser. A parser has access to information about how words can be grouped in a particular language, say, English, and it makes use of this knowledge to determine the structure of particular sentences that it encounters. The information that a parser has access to is usually formulated as a set of rules of the kind that will be described in chapter 2.

Semantic interpretation

Although grouping does not itself amount to interpretation, words are grouped together so that sentences can be correctly interpreted. The meaning of a sentence is determined by a further set of rules specifying the kinds of things that particular groups of words refer to, and what relations hold among those things. The language understanding system uses two kinds of information in interpreting sentences. First, it uses information about the meanings of particular words – the kind of information that is to be found in a dictionary, though this information may be organized very differently in the mind of a language user from the way that it is set out in, say, the *Oxford English Dictionary*. The other kind of information tells it how word meanings are combined to produce the meanings of phrases and eventually those of sentences. In fact it is wrong to stop at sentence meaning. Units larger than sentences – discourses and texts – have meaning that goes beyond that of their component sentences.

Model construction

In this book the term *semantic interpretation* is used in a narrow sense. The semantic interpretation of a sentence, for example, specifies the range of situations that that sentence could describe, but does not determine which one it actually describes in a particular use. Neither does it specify which of those situations are more likely than others. For example the sentence:

The man met the woman.

could be used to describe the meeting of any woman and any man. However, on a particular occasion when the sentence is used it will be about one particular meeting, and the sentence has not been fully understood until that meeting has been identified. Some such meetings are much more likely than others, primarily because of where people live and how mobile they are. This fact is irrelevant to semantic interpretation, though it may well affect how readily the sentence is understood in a particular context. From the semantic interpretation of its input, the understanding system must work out what particular situation, in the real or an imaginary world, a particular discourse or text is, or is most probably, about. That is to say it must construct some internal representation of that situation – a *mental model* of it.

Pragmatic interpretation

Finally the understanding system must decide what to do with the model it has constructed. An utterance might be, for example, a description that should be added to an overall model of the world, a question about how things are in the world, or a request to change them. Psycholinguists aim only to describe how the point of an utterance, and hence the *intended* response to it, is determined, and not whether a command, say, is actually obeyed. Pragmatic interpretation is made more complicated by the fact that what people mean – the message that they are trying to convey – is often different from what they actually say. To take an extreme case, they may say the opposite of what they mean to create an ironical effect. The language understanding system copes easily with these complications, but constructing an adequate theory of how it does so is difficult.

The major components of the language understanding system have now been mentioned. In the later chapters of this book each of these processors, and the facts that are known about how they work, will be discussed in more detail. However, a theory of language understanding must do more than simply describe each component of the system. It must also describe how the components act together to produce understanding. Although the subprocessors were listed in an order from, roughly speaking, early low-level processors to late high-level processors, there is no implication that they operate serially, with the output of one simply being passed on as input to the next. There may be feedback from 'later' processors to 'earlier' ones, and some of them may work in parallel. The question of the overall structure of the language processing system will be discussed in chapter 8.

Where do psycholinguistic theories come from?

Now that the scope of psycholinguistic theories has been indicated, the question arises as to where such theories come from. How is a theory of language understanding developed? The answer to this question is that, in a quite straightforward sense, theories can come from anywhere – their origins do not affect their status as scientific theories. This insight is usually attributed to the philosopher Karl Popper (1959). Before Popper, the predominant view among philosophers of science was that scientific laws are generalizations from known facts, produced by a procedure called *induction*. However, although scientists sometimes achieve theoretical insights by surveying data, they may equally well get them while soaking in the bath. Theories are thought up in many ways. There is no mechanical way of generating them from data. If there were, science would be straightforward, but boring.

Many psycholinguists are still influenced by the inductivist ideas that guided early work in psychology. They collect large amounts of data in the hope that the data will suggest theories. This approach has not been particularly successful. Another of Popper's insights explains why. Popper argued that, in scientific investigations, the role of data is in testing theories, and in testing them in a particular way – attempting to *falsify* them. According to Popper, scientific enquiry should proceed as follows. A prediction should be derived from a theory, and an experiment performed in an attempt to show that the prediction, and hence the theory, is wrong. The point of Popper's account is to contrast falsification with *confirmation*. It is impossible to prove a theory true by amassing confirmatory evidence. Further evidence may always show that the theory is false. The same is true of any generalization. For example, the claim that all swans are white cannot be proved by observing a large number of white swans (confirmatory instances of the generalization). A black swan might (and indeed did) turn up later and show the generalization to be false. A single piece of falsifying evidence disproves the generalization for good. Furthermore, any piece of evidence will be consistent with, and hence will partially confirm, many theories. The situation remains the same no matter how much evidence is collected. It is always consistent with many different theories. Falsifying evidence is quite different. One piece of falsifying evidence shows a theory to be wrong. Only by trying to *falsify* theories can definitive results be obtained.

Things are not quite as simple as Popper claims. In practice, one piece of falsifying evidence will not condemn a theory, for a number of reasons. The evidence may not be completely reliable. It may suggest a minor modification to the theory. Most importantly, as Kuhn (1962) and others have pointed out, there may be no other theory to replace it, and science cannot operate in a theoretical vacuum.

Although Popper's ideas about scientific practice are not exactly right, they provide a number of lessons for psycholinguists. First, any scientific theory must be testable, in the sense that there must be experiments whose results, if they came out a certain way, would show the theory to be wrong.

Second, once there are plausible theories, the primary use of experimental data is to test between rival theories. Those that make different predictions can be distinguished experimentally, at least in principle. Theories that do not are versions of the same theory in different guises. Third, the mere accumulation of data is largely a waste of time. Data are useful only in so far as they can distinguish between theories.

Popper's view of scientific enquiry is often described by saying that science proceeds by the hypothetico-deductive method. Scientists formulate hypotheses, it does not matter how, and then they make deductions from those hypotheses. Those deductions are then tested in experiments.

The use of statistics

The data from almost all psycholinguistic experiments are analysed using statistical methods. The reason is that it is virtually impossible to isolate the effect of an experimental manipulation from all of the other factors that influence language understanding. For example, how closely subjects attend to the experimental task varies from moment to moment, affecting how well they perform on different trials. Statistical tests allow the results of experimental manipulations to be picked out from this background of 'noise'. The smaller the effect and the more noisy the data the more difficult the effect is to detect. Once a prediction has been made about a particular experimental manipulation, or a combination of such manipulations, an experiment can be designed to see if the manipulation has the predicted effect or some other effect. A third possibility is that no effect of the manipulation will be detected in the experiment. The testing of such predictions again gives rise to an asymmetry. If an effect is *not* detected against a background of noise, then it may simply be that the experiment is not sensitive enough to pick it out. However, if an effect is found, then, with a certain degree of probability, it can be concluded that the effect is genuine.

Statistical tests also allow the results of experiments to be generalized. Traditionally, psychologists have generalized to *subjects* similar to those used in the experiment. However, the reader of the psycholinguistic literature will find an increasing use of *by-materials* (or F2) and *minF'* (min F prime) analyses (see Clark, 1973), which permit generalization to materials (words or texts) like those actually presented.

The ideas from this section and the last, when taken together, specify the conditions under which progress can be made in psycholinguistic research. The ideal experiment is one that finds strong evidence for the effect of an experimental manipulation. This effect should falsify the prediction of a theory, or better, falsify the prediction of one theory while upholding that of its principal rival. Thus one theory can be discounted, leaving another that, if not fully confirmed, is at least not falsified.

Problems with the experimental method

Although this book is written primarily from the psychological point of view, it does not endorse all aspects of psychological practice. A number of problems with the way psychologists work have been pointed out by practitioners of a different approach to the study of language understanding, that of AI. The most serious hindrance to progress in psycholinguistics is that its theories are often imprecisely formulated. Imprecise theories are difficult to test, not because it is hard to generate predictions from them, but because it is too easy. Rigorous deductions from such theories are almost impossible, but it is easy to persuade oneself that a certain prediction does follow from the theory. The problem is that if the prediction is falsified it is also easy to persuade oneself that it did not follow from the theory after all.

Another problem in relating theory and data arises because language understanding cannot be studied in a 'pure' form, but is always affected by factors such as motivation and attention. Experimental data, therefore, reflect not only the operation of the language processor, but also that of other psychological systems. To the extent that these extraneous effects cannot be eliminated, any predictions that are made depend on the availability of at least partial theories of how these other systems work. Similarly, within the language understanding system itself it is difficult to isolate and study a single subprocessor. To explain how subjects behave it may be necessary to have a theory of the entire understanding system.

These problems are not quite as serious as they at first seem. It is not necessary to know about the *internal* workings of cognitive processors that are not under direct study. All that is required is a specification of the relation between their input and their output. Nevertheless, an incomplete knowledge of this relation will still impose constraints on the conclusions that can be drawn from experimental data. A very clear example of the problem of isolating subprocessors of the language understanding system will be described in chapter 4 in the discussion of the Derivational Theory of Complexity.

Even if the operation of a subprocessor can be isolated, the interpretation of experimental results is still not straightforward. Problems arise because each subprocessor uses both a store of information and a set of procedures for manipulating that information. In any experimental task both the stored information and the procedures must be employed, and the contribution of each to the pattern of results may be difficult to disentangle. This problem could be avoided if there was independent evidence about either the set of rules that a processor used, or the way it used them. The effects of one would be known and hypotheses about the other could be tested.

One hope for psycholinguistics is that linguists' descriptions of language correspond to the information that is stored in the mind of a language user. Most linguists have followed Noam Chomsky (e.g. 1965) in making this assumption that grammars are mentally represented, though there have been some dissenting voices (e.g. Katz, 1981). An alternative to Chomsky's view is Stanley Peters' 'ecumenical' principle (discussed by Johnson-Laird, 1983, 167). Peters avoids a strong claim about the form in which linguistic knowledge is represented in the mind. Instead he holds only that the output of linguistic rules specifies what the language understanding system has to *compute*. A psycholinguistic theory must describe how the information is actually computed. Peters' view, though more probably correct than Chomsky's, provides a weaker constraint on psycholinguistic theory, since, if it is true, theories of particular linguistic subprocessors will still have two things to specify – how information is stored and how it is put to use.

It may seem from what has been said so far that the experimental method is so problematic that it is of no use in psycholinguistics. This view is very far from the truth. If it is used properly, and its results interpreted with care, it is a very useful tool. In the past twenty-five years, since the birth of modern psycholinguistics, progress has been rapid, despite the difficulties. However, progress has also been made by those favouring and employing the radically different approach of AI.

Artificial intelligence and computer modelling

It is sometimes argued (e.g. Sloman, 1978, 18) that psychological *experiments* are superfluous at the present time, because so many everyday observations remain unexplained. In the field of language understanding, for example, it is apparent that people understand text, yet there is no adequate theory of how they do so. More specifically no experiments are needed to show that people can readily determine when two expressions (for example, *the man* and *he)* refer to the same person or object, or that they can recognize when an action of a character in a story is an attempt to achieve a certain goal, yet it is not possible at present to say how such judgements are made. Given the assumption that these abilities are amenable to scientific study, it should be possible to model them in detail. However, psychologists, at least according to their detractors, have never attempted to provide such an account of how understanding is achieved. Many practitioners of AI (e.g. Sloman, 1978) have argued that before any experiments are performed to test between psychological theories of language processing, it is necessary to formulate a sufficiently detailed theory. They point out that if a computer were programmed to simulate language understanding, then, because of the nature of computers, every step in the comprehension process would have to be explicitly specified. Therefore a computer program for understanding language would automatically embody a theory of how comprehension *could* be achieved. It may not comprehend in the way that people do, but it would demonstrate the form that an adequate theory might take. It is sometimes further argued that because comprehension is such a complex process, it can be achieved in only a limited number of ways, which must all be similar to one another. Hence writing a computer program to understand language would be a major step towards a theory of how people comprehend.

Another argument for writing programs is that a program that simulated language understanding would have to include models of all the subcomponents of the processing system, and incorporate some idea of how they act together. The problem of what happens when the bits are combined cannot be ignored.

The main advantage of computer programs over most psychological theories is that a program must be, in some sense, formally precise. High-level programming languages, many of them specially developed for AI, provide building blocks for well-specified theories. Indeed many psycholinguists have recognized the usefulness of AI formalisms and incorporated them into their own theories. Linguistic formalisms are useful for a similar reason. Unfortunately the formal apparatus of programming languages does not, of itself, guarantee an insightful, or even a testable, theory of language understanding. Furthermore, some AI research goals have worked against the production of psychologically interesting theories.

Some of these goals stem from the fact that AI is in many ways more similar to engineering than pure science. The aim of an AI research project is often to produce an 'intelligent' machine with a practical application. Such a project is successful if it results in the writing of a program that produces realistic outputs. Even when no applications are likely, this measure of success is often used in AI. However, a working program is of psychological interest only if it is based on general explanatory principles about the way the mind works. It is difficult to deduce such principles from programs themselves, whose creators have often omitted to formulate them. The problem is made worse by the fact that, in order to make programs work it is usually necessary to include sections, called *patches,* to perform parts of the task that the programmer is either not interested in, or has no theory about. Such *ad hoc* simulation does not provide any kind of explanation, and obscures the way in which underlying principles contribute to the program's output. Furthermore, as Weizenbaum's (1966) ELIZA program, which simulates a Rogerian (non-directive) psychotherapist, demonstrates, realistic outputs do not indicate that any theoretically useful analysis of language understanding has been made.

AI's potential contribution to psycholinguistics is a set of theoretically interesting principles that govern the operation of the language understanding system. The usefulness of programming comes not from the fact that its end result is a program that can 'talk', but from the fact that, when programmers try to produce a principled model of a linguistic subprocessor, and not a patch to make a program work, they are forced to think carefully about the sequence of operations that the subprocessor performs to produce its output, which might be, for example, a (partial) parse tree. This approach is very different from that of the experimental psychologist, who simply looks for an effect of the manipulation of variables.

Programs and theories

Occasionally an AI worker (e.g. Schank, 1973) has claimed that a computer program is itself a scientific theory of, say, the way in which people understand language. A more plausible view (e.g. Isard, 1974a; Johnson-Laird, 1982b) is that a program is a model of a theory. Unfortunately, it is comparatively rare to find the theory set out in a standard scientific way with its principal tenets stated in a concise form. The result is that the theory embodied in a program is often difficult to grasp, and hence of limited use in explaining psychological facts. However, sometimes the theoretical claims are clear. For example, the theory might make a claim about the format in which linguistic rules are stored, and the program may contain many instances of rules stored in that way. Or the theory might state that a procedure of a certain kind is used to compute, say, surface syntactic structure from the rules of the grammar and the input sentence, and that procedure will be written into the program in a certain way. Pure, as opposed to applied, AI research should provide a set of principles that govern the operation of the language operating system. Working programs are useful for showing that such principles work in practice, but it is important that the principles themselves should be formulated as clearly and precisely as the program (cf. VanLehn, Brown and Greeno, 1984).

Empirical tests of programs

As has already been mentioned, most AI researchers test their programs by ensuring that they produce realistic outputs. The programs are then evaluated in terms of the range of inputs they can process, and how satisfactory their responses are. However, it is not necessary to model the whole of the language understanding system in order to test psycholinguistic theories. The main argument put forward for producing such global models was that, since the various parts of the understanding system interact with one another in comprehension, it might be misleading to study any one component in isolation. The evidence for interaction is not now as strong as it was when this argument was originally put forward in the early 1970s, but even if it were, the argument would still be fallacious. If the operation of one processor is affected by the output of another, only the *output* of that second processor need be known in order to test a model of the first. It is not necessary to know how the second processor works. Thus, even if the language processor is interactive, a more standard scientific approach can be adopted. The problem of understanding language processing can be split up into subproblems, and models of individual subprocessors can be tested, provided that two conditions are met. First, there must be a specification of the input that the processor receives, and the output that it produces. For example, the word recognition system receives as input perceptual information, and perhaps the output of other subprocessors. Its output is the identity of the word currently being examined. Second, relevant outputs of other processors must be known. These outputs may be identified either from common sense, or by appeal to linguistic theory. The problem of identifying what subprocessors the language understanding system contains is a difficult, but separate, issue.

Cognitive science – a synthesis

Neither experimental psychology nor AI provides a wholly satisfactory approach to the study of language understanding. In recent years many members of the two research communities have become aware of the advantages that the other has to offer. A new synthesis of the two approaches – cognitive science – is beginning to emerge, combining the best points of the two. Cognitive science includes not only cognitive psychology and

AI, but also linguistics and philosophy, from which psychology and AI have both borrowed formalisms and rules. Cognitive science recognizes the importance of formalisms and the importance of giving a detailed account of language understanding, but it eschews the idea of programming for programming's sake. It draws clear distinctions between pure and applied science, and between formulating underlying principles and solving practical problems using existing resources.

Throughout this book research in both artificial intelligence and cognitive psychology will be discussed, with a bias towards the latter. At the present time the way forward in psycholinguistics appears to be the way of cognitive science.

Summary

Psycholinguistics aims to understand the mechanisms of language use. For practical reasons there has been a strong bias towards studying comprehension rather than production, and, in some areas, a bias towards written rather than spoken language.

Language is about the world – or sometimes about a fictitious world – and the primary tasks of the understanding system are to work out first the situation that a particular linguistic input is about, and second, the point of that input – description, question, command, promise or whatever. Thus the understanding system must construct a representation of a part of the world corresponding to the current discourse or text – a mental model, and work out what it must do with that model. Several subprocesses contribute to this operation – word recognition, parsing, semantic interpretation, model construction and pragmatic interpretation. A theory of language understanding should provide models of the subprocessors responsible for carrying out these tasks, and an account of the way in which they act together to effect understanding.

There are two main approaches to the study of language understanding – that of experimental psychology and that of AI. Both approaches have their strengths and defects, and a combination of the strengths of the two is found in cognitive science. AI provides the formalism for constructing well-specified theories, and the idea that every detail of the process of language understanding should ultimately be spelled out. Psychology suggests that manageable problems should be tackled in a standard scientific way.

2

The contribution of linguistics

A detailed account of the way people use language – a psycholinguistic theory – presupposes a description of what they are using – that is to say an account of language in general, and of particular languages, such as English. The discipline in which language, as opposed to its use, is studied is linguistics, and psycholinguists have frequently borrowed ideas from linguistic theory in constructing their theories of comprehension. It is for this reason that a book on psycholinguistics has a chapter primarily devoted to the work of linguists. The linguistic theories that have had the greatest influence in psychology regard syntax, or the structure of sentences, as the most important aspect of language, and place less emphasis on semantics, or meaning. This chapter is, therefore, primarily about syntax. Questions about meaning will be discussed in chapter 5, before empirical work on comprehension.

The nature of linguistics is a matter of debate, even among its own practitioners – they do not agree about such fundamental matters as whether linguistics is a science. However, since about 1960 one school of linguistic thought, that of (transformational) generative grammar, has predominated, particularly in the United States, and has had the greatest impact on psycholinguistic research. This chapter will therefore consider only generative grammar and its offshoots.

The founding father of generative grammar, and still arguably the most important figure in linguistics, is Noam Chomsky. To psycholinguists Chomsky is important not only for his linguistic ideas, but also for his critique of earlier research in the psychology of language, and for his ideas about the relation between linguistics and psychology. Chomsky's views on these last two topics will be considered first, since they were directly responsible for the birth of modern psycholinguistics.

A simple model of language use

Chomsky pointed out that virtually all work in the psychology of language in the 1950s and before, implicitly accepted a particular view of language. The assumptions underlying that view seemed so natural that they were never questioned. First, there was a set of very general assumptions about the brain and the mind. The brain is of a finite size. It has a finite number of neurons, and there are limits on both the maximum rate at which neurons can fire and on the difference between rates of firing that is functionally effective. The brain can therefore be in only a finite number of functionally distinct states (that is states that can give rise to different behaviours). The mind is assumed to be dependent on the brain. Hence, there are only a finite number of different states of mind – a very large number, but a finite one.

Second, a number of assumptions about language and the way it is processed were made. Sentences consist of units strung together. These units are most conveniently thought of as words, but they could be phonemes (the smallest units of sound that can make a difference to meaning) or morphemes (the smallest meaning bearing units of language, that is word stems, prefixes and suffixes). The units are both produced and perceived sequentially. Hearing (saying) a word changes the hearer's (speaker's) state of mind from state s_i to s_j (where s_i and s_j are two of the finitely many states of mind, possibly the same one). Each word does not necessarily cause the same change every time it occurs, because it might be said or heard in different states of mind. The change depends directly only on s_i (and the word), and not on previous states, but the fact that the system is in the state s_i and not s_j when it hears a particular word is determined by the previous words that it has heard. Thus there appeared to be no problem in accounting for the way in which words make different contributions to sentence meanings in different contexts.

A refutation of the model

Could this account of language use, based on such readily acceptable generalities, be false? Chomsky showed that the answer to this question is 'yes'. He demonstrated that the account was wrong by formalizing it and applying mathematical techniques to deduce unacceptable conclusions from it. The full details of Chomsky's arguments cannot be reproduced here. The interested reader is referred to the original sources (for example, Chomsky, 1956). However, a brief sketch of the procedure that Chomsky employed can be given.

Chomsky began with an assumption about how to define a language. He proposed that its vocabulary should be listed, and then a statement made about which strings of vocabulary items are sentences of the language. Since languages such as English have indefinitely many grammatical sentences, any finite specification of which strings of English words are English sentences must be in the form of a set of rules. Chomsky called this set of rules a grammar, and he showed that corresponding to each grammar there is a machine that will generate, in an abstract sense, just those strings that are sentences of the language.

Given the account of language just set out, the following would be needed to construct such a machine:

(1) A vocabulary comprising a finite number of words.
(2) A finite number of states (of mind), including (a) some *initial states,* corresponding roughly to the state of mind 'I am about to say a sentence', and (b) some *completion states,* corresponding to 'I have just finished a sentence'.
(3) Rules that describe what happens when the machine is in a certain state and produces a given word. Each rule comprises two states and a vocabulary item. It is interpreted as follows: if the machine is in the first state, and it produces the word, then it will then be in the second state.

Figure 2.1 shows, in a standard format, a simple machine of this sort – technically known as a *finite state automaton*-capable of generating a few English sentences. The word written above an arc is output as the arc is traversed. So to generate the sentence *The boys eat cheese* the machine will successively be in states s_0, s_1, s_3, s_4, s_5. The complete set of sentences generated by this automaton is given in Table 2.1. To produce all (and only) the sentences

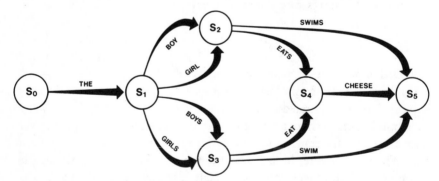

Figure 2.1 A finite-state automaton for generating English sentences

Table 2.1 The sentences generated by the finite-state automaton in Figure 2.1

The boy swims.
The girl swims.
The boy eats cheese.
The girl eats cheese.
The boys swim.
The girls swim.
The boys eat cheese.
The girls eat cheese.

of English a much more complicated machine would be needed, but there seems no difficulty in principle in constructing one.

However, Chomsky demonstrated that such a machine has important limitations. These limitations do not prevent such machines from producing certain sentences. The problem is rather that they cannot produce just the strings of words that are English sentences *and no others.*

Following Chomsky, an abstract argument will be given to demonstrate what these machines cannot do. Consider a very simple language with two vocabulary items α and β, and one rule for forming sentences: the strings of the language are just those that are 'mirror images' about their midpoint, for example, $\alpha\alpha$, $\alpha\alpha\alpha\alpha$, $\beta\beta$, $\alpha\alpha\beta\beta\alpha\alpha$, $\alpha\beta\alpha\alpha\alpha\alpha\beta\alpha$. It is a simple matter to show that no finite-state automaton can produce all and only the mirror image strings formed from αs and βs. The first step in the argument is to define the notion of *completion equivalence.* Look back to Figure 2.1, and consider the state s_2. There are two routes from s_0, the initial state, to s_2. That is to say there are two ways of beginning a sentence that can cause the machine to be in state s_2. They are: *the boy* and *the girl.* Any way of completing a sentence beginning *the boy* must also be a way of finishing a sentence beginning *the girl.* These two beginnings are, therefore, said to be *completion equivalent.* In this example there are two possible completions for these two beginnings, that is two sequences of words that takes the machine from s_2 to s_5, *swims* and *eats cheese.*

The remaining part of the argument builds on the notion of completion equivalence. Since finite-state automata have only a finite number of states, there can be only a finite number of sets of completion-equivalent beginnings of sentences in a language that such an automaton can produce, at most one corresponding to each state. However, in the mirror image language there are infinitely many completion equivalent sets. Consider the strings $\alpha\beta$, $\alpha\alpha\beta$, $\alpha\alpha\alpha\beta$, and so on. $\beta\alpha$ is a possible completion for the first of these, but for none of the others, $\beta\alpha\alpha$ for the second only, $\beta\alpha\alpha\alpha$ for the third only, and so on. There is no limit to the length of a sentence in the language, so there are infinitely many completion equivalent sets. Hence no finite state automaton can generate all *and only* the mirror image strings. It is a trivial matter to produce *all* of these strings. For example, a finite-state automaton with two states can generate all possible combinations of α and β, and it will produce the mirror image strings among the rest. The problem is in restricting the automaton to produce all *and only* those strings.

   What is the relevance of this abstract discussion to ordinary languages? Consider first a widely used language – that of arithmetic – which is in an important respect similar to the mirror image language, and which poses similar problems for generation by a finite-state automaton. In arithmetic expressions such as $(((4+5)/(3 \times 2))+10)$, every opening parenthesis '(' must be matched by a following closing parenthesis ')'. Only sequences of symbols that conform to this rule make sense. Although this property of arithmetical expressions is not identical to the mirror image property, it can be shown mathematically to have the same consequences. It follows that the set of sensible arithmetic expressions cannot be generated by a finite-state automaton.

   Chomsky argued that a number of English constructions have the same property as arithmetic expressions. For example, in sentences such as:

   She is more afraid than you are.

the *more* must be followed by a *than*. Such sentences can have sentential complements between the *more* and the *than:*

   She is more afraid that cats bark than you are.

and these sentences can in turn contain a *more. . .than* (or a *less...than,* or an *as. . .as*) construction:

   She is as certain that Bill is more dismayed that cats bark than you are as Fred is.

Although such sentences are comparatively difficult to understand, Chomsky argued that they should be classified as grammatical, and that the difficulty in understanding them should be explained in terms of limitations on psychological processing mechanisms. Several such attempts to explain this difficulty, which appeal, for example, to the limited capacity of short-term memory, will be discussed in chapter 4.

   Not everyone is immediately convinced by Chomsky's rejection of finite-state automata as models of sentence generation. However, such models have another serious failing, which was also pointed out by Chomsky, and which will be discussed shortly. They cannot account for the way words are grouped together in sentences.

Chomsky vs. Skinner – the birth of psycholinguistics

The finite-state model had been implicit in almost all psychological work on language, for example in Miller's (1951) experiments based on information theory (Shannon and Weaver, 1949) and, in a more extreme form, in Skinner's (1957) attempt to extend radical neo-behaviourism to language, in his book *Verbal Behavior*. It was in a review of this book that Chomsky (1959) first put forward his ideas on how psychologists should study language. The review dealt behaviourism a blow from which it was unable to recover – very few behaviourist accounts of cognitive functions have been published since.

Verbal Behavior is based on two related assumptions.

(1) Behaviour should be explained in terms of input/output (I/O) laws, relating what organisms (to use Skinner's term) perceive, to a functional analysis of their behaviour. What is perceived must be described in terms of its physical properties, and behaviour must be described in terms of its function rather than its form. For example, an appropriate description of an animal's response is 'depressing a bar'. A detailed account of how the bar was pressed is of no interest.

(2) No *intervening variables* enter into the explanation of behaviour. In particular an organism's mental state is not relevant to understanding what it does. Skinner argued that variables intervening between input and output had never been shown to have explanatory power in psychological theories.

Given these assumptions, the interpretation of finite-state automata put forward earlier, in which the states of the machine correspond to states of mind, cannot be the one that underlies Skinner's account of language behaviour. On his account the states must be describable in physical terms, and must be perceivable as stimuli by the language user.

What of *Verbal Behavior* itself? From what has been said so far it might be assumed that the book describes the results of a series of experiments, and provides a behaviourist analysis of them. Nothing could be further from the truth. The book is almost entirely speculative. Skinner intuitively identifies various kinds of verbal behaviour and suggests possible explanations for them in learning theory terms. There is no attempt to show how these claims might be tested, let alone any attempt to test them.

Chomsky's review of *Verbal Behavior* is abrasive in tone, and it may take several readings to overcome the idea that Chomsky is merely expressing his prejudices. However, it is well worth the effort, because Chomsky makes many points that are vital to the understanding of what would count as a real *explanation* of language behaviour. He admits that much of what Skinner writes is superficially plausible. But, he argues, the plausibility arises from an equivocation on the meaning of the central terms, *stimulus*, *response* and *reinforcement*. In studies of animal learning, stimuli, responses and reinforcers are, by definition, lawfully related. If an animal's response is not affected by a particular aspect of its environment, say the colour of a light, then colour is not the stimulus that produces the response. In the Skinner box, where the environment is strictly controlled and the function of a piece of behaviour can be readily identified, putative stimuli, responses and reinforcers can be tested to see if they do, in fact, enter into lawful relations. However, when Skinner discusses verbal behaviour, he uses these central notions quite differently. Sometimes he effectively equates them with concepts that have traditionally entered into accounts of verbal behaviour, such as meaning, and provides explanations that are plausible in so far as they are mere paraphrases of traditional ideas. At other times he identifies stimuli in a way that his own proscriptions forbid – in terms of the responses that they produce rather than their physical characteristics. He does so because it is relatively easy to identify linguistic responses (that is what people say), though often very difficult to decide what has produced them. For example, Skinner talks about the property of a picture that causes someone to remark on its beauty, but he cannot begin to describe this property in terms of physical attributes of the picture. This way of identifying stimuli makes the claim that verbal behaviour can be explained using concepts from learning theory circular, and hence untestable. It is always possible to name the stimulus that is lawfully related to response X: it is, of course, 'the stimulus for response X'.

To avoid this circularity Skinner would have to follow his own advice and identify stimuli in physical terms. In so far as he does so in *Verbal Behavior* his suggestions seem blatantly false. Chomsky argues that Skinner's programme must fail, because linguistic behaviour is not determined solely by characteristics of the environment. The internal workings of the 'organism' contribute to the causation of the behaviour. Any viable account of why people say what they say must appeal to beliefs, intentions, and other mental constructs that Skinner eschews. In addition Chomsky proposes that an account of verbal behaviour requires a specification of what a person must know in order to use a language.

Competence and performance

The classical position

Before Chomsky the dominant school in American Linguistics was Struc-turalism, of which the leading figure was Bloomfield. By the time he wrote his most influential book, *Language* (1933), Bloomfield had become a behaviourist and thought that linguistic theory was irrelevant to psychology. Chomsky takes a diametrically opposite view, claiming that linguists' discoveries correspond directly to what people know, in the sense of what they must have in their minds in order to use language. He refers to this idea as the 'rationalist' view of linguistic knowledge, identifying himself with such philosophers as Descartes and Kant, who believed that certain parts of our mental apparatus are innate.

Chomsky distinguishes two aspects of linguistic theory: Universal Gram-mar (UG) and grammars of particular languages. UG is a set of principles common to all languages. It defines the notion of a 'possible human language' and represents innate linguistic knowledge. It is because each child is born 'knowing' UG that it can acquire languages so quickly and with so little effort, despite their complexities. What must be acquired is the grammar of a particular language. The details of Chomsky's account of language acquisition will not be given here (see for example, Chomsky, 1972, 78–99), nor will the confusions that have been pointed out in Chomsky's views. What is of concern, however, is the relation that Chomsky sees between linguistics and psycholinguistics.

According to Chomsky, linguistics is part of theoretical cognitive psychology. It gives an account of 'the speaker-hearer's knowledge of his language' (1965, 4) – what Chomsky calls *linguistic competence*. However, linguistics does not explain how language is used on particular occasions. It describes only the relatively static knowledge stored in a special mental faculty called the language faculty. The explanation of language use is the province of psycholinguistics, which describes not only the processes that access and utilize knowledge stored in the language faculty, but also the way in which they interact with other psychological faculties and processes such as memory and attention. Psycholinguistics can thus explain devia-tions from the ideal in what Chomsky calls *linguistic performance* ('the actual use of language in concrete situations', 1965, 4).

Chomsky makes no distinction in principle between two kinds of devia-tion that a psycholinguistic theory must explain. First, there are those errors that people can readily correct, such as slips of the tongue, false starts, and failures of subject–verb agreement. Second, there are 'problems' that cannot be avoided – for example the difficulty in understanding centre-embedded sentences, such as:

The man the girl the woman met saw ran away.

Chomsky's attitude towards psycholinguistics has changed over the years. Initially he stressed the need for his ideas to be incorporated into a psychological theory that would replace the earlier approaches. He was pleased when George Miller produced experimental results that supported the idea of a transformational grammar as part of a theory of sentence understanding (see chapter 4). However, findings soon emerged that did not fit the Chomsky/Miller view. One possible interpretation of these data was that Chomsky's theory of grammar was incorrect. Chomsky then claimed that psycholinguistic data could never be used to refute a linguistic theory, since a theory of performance always comprised two parts, an account of the speaker/hearer's knowledge and a set of procedures for putting that knowledge to use. If psycholinguistic data did not confirm the predictions of a performance theory, it was not the competence theory that was wrong, but the account of how linguistic knowledge is used. It is a pity that Chomsky ever espoused a stronger view. If linguistic competence is characterized, as Chomsky claimed that it should be, as unconscious 'knowledge' of linguistic rules, a theory about this knowledge can be tested only by using tasks in which the mechanisms that use it do not affect the outcome. Otherwise it is impossible to determine the contributions of knowledge structures and processing structures to experimental results (cf. Anderson, 1976). Because Chomsky changed his mind, it is sometimes assumed that he made a cowardly retreat. The fact of the matter is that his earlier views were rather too rash.

Not all linguists agree with Chomsky about the relation between linguistics and psychology. Katz (1981), for example, propounds what he calls a 'Platonist' view of grammar. By using this label he means that linguistics should be independent of psychology. Montague, whose work on the semantics of natural languages will be discussed in chapter 5, was also a Platonist. He believed semantics to be a branch of mathematics, not psychology.

There are plausible arguments against the view that the rules people use in language processing are those discovered by linguists. Despite Chomsky's characterization of their discipline as part of cognitive psychology, linguists take no account of strictly psychological considerations. Their goal is to produce elegantly formulated grammars. But a concisely stated set of linguistic rules may not correspond to mental mechanisms, which are subject to processing constraints. A linguist's rules might require very complex computational procedures if they were to be incorporated into a language processor, whereas a slightly less elegant set of rules that had the same consequences for linguistic structure, might be computationally more tractable.

A further argument against identifying linguistic rules with rules in the mind can be made by comparing language use with other cognitive skills. Consider mental arithmetic. The formalism that is mathematically most satisfactory for describing the correct results of mental computations is number theory. But it is unlikely that number theory is mentally represented. Presumably people do mental arithmetic using a set of rules (addition tables, multiplication tables, and rules for 'carrying') that produce the same results in a simpler way. It is possible that the same is true in the realm of language understanding (cf. Sutherland, 1966).

These considerations suggest an alternative formulation of the competence/performance distinction, originally proposed by Stanley Peters (see Johnson-Laird, 1983, 167). On this view a linguistic theory specifies what the *results* of the mental computations of language production and comprehension should be. In technical terms, the linguistic theory specifies the *function,* in the mathematical sense, to be computed. Psycholinguistics has to determine which of the indefinitely many possible procedures the human language understanding system uses to compute that function.

Other views on competence and performance

Much has been written about competence and performance, though it is often difficult to understand and ultimately unenlightening. Fodor and Garrett (1966) clarified Chomsky's position by showing that, although a competence theory puts some constraints on possible theories of performance, it does not force the acceptance of any one theory. There are many ways in which the rules of a grammar could be used. Fodor and Garrett's own view, which will be discussed in chapter 4, was that one part of a generative grammar – the transformational component – is not part of the correct performance theory. However, the strongest conclusion that could legitimately be drawn from their experimental findings was that transformations are not used in *some* experimental tasks.

Watt (1970) put forward a theory that is essentially similar to Fodor and Garrett's, though he expressed it differently. Watt noted that any language has more than one grammar – in general it has indefinitely many. He hypothesized that the linguists' grammar for English and the mental grammar of English speakers are different, and that the mental grammar is the one that is used in comprehension and production.

A different view, which has been suggested several times (for example, Bever, 1970; Clark and Haviland, 1974), is that no clear distinction between competence and performance can be drawn. Bever was led to this conclusion by considering how linguists collect their data. They decide whether sentences are grammatical by thinking about them carefully, constructing systematic variants of them and consulting their colleagues about them. Chomsky has misleadingly called this procedure the 'method of linguistic intuitions' – linguists, and indeed all native speakers are said to have 'intuitions' about grammaticality which derive from their implicit knowledge of grammatical rules. Bever claimed that intuitions are another kind of performance, and should therefore be explained by a psycholinguistic rather than a linguistic theory. Bever's claim rests on at least two confusions. First, as Valian (1979) points out, Bever confused a method of collecting linguistic data (by using language in a particular way) with the import of those data (they are about language rather than its use). Second, Bever failed to recognize that the method of 'intuitions' is designed to overcome such performance factors as personal preference and failures of attention. Whether it is wholly successful is another issue (see Levelt, 1974, ch. 2).

Clark and Haviland (1974) argue that the study of language use will lead to an account of language itself, without an independent discipline of linguistics. All the evidence is against such a view. Psycholinguists have produced remarkably few *linguistic* insights, as opposed to ideas about processing. Furthermore, Clark and Haviland's argument is flawed in a number of ways. Its starting point is the observation that many facts about the use of language cannot be explained in terms of linguistic structure. They must be explained in terms of the context in which a sentence is uttered. Clark and Haviland argue that the most appropriate kind of explanation of these facts is a processing explanation. They then argue that a complete processing theory will explain everything that linguists attempt to explain, such as grammaticality judgements. They conclude that linguistics is redundant. However, it does not follow that structural factors are unnecessary in explaining language use simply because they do not explain it completely. Clark and Haviland's processing theory would have to include syntactic rules, for example. Furthermore, their assumption that all linguistic explanations are structural is false.

The arguments against Chomsky's competence/performance distinction are invalid. Valian (1979) claims that they are bound to be, because the *general distinction* between knowledge and its use is one that no empirical evidence could show to be false. However, she does not explain why this is so, and she provides only a cursory discussion of some apparently revelant AI literature. There are many AI programs that express knowledge – including knowledge of linguistic rules – in the form of procedures. In such programs, for example the augmented transition network (ATN) parsers discussed in chapter 4, it is difficult to distinguish clearly between knowledge of linguistic rules and other procedures that use those rules. To every ATN parser there corresponds a grammar, but this fact does *not* show that it makes sense to draw a sharp distinction in a performance theory between knowledge and its use, for two reasons. First, there is no obvious reason to prefer the grammar to the ATN – it is wrong to assume that the grammar is the canonical representation of the syntactic knowledge embodied in the ATN. Second, even if the grammar can be characterized independently of how it is used, it may not be possible to characterize the procedures for using it independently of the grammar. These issues are conceptually difficult, and Valian is probably right, but the last word on competence and performance has not been said.

Summary

A grammar determines which strings of words are sentences of a language, and specifies their syntactic structures. It is expressed in the form of a set of 'generative' rules. The intended sense of *generate* is an abstract one. A grammar is not an account of how speakers produce utterances when they talk, and it may not even reflect the way that linguistic knowledge is organized. A psycholinguistic theory specifies how linguistic knowledge is mentally represented. One view – that of Chomsky – is that the rules of grammar, as discovered by linguists, *are* stored in the mind. There is no decisive evidence on this matter. A psycholinguistic theory should also explain how linguistic knowledge is *used*. A further constraint on the theory is that it should be compatible with the rest of cognitive psychology so that, together with theories of memory and attention, it can explain why people make mistakes in understanding and producing language.

Generative syntax

Whether or not grammars are stored directly in people's minds, psycho-linguists need a detailed description of what is processed in language comprehension and production. Furthermore, the methods of describing languages developed in linguistics are useful in constructing psycholinguistic theories. For these reasons the remainder of this chapter is devoted to a survey of the major developments in generative syntax since the theory was first propounded by Chomsky.

One of Chomsky's abstract mathematical arguments against the use of finite-state automata (and the corresponding finite-state grammars) for the analysis of natural languages has already been outlined. Another of his arguments was that such devices do not capture the way that words in a sentence are grouped together. For example, in the simple sentence:

The boy met the little girl.

the and *boy* form a unit, rather than, say, *boy* and *met*. A natural way to group the words in the sentence is:

[The boy][met[the little girl]]

To make things clearer an outer set of brackets enclosing the whole sentence can be added. Each set of brackets can then be labelled with a name of the *constituent* that it encloses.

[[The boy]$_{NP}$ [met[the little girl]$_{NP}$]$_{VP}$]$_{S}$

The boy and *the little girl* are constituents of the same kind, noun phrases (NP). *Met the little girl* is a verb phrase (VP) in which the object noun phrase (*the little girl*) is grouped with the verb (*met*) to form a constituent that denotes an action. Another, more common, way of displaying the information conveyed by the labelled bracketing is a hierarchical tree. In the tree shown in the following diagram an extra layer of structure has been included – the lexical categories of the words. This structure can be displayed in labelled bracketing by additional sets of brackets.

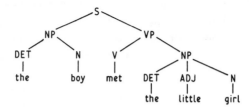

Chomsky formalized the idea of dividing sentences and phrases into parts using the notion of *phrase-structure rules*. A phrase-structure (PS) rule states (i) that a complex expression, typically but not always a phrase, (the item on the left-hand side of the rule) is made up of one or more other expressions, which may be phrases or single words (the items on the right-hand side of the rule), and (ii) that the items on the right-hand side of the rule occur in a particular order. Some phrase-structure rules for English are shown below, together with an indication of what they mean. The arrow (→) can be read as 'is made up of'. Note that a PS rule may be used several times in the description of a single sentence.

S   → NP VP   Sentence → Noun Phrase   Verb Phrase
NP → DET N   Noun Phrase → Determiner   Noun
VP → V   Verb Phrase → Verb
VP → V NP   Verb Phrase → Verb   Noun Phrase

Since there is only one constituent on the left-hand side of a PS rule the branches of the tree can never meet up again. Chomsky argued that, as well as capturing our intuitions about the grouping of the words in a sentence, phrase-structure analysis explained a wide range of syntactic facts that native speakers are not directly aware of.

Structuralists had previously employed the technique of *immediate constituent analysis*, in which sentences were divided up into phrases. However, Chomsky's use of phrase-structure rules was radically different from the structuralists' use of immediate constituent analysis. He regarded phrase-structure rules as *generating* skeletons of sentences called *phrase markers* – hence the term *generative grammar*. It should be emphasized that Chomsky used the term *generate* in an abstract sense. By generation he did not mean language production.

Since a phrase marker is a skeleton of a *sentence,* it is generated by starting with a rule for rewriting S(entence), (for example S → NP VP), and then expanding the *daughter* nodes of the S (i.e. the NP and the VP that make up the sentence) using further phrase-structure rules, and so on, until lexical categories (N, V, ADJ, DET and so on) are reached. Other rules, to be described below, may also be applied to the phrase markers to produce further phrase markers. Actual sentences are generated by inserting words into phrase markers, and performing certain 'tidying up' operations, which ensure that, for example, words have the right endings. The simplest method of lexical insertion is to use PS rules of the form N → *boy*, V → *kick*.

A generative grammar provides a finite, principled account of which strings of English words, out of indefinitely many possible strings, are sentences of the language, and which are not. However, Chomsky was not content with producing a generative grammar for each language. He also set himself the more general goal of defining the notion of a possible human language.

Chomsky hoped to achieve this goal by stating a set of principles common to all grammars. He claimed that these principles were part of the genetic endowment of each human being. One principle that he proposed was that all grammars include a set of phrase-structure rules. A more specific principle, formulated later, was that every language had as its basic rule for expanding S either S → NP VP or S → VP NP.

Further considerations led Chomsky to conclude that PS rules were not, by themselves, sufficient to account in a principled way for English syntax. For example, he wished to explain certain syntactic generalizations about active sentences and their corresponding passives.

Sincerity frightens John.
John is frightened by sincerity.

If, as in the above examples, the direct object of the active must be animate, then the subject of the passive must also be animate. If the active is anomalous:

John frightens sincerity.

so is the passive.

Sincerity is frightened by John.

To explain these facts Chomsky proposed a *syntactic* relation between actives and passives – roughly speaking, a relation between *complete sentences,* not phrases and their parts. More precisely, the relation holds between *phrase markers.* This kind of relation cannot be expressed by PS rules, so Chomsky introduced a new kind of syntactic rule, the *transformation.* Such a rule takes one phrase marker, for example one that provides the skeleton of an active sentence, and produces another phrase marker, for example one corresponding to a passive. A transformation is, therefore, a rule that produces one tree structure from another.

The details of Chomsky's theory of grammar have changed over the years. The versions that had most impact on psycholinguistics were those of *Syntactic Structures* (1957) and *Aspects of the Theory of Syntax* (1965). In *Syntactic Structures* Chomsky proposed a fairly small set of phrase-structure rules that generated a set of *kernel strings*, corresponding closely to simple (that is one clause) active affirmative declarative sentences. A small set of obligatory transformations, ensuring, for example, that auxiliary verbs had the correct endings, converted kernel strings into such sentences. Apart from the obligatory transformations, there were two sets of optional transformations. The first set included Negation, Passivization and Question-formation. They operated on one kernel string to produce further single-clause sentences.

The others, the so-called generalized transformations, produced multi-clause sentences by combining several kernel strings. Again the obligatory transformations tidied up surface details. In addition to the PS rules and transformations a set of *morphophonemic rules* specified how the sentences were pronounced. Little was said about meaning in *Syntactic Structures*. In 1957 Chomsky adhered to Bloomfield's doctrine that semantics could not usefully be studied.

The theory of *Syntactic Structures* was the one on which Miller based his early psycholinguistic experiments. Chomsky himself, however, soon became dissatisfied with its errors and omissions. It was replaced by what he immodestly dubbed the 'Standard Theory' of 1965. According to Standard Theory a grammar specifies the relation between the sounds and the meanings of a language. This formulation of the role of a grammar raises two questions. First, what change of mind is indicated by the reference to *meaning*. This question will be answered shortly. Second, what is the connection between this new conception of a grammar and Chomsky's previous claim that a grammar should generate all and only the sentences of the language? The answer to this second question is straightforward. Chomsky intends to relate sounds and meanings by generating in the syntax all and only the sentences of the language, and then associating with each sentence a sound and a meaning. A grammar therefore has three components, syntax, semantics and phonology. Only the syntax is generative, the other two components *interpret* sentences generated by the syntax.

The 1965 theory differs in many details from that of 1957. The most important of these are, first, that the generalized transformations are replaced by additional PS rules, in which the symbol S appears on the right-hand side. For example, the rule NP → NP S generates an underlying clause corresponding to a relative clause, immediately to the right of its head noun phrase. The structure underlying:

The man I saw left.

is (ignoring some details):

This change is often described by saying that in Standard Theory the *recursive power* of the syntax lies in the base (that is the set of PS rules). By recursion is meant that in the expansion of one S, or any other category, another item of the same category may be expanded as a proper part of the first. Second, in Standard Theory, lexical insertion rules are not PS rules. Third, in complex sentences, transformations are applied first in the most deeply embedded clause, then in the next most deeply embedded and so on (*cyclic* application of rules). Fourth, many, or perhaps all, transformations are ordered with respect to each other. Passivization, for example, must always be applied before Negation if both occur in the derivation of a clause. Fifth, transformations do not change meaning.

This last point is closely related to Chomsky's change of mind about semantics. In *Syntactic Structures,* transformations such as Negation did change meaning, in the sense that the affirmative and negative sentences derived from the same kernel string did not convey the same information. However, Katz and Postal (1964) showed that an integrated theory of syntactic, semantic and phonological descriptions would be simpler if transformations did not change meaning. This suggestion depended on the fact that, in the years since 1957, a semantic theory had emerged that was compatible with generative syntax – that of Katz and Fodor (1963), which will be discussed in chapters 6 and 7. Standard Theory specifies that a grammar is organized as follows: the phrase-structure rules and lexical insertion rules, which together make up the *base* component of the syntax, generate structures in which the subject and all the objects of each verb are explicit. This structure is called the *deep structure.* Transformations apply to deep structures to produce *surface structures,* in which words and morphemes occur in the order in which they are pronounced. Because each clause in deep structure has a canonical configuration, semantic interpretation is straightforward, and since transformations do not change meaning, the semantic interpretation of a surface structure is the same as that of its deep structure. Phonological interpretation takes place at surface structure, producing the sound pattern of the sentence.

If transformations do not change meaning, then any difference in meaning between two sentences must be paralleled by a difference in deep structure. For example, the deep structure of an affirmative sentence must be different from that of its corresponding negative, that of a question different from its corresponding declarative, and so on. Chomsky proposed that such differences should be expressed by transformational markers in deep structure that trigger transformations in the derivation of surface structure.

The concept of deep structure is an important one in Standard Theory. Deep structure is a level of syntactic representation with a number of properties that need not necessarily go together. Four important properties of deep structure are:

(1) Major grammatical relations, such as *subject of* and *object of,* are defined at deep structure.
(2) All lexical insertion occurs at deep structure.
(3) All transformations occur after deep structure.
(4) Semantic interpretation occurs at deep structure.

The question of whether there is a single level of representation with these properties was the most debated question in generative grammar in the years following the publication of *Aspects.* One part of the debate focused on whether transformations preserve meaning. Consider the following active and its corresponding passive.

Every man loves some woman.
Some woman is loved by every man.

Although both sentences are potentially ambiguous (Johnson-Laird, 1970), the natural interpretation of the first is that for each man there is some woman or other, not necessarily the same for each man, whom he loves. The natural interpretation of the second is that there is one particular woman whom every man loves. The two sentences have different preferred meanings, but their deep structures differ only in the presence or absence of the Passive tag, which does not usually account for such differences in meaning. Therefore, transformations do not always preserve meaning.

As it became clear that there was no level of syntactic representation with all the properties ascribed to deep structure in Standard Theory, two alternative schools of thought emerged – Generative Semantics (GS) and Extended Standard Theory (EST). EST was Chomsky's response to the problems of Standard Theory. In EST deep structures are less deep – they look more like surface structures, and some aspects of meaning are determined by levels other than deep structure, notably by surface structure. On some versions of EST (for example, Jackendoff, 1972) semantic interpretation can occur at any stage in the derivation from deep structure to surface structure. However, in EST semantics remains interpretive. Generative power remains in the syntax.

GS was developed by Ross, Lakoff, McCawley and others, who had been students of Chomsky's in the 1960s. GS retained the idea that every difference in meaning is reflected in underlying structure. For example, it postulated different underlying structures for actives and passives with *every* and *some,* such as the examples discussed above. In GS, underlying structures are more complex and more abstract than in Standard Theory. Furthermore, they contain semantic primitives, that may be assembled and converted into lexical items at any stage in a derivation. Generative semanticists therefore claimed that in GS there was no distinction between syntax and semantics, and that the generative component of grammars was semantic.

GS was at one time more popular than EST, and Chomsky attempted, implausibly, to show that the two were notational variants. However, GS never produced grammars to rival that of *Aspects.* Its practitioners became obsessed with discovering subtleties of meaning to incorporate into underlying structure, without considering whether they were best represented structurally. Fairly suddenly, in the mid-1970s, people stopped working in the GS framework. It was subsequently realized that GS, despite its name and the claims of its proponents, was a *syntactic* theory – that is a theory about the structure of sentences. It did not explain the kinds of facts that a semantic theory should (see chapter 5).

A parallel development to GS was Fillmore's (1968, 1971) *case grammar.* This theory had few adherents among generative linguists, though its ideas parallel some other schools of linguistic thought, and it has been influential in both psychology and AI. In Standard Theory grammatical relations, such as *subject of, direct object of* and *indirect object of,* are defined in terms of deep structure configurations. For example, the subject of a deep structure clause (S) is the NP that is immediately dominated by S node, and the direct object is the NP that is immediately dominated by the VP. In English, subject and direct object therefore occur in deep structure clauses in the positions shown in the following diagram.

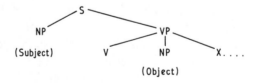

Fillmore proposed that a wider set of relations, such as agent, object and instrument, should be represented by syntactic primitives. Because these relations are based on meaning rather than structure, case grammar, violates Chomsky's *formal autonomy principle,* which states that syntactic concepts should be defined without reference to semantic notions. In a case grammar, AGENT, OBJECT, INSTRUMENT are syntactic categories, and a sentence such as:

John broke the window with a hammer.

has the following underlying structure, shown somewhat simplified in the diagram.

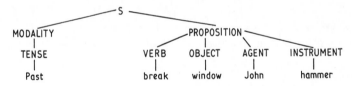

Case grammar recognizes the central role of the verb in the sentence and represents the things denoted by NPs and PPs in surface structure as being in various *case relations* to it. As in Standard Theory a series of ordered transformations converts underlying structures into surface structures.

It was claimed that case grammar had three main advantages over Standard Theory.

(1) Each case has a consistent semantic interpretation, unlike traditional grammatical relations such as *subject of* and *direct object of*.

(2) Underlying representations of the kind shown in in the last diagram, together with a specification of which cases are optional in surface structure (in this instance AGENT and INSTRUMENT), explain relations between the meaning of sentences such as:

John broke the window with a hammer.
John broke the window.
The window was broken with a hammer.
The window broke.

(3) Certain kinds of ungrammaticality can be explained, if it is assumed that only instances of the same case can be conjoined. For example, the following attempt to conjoin an AGENT and an INSTRUMENT is predicted to be ungrammatical by this stipulation.

John and a hammer broke a window.

These advantages were not enough to establish case grammar as a serious rival to EST and GS. Each point was countered by adherents of EST, who also showed that case grammars had serious defects. First, the counters:

(1) Correct semantic interpretation rules for the sentences that case grammar handles well can be provided in the Standard Theory framework. Lack of agreement among case grammarians about the number of cases

needed in a case grammar, and about the interpretation of those cases, considerably weakens their claims.

(2) The meaning relations mentioned under (2) above can be captured in Standard Theory by rules called *lexical redundancy rules.* These rules relate the various structures in which a verb such as *break* can appear.

(3) The case grammar predictions are wrong. Some sentences in which an agent and an instrument are conjoined are acceptable.

John and his trusty sword have routed the enemy.

Case grammar suffers from two major problems, apart from the lack of agreement about what cases are needed.

(1) Its new syntactic categories (e.g. AGENT) are dissimilar to the standard categories (NP, VP, and so on.), in that no transformations that have ever been proposed, even by case grammarians, make reference to them. This fact suggests that it may be misleading to group them with standard syntactic categories.

(2) Every case grammar has one case for those NPs whose relation to the verb cannot be classified positively. This case has no systematic semantic interpretation.

Unlike case grammar and GS, EST, renamed first REST (Revised Extended Standard Theory) and later GB (Government-Binding theory, Chomsky, 1981), is still being actively pursued by Chomsky and others. The major recent changes to the theory are to its transformational component. Many phenomena that were formerly explained by transformations no longer are – transformations do less work in REST than in EST. Furthermore, the transformations that remain are formulated more generally, and have names such as NP-movement, or, in GB, Move α (where α is any constituent), rather than more specific names such as Passivization. In REST and GB the 'tidying up' rules are renamed *stylistic rules*, and are no longer classified as transformations. An important shift of emphasis in GB is from rules, which, as in the case of Move α, now have little specific content, to sets of *principles* constraining the application of those rules. Two such sets of principles are the theories of government and of binding.

The semantic component of GB is also different from that of EST. Semantic interpretation is effected by rules that work on the output of transformations. These rules produce a representation called *logical form.* However, the majority of work in the REST framework continues to be on syntax, and the details of the semantic interpretation rules have not been worked out.

Reducing the power of the transformational component of grammars has been one of the main aims of syntacticians in the 1970s. Peters and Ritchie (1973) showed that transformational grammars were, in a sense, too powerful to be tested empirically. They proved that every natural language is bound to have a transformational grammar, so Chomsky's claim that the grammars of all languages are transformational has no testable, and hence no explanatory, content. To explain what is special about human languages, it is necessary to discover further restrictions on the kinds of grammars they can have.

Recently it has been suggested (by Brame, 1978; Kaplan and Bresnan, 1982; Gazdar, 1981, 1982; and in unpublished work by Stanley Peters) that the transformational component of grammars can be eliminated and syntactic structure captured by a (somewhat extended) set of PS rules. The most easily accessible of these accounts is Gazdar's, which will be discussed here.

Gazdar analyses natural language syntax using *Generalized Phrase-Structure Grammars* (GPSGs). Such grammars have two major advantages over transformational grammars. First, they have almost all of the properties of simple PS grammars (grammars comprising sets of PS rules). In particular, they are less powerful than transformational grammars, and provide genuine constraints on the set of possible natural languages. Second, because many computer-programming languages are phrase-structure languages (i.e. languages that have phrase-structure grammars) much is known about how to parse such languages, whereas the theory of parsing for transformational grammars is less well developed, and the few results that have been established do not suggest psychologically plausible models.

If natural languages have GPSGs, how are the phenomena that led to the introduction of transformations accounted for? There are two main ways in which this goal is achieved. The first is applied to constructions that were explained in Standard Theory by transformations operating within a single clause. An example is dative-shift, exemplified by:

John gave Mary the book.

In Standard Theory such a sentence is derived by a transformation called Dative Movement from the same underlying structure as:

John gave the book to Mary.

In REST a *lexical redundancy* rule states that certain double object verbs occur in two syntactic environments:

< __NP PP[to] >
< __NP NP >

A similar treatment is adopted in GPSG. Related pairs of sentences, such as the ones above, are then assigned the same meaning by the semantic component of the grammar. This component is typically a Montague-style semantics of the kind discussed in chapter 5. GPSGs have been associated with a much more rigorous approach to semantic interpretation than transformational grammars.

A more complex construction that is limited to a single clause is the passive. Chomsky continues to generate passives transformationally, though treatments of passivization using lexical redundancy rules have been proposed (for example, Bresnan, 1978). In Gazdar's (1982) GPSG treatment the relation between the meanings of actives and passives is explained semantically, but a redundancy rule, this time at the phrasal level, is also included in the grammar to capture some syntactic generalizations about passives. Since the relation between actives and passives is a meaning relation, its treatment purely in terms of structure, for example in Standard Theory, has always seemed odd.

The second method of dealing with 'transformational' phenomena in GPSG is applied to those constructions containing *unbounded dependencies*, in which syntactic relations hold between items in different clauses of the same sentence. Unbounded dependencies are found in constructions such as questions and relative clauses. Below are some WH-questions that illustrate the potential unboundedness of the dependency between the questioned element, *which book,* and the *t*, or *trace*, which indicates the position where *book* would be in a corresponding declarative clause (that is as the direct object of the verb *read*). For example, corresponding to the final clause *you read* in each of the examples is the declarative clause *you read the book.* On a transformational analysis *book* is generated by PS rules at the position where the trace is indicated, and is moved to the front of the sentence. In the successive examples the *t* is located in more and more deeply embedded clauses, while *which book* remains in the outermost clause. The distance between the two can be increased indefinitely.

Which book have you read *t* ?
Which book did you say you read *t* ?
Which book did you say Frank recommended that you read *t* ?

In GPSG category names such as S, NP, VP can be 'annotated' with sets of features – simple examples are [singular], [plural], [masculine], [feminine]. A more complex feature of, say, an S can be that it has an NP 'missing' from inside it. Thus in the question *Which book did you read?* the embedded clause *you read* has no NP for its direct object – the clause is, syntactically, an S with an NP missing. If an S lacks one of its NPs then one of its immediate constituents (the NP or the VP) must also lack an NP. If it is, say, the VP, then that too must have an NP missing somewhere inside it, and so on. Thus the dependency can be carried down as far as is required into embedded clauses. At some point an NP that would be present in a declarative clause can simply be omitted. An unbounded dependency has then been created from the WH-phrase at the beginning of a WH-question, to the point at which the constituent is missing. GPSG must avoid claiming that *you read* on its own is a grammatical sentence. Therefore, to complete the GPSG analysis of unbounded dependencies, rules are needed to say where 'incomplete' constituents can occur. For example, one such rule will say that a WH-question has a special kind of S node, one with an NP missing, as one of its daughters.

S[WH-Question] → NP[+WH] S[NP missing, inverted]

This rule is used to generate structures such as:

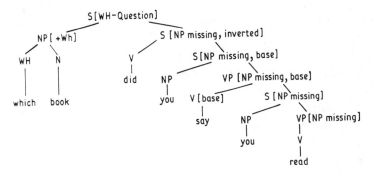

A rule such as

S[NP missing] → NP VP[NP missing]

is a generalization of S → NP VP. This fact is captured not in the GPSG itself, but in a grammar for the grammar. Stating generalizations in this way allows a considerable simplification of the grammar itself.

GPSGs are important for for two reasons. First, GPSG is a promising framework for describing natural language syntax. Second, GPSG forms a plausible basis for a psychological theory of parsing. A GPSG assigns to each (structurally unambiguous) sentence just one syntactic structure. The PS rules of the grammar therefore define possible *surface structure* configurations, and hence the parser can make direct reference to these rules. In transformational grammar the PS rules produce deep structures. Surface structure configurations may not conform to these rules, though in GB (Chomsky, 1981) they generally do.

Summary

Linguistic theory is important to psycholinguists primarily because it provides a formalism in which to describe languages. Whether linguistic knowledge stored in the mind corresponds to linguists' grammars is a further question. Chomsky claims that it does, but certain general considerations cast doubt on this claim. In particular, the constraints of elegance and simplicity on the formulation of grammars are unlikely to have parallels in the way the mind works, because of the other influences on mental processing, such as the need to operate in real time and with finite resources.

Chomsky is, from the psycholinguists' point of view, the most important figure in linguistics. He introduced a new degree of precision into linguistic argument, which enabled him to prove that an account of linguistic behaviour based on finite-state automata is, in principle, inadequate. He undermined Skinner's attempt to apply neo-behaviourist learning theory to verbal behaviour, and he introduced the idea of a generative grammar that could form part of a model of language use. In attempting to clarify the relation between linguistics and psycholinguistics, and to protect linguistics theories from refutation by psychological data, Chomsky distinguished between competence, or knowledge of language, and performance, or its use.

Chomsky's linguistic theory has changed considerably since *Syntactic Structures* was published in 1957, but certain aspects of it remain constant. The theory has two parts: Universal Grammar – the study of what all languages have in common, and grammars of particular languages. The most important part of a grammar is its syntactic component, which generates sentences. Semantics and phonology interpret syntactic structures. The underlying syntactic structures of sentences are produced primarily by PS rules. Related sentences, such as actives and their corresponding passives, have the same or very similar underlying structures, but are converted into different superficial forms by transformation rules.

There have been a number of alternatives to Chomsky's Standard Theory and subsequent developments of it. Generative Semantics was important in linguistics, but had little impact in psychology. Case grammar continues to be used in AI and psychological semantics, despite its lack of appeal to linguists. An important new development is Generalized Phrase-Structure Grammar. Unlike previous rivals to Standard Theory GPSG is formally more rigorous and psychologically more plausible. In particular it should be easier to construct well-specified theories of parsing within the GPSG framework.

3

Recognizing words

In chapter 1 the major subprocesses of language understanding were identified. The first of these to be examined in detail is the recognition of individual words. The problem of identifying words arises *only* in comprehension, and not in production. The corresponding problem in production is the selection of lexical items to express particular meanings. There has been comparatively little work on this topic. Some of it will be mentioned briefly in chapter 9.

Word recognition is an early process in comprehension, in the sense that the language understanding system has to decide which words are present before the structure or meaning of a linguistic input can be computed. The processes that identify words are inevitably somewhat different for spoken and written language, primarily because of the different temporal properties of speech and writing. Furthermore, some kinds of written language are more difficult to process than others. Recognizing words in cursive script is, in general, harder than identifying printed words. Most of the experiments discussed in this chapter use printed words or analogous computer displays. Such words are easier to analyse than cursive script for three main reasons. First, the problem of segmenting the input into words is relatively trivial, since spaces, new lines and hyphenation provide information about where one word ends and another begins. Such clues, though present in cursive script, are harder to identify. Second, there are in printed words equally obvious cues that show which line segments belong to which letters. Third, type founts are designed so that all characters are visually distinct. Because the major questions about recognition are not about segmentation or the resolution of perceptual ambiguities, cursive script is generally avoided in word recognition experiments and, since most studies examine the identification of single words, the problem of finding word boundaries is rarely relevant.

The emphasis on written word recognition in this chapter reflects the comparative neglect of spoken word recognition in the psycholinguistic literature. An important exception is the work of Marslen-Wilson (see for example Marslen-Wilson and Tyler, 1980).

The mental lexicon

The usual goal of reading or listening is to derive meanings from visual patterns or sound patterns. If this goal is to be achieved, incoming perceptual information must activate stored knowledge about words that are presented. The mental state of knowledge about words is referred to as the *mental lexicon*, as it contains the same kinds of information that are found in a good dictionary, although the mental lexicon and, say, the *Oxford English Dictionary* are organized very differently. The mental lexicon specifies how a word is spelled, how it is pronounced, its part of speech and what it means. However, it is convenient to think of the lexicon itself as containing not the meanings of words, but rather *pointers* to those meanings. The way in which word meanings are mentally represented is discussed in chapter 6. The representations are considerably more complex than those in an ordinary dictionary, and do not directly affect the process of word recognition. It would be an unnecessary complication to include them in a system for identifying words.

Two kinds of information are used in word recognition: perceptual and contextual. The perceptual information, in the case of written words, comes from a pattern recognizer that detects such things as straight lines and curves, their relative positions and possibly the overall shape of words. Contextual information comes from the preceding part of the current discourse or text, from pictures associated with the words (for example, in advertisements), from objects in the real world (for example, in scenes that are being described) and from shared knowledge, including knowledge of cultural norms. The question that theories of lexical access and word recognition attempt to answer is: how are these two kinds of information used to determine what words are being looked at (or heard)?

Lexical access and word recognition – definitions

The terms *lexical access* and *word recognition* are frequently used as though they were interchangeable. However, they have different meanings, and it is important to distinguish between them. *Lexical access* is the retrieval of a word from the lexicon on the basis of perceptual and contextual information. That word then becomes a *candidate* for the identity of the current input. *Word recognition* is achieved when there is only one remaining candidate, and the input has been identified. In the two main classes of model to be discussed below, words are accessed only when there is sufficient information to identify them accurately. Therefore lexical access and word recognition occur simultaneously. However, there are models that propose a different relation between access and recognition. In particular, a set of several candidate words could be *accessed* from the lexicon, before one of them was finally *recognized* as the word presented.

Experiments on word recognition

Experimental techniques

In the study of word recognition two principal experimental paradigms have been used – lexical decision and pronunciation. In lexical decision experiments subjects are presented with strings of letters, such as *blink* or *brast*, and have to decide as quickly as possible whether those strings are words. Lexical decision is considered to be an appropriate method for studying word recognition, because in order to perform the task subjects need only access their mental lexicons. No further processing of the letter strings is required. For example, it is not necessary to determine the meaning of the string, if it is a word. This fact is best illustrated by considering how lexical decisions could be made in an unfamiliar language, say Finnish, using a printed dictionary. The task can be performed even though the definitions in the dictionary cannot be understood. The correct answer is 'yes' if the letter string is in the dictionary, and 'no' if it is not – assuming that all words are in the dictionary. This thought experiment illustrates another point. The task is only possible because the organization of the dictionary is known – the words are written in the Roman alphabet and the entries are arranged alphabetically. Similarly the word recognition system depends upon the organization of the mental lexicon, and the way perceptual inputs are categorized.

Recently doubts have been raised about whether results obtained in the lexical decision task reflect only the process of lexical access. Although lexical access is sufficient to perform the task correctly, there is evidence that subjects in lexical decision experiments engage in other processing. It has even been mooted (e.g. Henderson, 1982) that some of the principal findings in lexical decision, such as the frequency effect discussed below, should be explained in terms of things that happen after lexical access, for example checking the output from the lexicon against the perceptual input. Such a view is not entirely new (see for example Goldiamond and Hawkins, 1958).

An alternative to asking subjects to make lexical decisions is to ask them to pronounce strings of letters. In the pronunciation task subjects have to say out loud words or non-words, and the time they take to begin speaking is measured. The task is a little less useful for studying lexical access than lexical decision, because, at least for some words, it may not be necessary to access the lexicon in order to pronounce them. There may be a non-lexical way of pronouncing non-words and regular words, using pronunciation rules. Alternatively all letter strings – both words and non-words – could be pronounced on the basis of lexical analogies. This issue is discussed below under the head of phonological recoding. The pronunciation task is particularly useful for addressing questions about the effect of the sound of a written word on its identification.

The basic findings

Any model of word recognition must explain the following well-established findings.

(1) *The frequency effect* (e.g. Rubenstein, Garfield and Millikan, 1970; Forster and Chambers, 1973). Common words, such as *door*, are responded to more quickly in the lexical decision and pronunciation tasks than are uncommon words, such as *cask*, even when the words are matched for length – most long words are used relatively infrequently.

(2) *Word/non-word effects* (e.g. Rubenstein, Garfield and Millikan, 1970; Stanners and Forbach, 1973). Letter strings such as *xgyz* that could not possibly be English words produce very fast 'no' responses in a lexical decision experiment, and are probably rejected without any attempt to access the lexicon. However, it takes slightly longer to reject non-words, such as *nint*, that could be words but that happen not to be (i.e. non-words that conform to the rules of English orthography), than to accept infrequent words. Furthermore, the greater the similarity between a non-word and real words, the harder the non-word is to reject (e.g. Coltheart, Davelaar, Jonasson and Besner, 1977).

(3) *Context effects* (e.g. Meyer and Schvaneveldt, 1971). One source of information used in recognizing words is context. Words are identified more quickly in context than out of context, though there is some debate about which kinds of contexts affect *lexical* processing. There is no doubt, however, that simple word associations speed word recognition. If a subject sees the words *bread butter*, presented either together or one after the other, then lexical decision on both of the words, if they are presented together, or on *butter*, if it follows *bread*, is faster than it would have been if the words were unrelated, for example *nurse butter*, or if the context had been neutral, for example *xxxxx butter*, or *ready butter*.

(4) *Degradation*, or *stimulus quality*, *effects*. If a letter string is made difficult to see, either by superimposing a pattern of dots or squiggles over it or

by making it faint, then lexical decision is not surprisingly slowed down.
(5) *Word-superiority effects* (e.g. Reicher, 1969; Wheeler, 1970). It is worth
mentioning finally these rather misleadingly named effects. It is easier
to recognize a letter in a word (for example, *a* in *bland*) than a letter
presented alone or in a string of Xs. Although there are a number
of possible explanations for this finding, it at least suggests that words
are *not* recognized by identifying their component letters, and then
performing an alphabetical look-up in the mental lexicon. On the
simplest account, if letters are identified before words, then they should
be recognized just as quickly on their own as in words.

Models of lexical access

Two major classes of model have been proposed to account for how words
are recognized – direct access models and search models.

Direct access models

The concept of direct access   The most well-known model of this class is John
Morton's (1969, 1979) *logogen* model (see Figure 3.1). It is called a *direct*

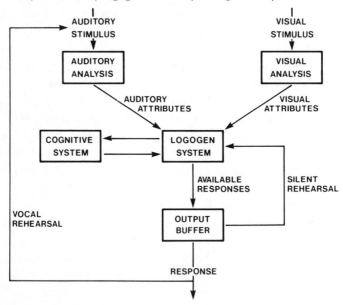

Figure 3.1 The logogen model
(*Source* Morton, 1970)

access model because perceptual information feeds directly into a set of feature counters, called logogens, that forms the heart of the word recognition system. There is one logogen corresponding to each word, or perhaps morpheme, that the person knows. If the perceptual input contains a feature of a particular word, then the feature count of its logogen is incremented. for example, whenever low-level visual analysis identifies the feature 'curve at left-hand end of word', the feature count of all the logogens for words beginning with C G O Q goes up, if the word is in capital letters. Each logogen has a threshold level at which it 'fires'. The threshold is set so that it is reached only if it is almost certain that the input is the word corresponding to the logogen. When the logogen fires the corresponding word is made available as a response, and all the logogens return to their *resting level* (zero feature count), though this process takes some time. In this original version of the model once a logogen fires, a word has been recognized and the logogen system prepares for the next input.

The logogen model's account of the basic findings   To account for the frequency effect it is assumed that logogens have different thresholds – those for frequent words being lower than those for infrequent words. The model itself does not attempt to explain how these differences arise, but one possibility is that when a language is being learned, a logogen's threshold is slightly reduced each time it fires (c.f. Morton, 1970, 207). The more frequent a word is, the more often it is encountered, and the lower its threshold becomes.

The simple logogen model has difficulty explaining non-word effects. As described so far the model has no mechanism for producing 'no' responses in lexical decision. The reason for this 'omission' is that the model was originally formulated to explain recognition of very briefly presented words, not decisions on letter strings. When a word is presented for such a short interval that it is not properly seen, no logogen fires, and no response is made.

One way of rejecting non-words using a logogen system is to set a *deadline*. If no logogen has reached threshold by the deadline, the response is 'no'. Coltheart *et al.* (1977) argued that the deadline cannot be constant – a constant deadline implies that all non-words should take the same amount of time to reject. In fact rejection time depends on the similarity of the non-word to actual words. Coltheart *et al.*'s own suggestion is that the deadline is varied during the identification of a word. It starts at a low value, but is increased as the activation in the logogen system increases – if there is a lot of activity, the stimulus is probably a word, and 'no' response should be made with caution. Forster (1976) suggests an alternative explanation of non-word decision times within a word detector model. He argues that it is necessary to assume that non-words, and by implication real words also, activate a *number* of logogens to threshold level. The input is then checked more thoroughly to see if it matches any of these words. In this version of the logogen model, word recognition does not occur solely by direct access to the lexicon. A search process is also required before a final identification is made.

To account for context effects it is assumed that contextual information, as well as perceptual information, can increment the feature counts of logogens. This increases occurs *prior to* the presentation of the word whose recognition will be speeded. According to Morton the output of the logogen system is passed to a separate 'cognitive system', which constructs and updates a representation of context. The cognitive system is able to compute both associative and sentential or textual context. Its representation of context can be used to predict the words that are likely to occur next and, hence, to increment the feature counts of the corresponding logogens. The result of this *priming* is that the amount of perceptual information required to make those logogens fire to the next input, and hence the time taken for them to reach their thresholds, is reduced.

The simplest account of stimulus quality effects in the logogen model is that degradation slows down the rate of feature extraction from the stimulus. An alternative suggestion is that degradation has its effect at an earlier stage, making more difficult the preprocessing that 'cleans up' the stimulus prior to feature extraction (Mitchell, 1982, 61–2).

Some predictions from the logogen model　So far it has been shown how the logogen model explains previously established findings. To *test* the model it is necessary to make predictions about, for example, what happens when context, frequency and stimulus quality are varied together in lexical decision experiments. However, in fairness to Morton, it must be mentioned that he still thinks that the logogen model's primary application should be to threshold tasks, and that in predicting or explaining the results of lexical decision experiments the logogen system need not play a major role. (cf. Morton, 1982).

In order to derive these predictions first note that in the logogen model the effects of frequency and of context are produced in the same way. To recognize a high frequency word less perceptual information is required than to recognize an otherwise similar low frequency word. Similarly less information is needed to recognize a word in context than out of context. Thus frequency and context should show similar *patterns of interaction* with stimulus

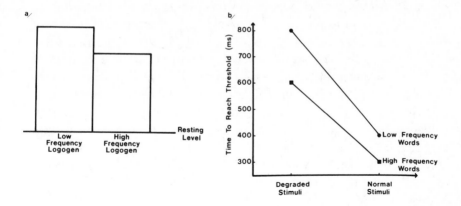

Figure 3.2 The interaction between frequency and stimulus quality in the logogen model: (a) logogens (b) predicted times for logogens to reach threshold

quality. Consider Figure 3.2a. Assume that, if the words are clearly visible, it takes the high frequency logogen 300ms to gather enough information to reach threshold, and the low frequency logogen 400ms. If degradation slows the rate of feature extraction by half, the two logogens will take 600ms and 800ms respectively to fire, when the words are hard to see. Thus a frequency effect of 100ms when the words are clear has been increased to one of 200ms for degraded stimuli, and a statistical interaction between frequency and degradation is predicted (Figure 3.2b). By a parallel argument, an interaction is predicted between context and stimulus quality (see Figure 3.3). Furthermore, if the main effect of context is of the same size as

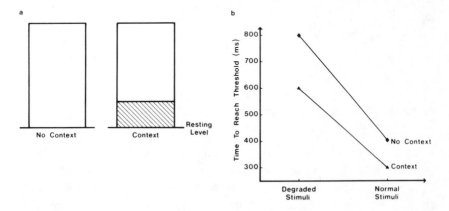

Figure 3.3 The interaction between context and stimulus quality in the logogen model: (a) logogens (b) predicted times for logogens to reach threshold

the main effect of frequency (which was 150ms, averaged across the two presentation conditions in the above example), then the interaction should also be of the same magnitude.

If degrading the stimulus slows down perceptual clean-up, then additive effects are predicted in both cases – making the stimulus difficult to see should delay the identification of any word by a fixed amount. Thus whichever assumption is made about the effect of stimulus quality, the logogen model predicts that context and frequency interact in the same way with degradation. Becker and Killion (1977) tested this prediction experimentally, and found that it was not correct. Context and degradation produced the kind of multiplicative effect illustrated in Figure 3.3b, but the effects of frequency and degradation added together. More recently Norris (1984) has demonstrated that frequency and stimulus quality can interact. However, it remains true, contrary to the prediction of the logogen model, that the interaction of context and frequency is larger and more robust.

When frequency and context are varied together their effects should, according to logogen model, be additive (see Figure 3.4). An association

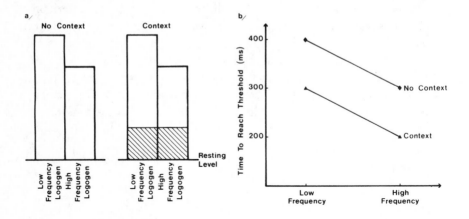

Figure 3.4 The interaction between frequency and context in the logogen model: (a) logogens (b) predicted times for logogens to reach threshold

of a given strength, as measured in word association norms (e.g. Postman and Keppel, 1970), reduces the amount of perceptual information required to identify the current word by a fixed amount, for both high frequency and low frequency words. The time taken to reach threshold is therefore decreased equally by context for any logogen. This prediction was supported by the results of Schuberth and Eimas (1977).

Search models

The concept of search   The second class of word recognition model denies that perceptual information has direct access to lexical entries. Instead, such models claim that the visual or auditory input is used to make a *search* through all or part of the lexicon. A pure *search model*, in which the whole of the lexicon is searched every time a word is encountered, has never been seriously proposed. The kind of model now under discussion is therefore sometimes referred to as a *mixed model*, since the set of items to be searched is first selected in some other way.

The two main versions of the mixed model are Ken Forster's (1976, 1979) search model and Curt Becker's (1976) verification model. Forster's model illustrates the idea of search more clearly, and it is this model that will be discussed in detail (see Figure 3.5). According to Forster, words are recognized in the following way. In contrast with direct access models, a complete perceptual representation of the input is first constructed. This representation contains the featural information that, according to Morton, is fed directly into logogens. In order to discover which word the perceptual representation corresponds to, it is compared with representations of what words look like or sound like, stored in *access files*. The comparisons are made one after the other in an order that is determined by the listing of the entries in the access file – that is to say the access files are searched for a match. The access files are peripheral to the mental lexicon itself, and allow entries in it to be retrieved. There are three access files, the orthographic for recognizing written words, the phonological for recognizing spoken words, and a syntactic/semantic access file used in language production. This last access file allows words with given syntactic and semantic properties to be located for insertion into sentences. The entries in the access file are searched in order, and when a match is found, information becomes available from the corresponding entry in the *master file* or mental lexicon proper. This entry contains all the information about the word, duplicating much from the access files. As was mentioned above, information about the meaning of a word may be stored only indirectly, in the form of a pointer to a location in semantic memory. Forster's model is not a pure search model. He proposes that the access files are subdivided into *bins*. Only one bin need be searched to find a word, and access to the appropriate bin is direct. However, Forster proposes that when a non-word is presented almost all of the bins may be searched. One way in which the access files used in word recognition could be divided up into bins is by initial letter or sound, though Forster does not commit himself on this question.

Figure 3.5 Forster's search model
(*Source* Forster, 1976)

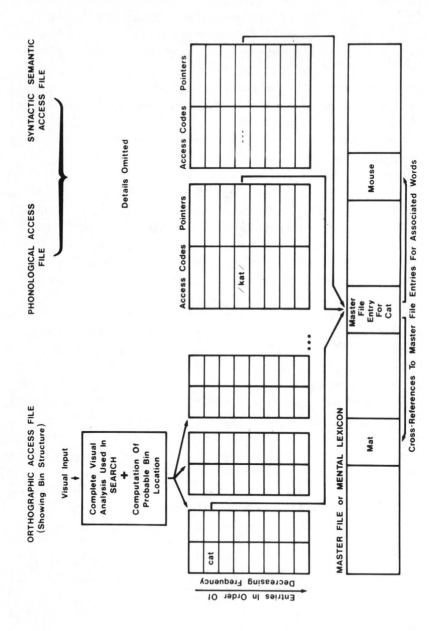

The search model's account of the basic findings The search model accounts for the frequency effect by assuming that entries in the bins are arranged in order of frequency. Therefore an input is compared with high frequency words first, and if it matches one of them the master file is accessed quickly. Low frequency words, which require many comparisons before a match is found, take longer to recognize, since the comparisons are made sequentially and each one takes time. To decide that a letter-string is a non-word takes longer still, since every word in at least one of the bins must be searched, and a 'no' response is made only if no match is found. Non-words similar to real words are especially difficult to reject, because it takes a comparatively long time to decide that, say, the input *huamn* does not match the access file entry *human*. The similarity might even be sufficient to activate the master file entry for *human*, producing either a false alarm, or a further delay while checks are made that reveal the mismatch.

Context effects are less successfully explained by the search model. Forster assumes that there are connections in the master file between strongly associated words, and that when a word is accessed, related words are primed as candidates for the next word to be presented. Effectively a new list of words is created, to be searched at the same time as a bin in one of the access files. As soon as a match is found in either list, the master file is accessed. Since the list of associated words is likely to be shorter than a bin, a word presented in context will probably be recognized because it matches one of the list of associated words. Recognition is therefore quicker than it would have been with no context, when the system would have to wait for a match in the bin. There is no mechanism in the search model for non-associative sentential context to aid word recognition. Although a number of studies have found effects of this kind of context (e.g. Fischler and Bloom, 1979; Stanovich and West, 1979), Forster has suggested an alternative explanation of these results (see chapter 8), and claimed that context effects on lexical access arises only from word associations.

In the search model stimulus quality has its effect at an early stage in lexical access. It influences the time taken to produce a perceptual representation of the input.

Some predictions from the search model For the logogen model it was comparatively easy to predict what happens when frequency, context and stimulus quality are varied together. The corresponding predictions for the search model are less obvious, for two main reasons. First, context produces its effect in a complex fashion. Second, Forster presented his version of the 'predictions' after the discovery (e.g. Schvaneveldt, Meyer and Becker, 1976) that context and degradation interact (as in Figure 3.2b), and hence he proposed a *post hoc* explanation of this result, rather than deriving what seem to be the obvious predictions from the search model. There are, however, a number of other predictions that do follow straightforwardly from the model. For example, the effects of frequency and degradation should add together, since degrading the stimulus delays the start of the search by a fixed amount of time, until perceptual analysis is completed. This prediction is compatible with the findings of Becker and Killion (1977). Another obvious prediction is of a larger context effect for low frequency words than for high frequency words. The search in the access file takes longer for an uncommon word, so when it is presented in context, such a word will almost always be found first in the list of associated words, rather than in the access file. On average, context speeds the recognition of such a word by a large amount. High frequency words, however, are reached comparatively rapidly in the access files, and context has less of a chance to speed their identification. This prediction was not borne out in the results of Schuberth and Eimas (1977).

On the question of context and degradation, the most obvious prediction is that degradation delays the start of both searches and, therefore, always delays word recognition by a fixed time. However, Forster claims that he can predict the interaction found by Schvaneveldt *et al.* (1976) and by Becker and Killion (1977) in the following way. He first argues that the primary use of associations is in language production, not comprehension. Associated words are likely to be required either to convey different aspects of the same theme or as alternative ways of expressing the same message. Forster then claims that the production system can be used as a back up in word recognition, though he does not say exactly how. This back up is most useful when words are difficult to identify, and hence context has a bigger effect with degraded words.

Inhibitory effects in word recognition

Both the logogen model and the search model provide accounts of the basic findings in word recognition that are fairly satisfactory in broad outline, if incorrect in some of their details. They have advanced our thinking about word recognition and stimulated further experiments. This research has in turn produced new problems for the models, and indicated the directions in which they need to be extended.

One question that has been widely investigated is whether there are inhibitory effects of context on word recognition. That is to say, can an inappropriate context slow down the identification of a word compared with a neutral context? Such effects have been reported in several experiments, though neither model has any mechanism to explain them. It might be thought that the logogen model could handle such effects by allowing feature counts to be decremented as well as incremented. However, there is a problem in deciding which logogens are to be decremented in a given context – a problem that has no satisfactory solution in the case of sentential context. Modifying the search model to cope with inhibitory effects is even more difficult.

Neely (1977) studied two kinds of context – associations between categories and their instances, such as *bird* and *robin*, and what he called 'cognitive' associations. This second kind of association was established in the experiment by telling the subjects that the word *body* would usually be followed by part of a building (for example, *door*), and vice versa. Both kinds of association produced both facilitatory effects and inhibitory effects (on the small percentage of trials on which a word from the expected class did not follow the prime, for example, *bird arm*). Neely also varied the time between the presentation of the two words, so that he could investigate the time course of facilitatory and inhibitory effects. With category-instance associations the facilitation began to act very quickly, whereas all the other effects were comparatively slow in their onset. Neely therefore argued that two different kinds of processes produce contextual effects. He identified them with the automatic and conscious processes postulated in two-process theories of attention (e.g. Posner and Snyder, 1975). He argued that pre-established word associations produce automatic speeding of lexical access, but the other effects were mediated by conscious computation of what word was likely to come next.

Another experiment that demonstrated inhibitory effects in lexical access was carried out by Antos (1979), who also explained his results in the two-process framework. Antos used instance-category associations (e.g. *apple fruit*) so that subjects could make a highly accurate prediction of what word they were going to see. This procedure can be contrasted with the use of category-instance associations, where strong predictions cannot be made, because a category has many instances. On a small number of catch trials Antos followed an instance by an inappropriate category. On these trials recognition of the category was slower than in a neutral condition (*neutral fruit*), even at delays as short as 200ms. This result suggests that there may be an automatic component to inhibition when strong predictions can be made, but Antos argued that the detailed pattern of his results could not be explained in terms of automatic processes only.

Some recent theoretical developments

The most common way of accounting for inhibitory effects in word recognition is to follow Neely and Antos and add an attentional component to one of the models. The explanation of the effects then proceeds in terms of automatic and conscious processing. The two-process theory claims that information in the focus of attention is processed 'automatically', whereas shifting of attention requires conscious effort. One way of thinking about the application of this theory to word recognition is to imagine a revised logogen model in which the logogens are surveyed by an 'inner eye'. In this model a word is not recognized when a logogen fires, but only when the eye *sees* which logogen has fired. Only in its focus of attention ('foveal vision') can the eye determine accurately which logogen has fitted. If a logogen fires in a part of the system to which the eye is not attending ('peripheral vision'), it knows roughly where it must shift its attention, but it cannot tell, until it does so, which logogen has fired. Shifting of attention takes time, and word recognition is delayed. In Antos's experiment, the priming word *apple*, for example, will cause the eye to focus its attention on the area of the logogen system containing *fruit*, when the next word is presented, since priming is from instances to categories. If the next word is *fruit*, then it will be recognized quickly compared with the case of a neutral context, when the inner eye has no particular focus of attention. However, if an inappropriate word such as *arm* is presented, recognition will be delayed. The *arm* logogen fires in the normal way, but no response can be made until attention has been focused on the right part of the lexicon, and attention cannot be shifted until the logogen fires.

An alternative, and in many ways more elegant, account of inhibitory effects in word recognition is outlined by Norris (1982). Norris makes use of the distinction, made at the beginning of this chapter, between lexical access and word recognition. He assumes that in the course of word recognition the lexicon continuously outputs all those words that are consistent with the perceptual analysis so far performed. These candidate words are then checked against a representation of context, to see how well they fit with it – hence the name of his model of word recognition, *the checking model*. It should be noted that a mechanism of checking against context is, in any case, required in the word recognition system, for resolving lexical ambiguities. Context acts not in an all or none way, but by increasing or decreasing the amount of perceptual evidence that is required to recognize a word in an inappropriate or an appropriate context respectively. When sufficient evidence has been gathered, recognition occurs. Both inhibition and facilitation are produced by the same mechanism of changing the recognition criterion. For this reason the model is said to belong to the class of *criteria bias models*. The logogen model is also a criteria bias model. In that model context also has its effect by changing the amount of perceptual information that is required to identify a word.

Marslen-Wilson and Tyler's (1980) cohort model for the recognition of spoken words also assumes that early perceptual analysis makes a set of candidate words available. However, in this model analysis starts at the beginning of the word, and proceeds 'from left to right'. Words that are inappropriate in the context are eliminated from the candidate set. These aspects of the model give rise to two major problems. First, since the initial set of candidate words is selected on the basis of the first phoneme in a word, the model cannot account for the recognition of words that are mispronounced at the beginning (for example, a drunk saying *shigarette* instead of *cigarette*). Second, because words that do not fit with the context are dropped from consideration, the model predicts that words cannot be recognized in inappropriate contexts (cf. Norris, 1982). The way candidate sets are used in the cohort model is, therefore, less satisfactory than the way they are used in the checking model.

Two further issues

Phonological recoding

So far it has been assumed that, when a word is presented visually, lexical access depends solely on the *visual* features of the word. However, this assumption has frequently been questioned. Spoken language is prior to written language – both in the development of the species and of the individual – and learning to read is, at least initially, learning that certain visual patterns correspond in an orderly way to words already in the speaking vocabulary. One suggestion is that what is learned is a set of rules – called grapheme–phoneme correspondence (GPC) rules – that translate letter patterns into the sound patterns produced by the auditory analysis of spoken words. Perhaps all reading depends on such translation, and the mental lexicon can only be accessed via sound patterns. This proposal is known as the *phonological recoding hypothesis*.

Phonological recoding is *not* the same as hearing what is being read 'inside the head'. The existence of an inner voice, reported by many readers, is irrelevant to this issue, first because there is no reason why GPC rules should produce the illusion of hearing sounds, and secondly because these sounds could be produced in a different way. Visually presented words could access the lexicon on the basis of their visual features, and the sounds of the words read out of the lexicon subsequent to lexical access (cf. Crowder, 1982, 186--91). Evidence for phonological recoding must come from experiments that show that the sound of a visually presented word or letter string affects the way it is accessed, for example in lexical decision or pronunciation. A number of such findings have been reported.

Rubenstein, Lewis and Rubenstein (1971) compared lexical decision times for two kinds of pronounceable non-words, ordinary non-words, such as *shart*, and *pseudohomophones*, such as *brane*, which sound like real words. Pseudohomophones took longer to reject, suggesting that their sound patterns had activated lexical entries for the corresponding real words, and that this activation had to be suppressed in order to produce the correct 'no' response. Although there were few errors in classification of the non-words, the eventual 'no' decision took longer to make. However, there are a number of problems with the Rubenstein *et al.* study. Clark (1973) argued that a correct statistical analysis of the data showed that the effect was restricted to a subset of the pseudohomophones, and recently Taft (1982) and Martin (1982) have demonstrated that the pseudohomophone effect can be explained in terms of visual similarity rather than sound similarity – pseudohomophones *look* more like real words than do other non-words.

Meyer, Schvaneveldt and Ruddy (1974) asked subject to perform simultaneous lexical decisions on pairs of visually similar words that sounded either the same, for example *set wet*, or different, for example, *few sew*. The decisions for the rhyming pairs were faster, indicating again that the way a word sounds affects lexical access – in this case perhaps because the lexicon is arranged in terms of sound.

MacKay (1972) presented words very briefly, and asked subjects to detect misspellings. If the subjects were told what word they were supposed to be seeing, they were fairly good at detecting misspellings that sounded different from the target word, for example *wark* for *work*. However, misspellings that did not change the sound, *werk* for *work*, were hard to spot. McCusker and Gough (reported in Gough and Cosky, 1977) showed that, in a spelling error detection task, *werk* was also more difficult to detect as a spelling error for *work* than was *wark*. However, spelling checks may occur after lexical access, and may therefore be influenced by phonological information read out of the lexicon.

These experiments show that the way a written word sounds, as opposed to the way it looks, affects its behaviour in tasks in which the lexicon is accessed, such as lexical decision and reading. However, they provide only indirect evidence for phonological recoding, since subjects may undertake processing subsequent to accessing words from the lexicon. For example, it has been suggested (by Forster, 1976, among others) that, after lexical access, *post-access checks* are performed to confirm that the stimulus does correspond to the word accessed. Perhaps the sound of a visually presented word is important only after the word has been retrieved from the lexicon, and does not affect the retrieval itself. This kind of explanation of the results discussed so far would be consistent with other evidence that conflicts with the phonological recoding hypothesis. For example, in its purest form, the hypothesis predicts that the following should be read without any difficulty:

Two bee oar knot to bee.
Pas de leur rhone que nous.

If only the sound was important, then these two strings, which sound like English sentences, should not be hard to understand, which they clearly are. However, this anecdotal evidence is not very telling. Even in the first case, where the written words are English rather than French, the difficulties can be explained by post-access spelling checks that fail before any message has been apprehended. Real evidence against the phonological recoding hypothesis must come from experimental studies.

Baron (1973) asked subjects to classify phrases as either sensible or otherwise, and measured the time that they took. He compared phrases that sound sensible, such as *tie the not*, and ones that do not, such as *new I can't*. In both cases the correct answer is no, this is not a sensible phrase. Baron found no differences between the two kinds of phrase, though the phonological recoding hypothesis would predict more errors and/or longer classification times for phrases that sound sensible. However, it is unwise to draw a strong conclusion from this null result.

Forster and Chambers (1973) showed that subjects were quicker to name words than phonologically regular non-words. If words are named by recoding them phonologically, as non-words presumably are, there is no reason to expect this difference.

Perhaps the most telling evidence against any simple form of the phonological recoding hypothesis was provided by Kleiman (1975). He argued that if the sound of a word is important for classifying it, then there should be interference if the subject has to speak while making the classification, because both tasks will be competing for the limited resources of the phonological system. As an interfering task Kleiman chose digit shadowing – subjects had to repeat a series of digits presented to them over headphones. This task interfered with rhyming judgements, but not with visual similarity judgements or semantic relatedness judgements. The semantic judgements require lexical access, but, unlike the rhyming judgements, they do not require the sound pattern of the word to be retrieved. On the basis of these results Kleiman argued that phonological recoding was not always necessary for lexical access. To accommodate other findings Kleiman proposed the *dual access hypothesis* for visually presented words. This hypothesis states that such words can access the lexicon in two different ways, either by phonological recoding or by direct visual access (see Figure 3.6). Kleiman argued that lexical access via a phonological code was a reading strategy rarely used by the college students who served as subjects in his experiments. However, Coltheart (1978) claims that, in cases where the meaning of a word must be accessed, both methods are commonly used.

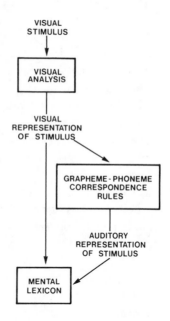

Figure 3.6 The dual access model

The dual access theory enjoys widespread popularity, despite the possibility that the sound of visually presented words may not affect lexical access itself, but only subsequent processing. This possibility is suggested by a number of observations. An experiment by Stanovich and Bauer (1978) showed that one phonological effect in visual lexical decision – words with regular spellings are recognized more quickly than irregular words – disappeared if subjects were required to react more quickly than they normally would. To encourage rapid responding subjects were given visual feedback ('fast' or 'slow') to indicate whether they had met a deadline. One explanation of this result is that when responding is speeded, there is no time for post-access checks. If this explanation is correct, phonological effects in lexical decision must occur at the time of these checks, and not during lexical access.

Levy (1978) showed that concurrent vocalization interfered with the understanding of connected prose only if subjects had to remember the exact wording of what they had read (for example, to detect synonym substitutions), and not if they had to detect only meaning changes. Levy interpreted this result to mean that, although phonological codes are used in comprehension, they are generated after lexical access, and are used to aid short-term retention of what has just been read. Similarly Slowiaczek and Clifton (1980) found that vocalization did not affect comprehension of single words, but it did affect the ability to relate one word to another.

Recently an alternative to the dual-access theory has been proposed by Glushko (1979) and by Kay and Marcel (1981). It is also discussed by McClelland and Rumelhart (1981; Rumelhart and McClelland, 1982) as a motivation for and elaboration of their model of letter recognition, which uses McClelland's (1979) idea of processes in cascade (that is a set of processes working simultaneously with the output of 'earlier' processes being fed continuously to 'later' ones). The theory is sometimes referred to as the *analogy theory*, as it claims that all letter strings, both words and non-words, are pronounced with reference to lexical entries for words with 'similar' spellings. One of the main problems in formulating the theory is to provide a satisfactory definition of similarity. The theory claims that there is only one route, not two, by which visually presented words access the lexicon. When a word is presented, information is fed into a system that performs analyses at three levels – features, letters (at particular positions in words, for example, 'a' as the third letter of a six-letter word) and words. Each feature or letter that is present counts as perceptual evidence for all the words of which it is a constituent, just as in the logogen model the presence of a feature counts as evidence for every word that has that feature. As in the logogen model, all entries that include the component are partially activated. However, unlike the logogen model, words that do not contain the features are inhibited.

The model accounts straightforwardly for phonological effects in visual word recognition, particularly in pronunciation experiments. Consider the English word-endings *-ope* and *-ove*. The first is always pronounced in the same way. Therefore when a word ending *-ope* is presented, every lexical entry that is activated provides the same information about its pronunciation, and hence there will be little delay in starting to speak. Similarly, a non-word ending in -*ope*, such as *gope* will be pronounced quickly. However, -*ove* is pronounced in at least three different ways in English, as in, for example, *move*, *cove* and *love*. When a word or non-word ending in -*ove* is presented, there will be conflicting information about how to pronounce it, and it cannot be spoken until the conflict is resolved. The model therefore predicts two effects in pronunciation. First, the *regularity effect* – words that are pronounced irregularly should be more difficult to say than those that are pronounced regularly. This effect is well established. It was investigated, for example, in Stanovich and Bauer's experiment. The effect is predicted because an irregularly pronounced word will activate lexical entries for regular words with similar spellings. Since, by definition, more words have the regular than the irregular pronunciation, there will be a tendency to regularize the pronunciation of irregular words. This tendency will manifest itself as either a mispronunciation or a delay in starting to speak until the mispronunciation is rejected. The analogy model has no plausible explanation of why the effect should disappear under speeded responding. The second effect predicted by the model is the *consistency effect* for both words and non-words. Letter strings that contain patterns, such as -*ope*, that are always pronounced in the same way should be easier to say than words that are themselves pronounced regularly, but that have 'visual neighbours' with other pronunciations. For example, there should be a delay in starting to say the regular word *mint* because there is one English monosyllable ending -*int*, *pint*, that is pronounced differently. Glushko (1979) reports consistency effects for both words and non-words.

Recent experiments suggest that both the regularity and consistency effects are restricted to smaller classes of words than simpler versions of the analogy model predict. Parkin (1984) showed that the regularity effect is confined to true exception words, and is not obtained with words such as *love*, which have an unusual but not unique spelling-to-sound correspondence (cf. *glove*, *shove*, and so on). Seidenberg, Waters, Barnes and Tanenhaus (1984) found that both the regularity and the consistency effects are restricted to uncommon words. Seidenberg *et al.* interpret their results as support for the more complex Rumelhart and McClelland version of the analogy theory, in which the rapid activation of high frequency words inhibits that of visually similar words more successfully than the slow activation of low frequency words.

Lexical ambiguity

In both spoken and written language some words are ambiguous. When such a word appears, the intended sense must be selected in order to interpret correctly the message of which the word forms part. A question that theories of lexical access must address is therefore whether all meanings of an ambiguous word become available when it is encountered or just one. Psycholinguists have suggested four answers to this question.

(1) The theory of *context-guided lexical access* states that contextual information ensures that only the relevant meaning of the ambiguous word is accessed. This theory is intuitively plausible, since ambiguities in sentences such as:

The farmer put the straw on the pile beside his threshing machine.

are seldom noticed, except in the context of a discussion of ambiguity (*straw* has several meanings). However, a major problem for the context-guided theory is that it is difficult to see how context could guide access in the required way. The relevant context often follows an ambiguous word, yet the word is identified when it is encountered.

(2) The *ordered access theory* of Hogaboam and Perfetti (1975) claims that when an ambiguous word is encountered its meanings are accessed serially in order of their frequency – the most common is accessed first, then the next most common, and so on. As each meaning is retrieved, it is checked against the context to see if it fits. If it does, it is accepted, if it does not, the next most frequent meaning is tried. This theory predicts that when ambiguous words have their most frequent meaning they are no harder to process than matched unambiguous words. But when they have their less frequent meaning they should take longer to interpret than control words.

(3) The *multiple access theory* states that when an ambiguous word is encountered all its meanings are accessed, and a choice is made among them when context allows. No single meaning is selected at the time the word is first processed. Just as the context-directed access theory is intuitively plausible, this theory is intuitively implausible, since alternative meanings of an ambiguous word are not usually noticed. However, as a theory of how context has its effects, it is more plausible than the guided access theory, particularly in cases where most of the context comes after the ambiguous word.

(4) A revised version of the multiple access theory has been proposed by Garrett and his colleagues (Garrett, 1970; Lackner and Garrett, 1972; Bever, Garrett and Hurtig, 1973). This revised theory claims that all meanings of an ambiguous word are accessed when it is

encountered, but that the ambiguity is always resolved by the end of the clause in which it occurs, even if this entails making an arbitrary decision about the intended meaning.

Evidence for multiple access   In the 1960s and 1970s the multiple access theory, either in its original form or its revised form, received support from a variety of studies. For example, MacKay (1966) showed that subjects took longer to start completing a sentence fragment containing an ambiguous word:

  After taking the right turn at the intersection, I . . .

than a corresponding fragment with an unambiguous word:

  After taking the left turn at the intersection, I . . . .

This result suggests that two meanings of the ambiguous fragments are being considered. In support of the revised version, Bever, Garrett and Hurtig (1973) found that such effects were much stronger in the clause in which the ambiguity occurred – if subjects had to start their completion after *at the* rather than after *I*.

The multiple access theory also received support from a series of experiments using the *phoneme-monitoring* technique. In such experiments subjects listen to sentences over headphones, and have to press a button as soon as they hear a word beginning with a specified sound, such as /b/ (here, and elsewhere, letters or words between oblique lines stand for their sounds). It is assumed that the time taken to respond to the target phoneme is a measure of local processing difficulty. Foss (1970; Foss and Jenkins, 1973) asked subjects to monitor phonemes following ambiguous and unambiguous words, for example *straw* and *hay*, respectively, in:

  The $\left\{\begin{array}{l}\text{farmer}\\\text{merchant}\end{array}\right\}$ put his $\left\{\begin{array}{l}\text{straw}\\\text{hay}\end{array}\right\}$ beside the machine.   (target /b/)

The result was that even with the stronger biasing context (*farmer* rather than *merchant*) subjects took longer to respond after the ambiguous word *straw* than after the matched unambiguous control word *hay*. Further experiments confirmed and extended these findings; Cairns and Kamerman (1975) showed that the effect lasted for about two words after the ambiguous word, and Swinney and Hakes (1976) found that the effect disappeared with strongly biasing contexts. However, all of these results were brought into question by Mehler, Segui and Carey (1978). Mehler *et al.* showed that the differences found by Foss and Jenkins disappeared if the ambiguous words and the controls were properly matched for length, and that the differences were in the opposite direction if the ambiguous words were longer than the controls. In the original experiments, which had all drawn on the same pool of materials, the ambiguous words were probably shorter. The subjects had therefore had less time to process the ambiguous words before they heard the target phoneme, so it was not surprising that the processing load was higher just after the ambiguous words, and that phoneme-monitoring was slower.

Mehler *et al.*'s findings did not refute the multiple access theory. The sentence completion results still provided support for it, as did experiments by Lackner and Garrett (1972) and MacKay (1973). These studies used a selective attention technique known as *dichotic listening* in which subjects hear two messages, one over each channel of a pair of headphones, and are instructed to attend to only one of them. In such experiments people are in the main unable to report what was presented on the unattended channel. Subjects attended to an ambiguous message, such as:

The spy put out the torch as our signal to attack.

The unattended message, which was presented 'subliminally' to the other ear, disambiguated the ambiguous verb-particle combination *put out*, which is probably represented in a single lexical entry. It was either

The spy extinguished the torch in the window.
OR The spy displayed the torch in the window.

The subjects' task was to paraphrase the attended message, and their performance was strongly affected by the unattended message. The fact that they could be biased towards either meaning suggests that both meanings are accessed.

Evidence for selective access   Not all experimental evidence has favoured multiple access. Schvaneveldt, Meyer and Becker (1976) asked subjects to make three successive lexical decisions on sequences such as:

save	bank	money
river	bank	money
day	bank	money

Lexical decision on *money* was speeded when the relevant meaning of *bank* had been primed, as in *save bank*, but not when the wrong meaning had been, *river bank*. Performance on the *day bank* trials was intermediate, presumably because the relevant meaning of the ambiguous word was accessed on some, but not all, occasions. Schvaneveldt *et al.* concluded that only one meaning of the ambiguous word becomes available, but their experiment produced no evidence for ordered access.

Hogaboam and Perfetti (1975) provided support for their frequency-ordered access model by showing that people are slow to detect ambiguities when an ambiguous word occurs in its most frequent sense, for example *letter* in:

The jealous husband read the letter.

With less frequent senses, for example in:

The antique typewriter was missing a letter.

the ambiguity is detected fairly quickly, suggesting that the most common meaning has already been brought to mind. Holmes (1979) obtained comparable results in a comprehension task, in which common and uncommon meanings of ambiguous words were compared with unambiguous high or low frequency synonyms of the senses. The results were that comprehension times for sentences with low frequency senses of ambiguous words were longer than those for sentences with high frequency senses of the same word, but there was no corresponding difference when the synonyms were substituted. A similar pattern of results was obtained when the relevant context followed the ambiguous word as when it came before. These results suggest that additional processing is required when ambiguous words are used with their less frequent meanings. According to the ordered access theory, this extra processing is the consideration and rejection of the more frequent meaning.

Some recent studies   Although the phoneme-monitoring experiments proved to be flawed, phoneme-monitoring has an important advantage over the techniques that provide support for frequency-ordered access – it provides an on-line measure of what happens when an ambiguous word is encountered. The classification and comprehension experiments of Hogaboam and Perfetti and of Holmes can indicate only how long it takes to make a judgement about a complete sentence. For this reason the results obtained using the new on-line technique of cross-modal priming are of great importance. In this technique subjects listen to sentences over headphones while watching a screen. At certain points in the sentence, letter strings appear on the screen, and subjects have to pronounce or make lexical decisions about these strings. Lexical decision should be speeded if the word that has just been heard is related to the one presented for lexical decision. This technique finds ready application to the study of ambiguity. After an ambiguous word has been heard, words associated with its different senses are presented on the screen. If the multiple access theory is correct, words related to all the senses of an ambiguous word should be responded to more quickly, but if access is ordered by frequency, then, in an appropriate context, only words related to the high frequency meaning will be recognized faster.

The experiments just outlined were performed by Swinney (1979) and by Tanenhaus, Leiman and Seidenberg (1979). In Swinney's experiment subjects heard passages such as:

> Rumour had it that, for years, the government building had been plagued with problems. The man was not surprised when he found several (spiders, roaches, and other) bugs [1] in the corner [2] of his room.

The words in parentheses were either omitted to produce a context that was neutral between the two meanings of the ambiguous word *bugs*, or included to provided a context that strongly favoured its more frequent meaning. [1] and [2] are the points at which items were presented for lexical decision. Decision times were compared for words related to the frequent and the infrequent meanings of the ambiguous words and for matched unrelated words. Words of the three kinds for the above example are *ant, spy* and *sew*. The results of the experiment were that 'cross-modal priming' was obtained at point [1] for both *ant* and *spy*, even with the strongly biasing context. However, by point [2] only *ant* was identified more quickly in the biasing context. These results suggest that when an ambiguous word is encountered all its meanings are initially accessed, but that context is very quickly able to select the appropriate one. Tanenhaus *et al.* obtained similar results in pronunciation, a finding that is of importance because of the possibility of postlexical effects, and in particular backwards priming, in the lexical decision version of the experiment (see Seidenberg, Waters, Sanders and Langer, 1984).

How, if at all, can Swinney's results be reconciled with Holmes's? The answer to this question depends on the fact that Holmes's results do not reflect what happens when an ambiguous word is encountered. As Swinney's results show, given an appropriate context, an irrelevant meaning of an ambiguous word can be eliminated before the end of the clause in whch it occurs. Holmes's results probably reflect the ease or difficulty with which judgements can be made about the unambiguous representation that has been constructed at the end of a sentence. Low frequency senses of ambiguous words produce longer latencies because more evidence is required that a low frequency sense is intended.

Finally, why do most lexical ambiguities go unnoticed, if all the meanings of an ambiguous word are accessed? The answer is that the processes that resolve ambiguities are largely unconscious, so we never become aware of the rejected senses.

Summary

The word recognition component of the language understanding system has to identify the words that are presented to it, and to make available information about their syntactic and semantic properties. Its primary source of information is perceptual, but it may be helped in its decision-making by contextual information. A theory of word recognition has to explain a number of well-established findings about the effects of word frequency, stimulus quality and context. It must also show how letter strings that have no entry in the mental lexicon are classified as non-words.

Two kinds of processes have been suggested as mediating word recognition: direct access of perceptual and contextual information to feature counters, and search through a set of lexical entries until a match is found. All viable models utilize both kinds of processes, but Morton's logogen model focuses on direct access, whereas Forster's model emphasizes search. Although both models can explain many experimental findings, each has problems in accounting for the full range of results. In particular, neither model can give a satisfactory account of inhibitory effects of inappropriate context. Several attempts have been made to amend the models to encompass these findings. The most common method is to add an attentional component to them. However, Norris has proposed a model that does not require assumptions about attention.

Two further issues are whether written words are translated into a phonological code before lexical access, and what happens when an ambiguous word is encountered. Although phonological recoding does not always occur, there is much evidence to suggest that the sound of a word sometimes affects the way it is processed. The standard explanation of these results is the dual access theory of Kleiman, but a recent alternative is the analogy theory, which does not incorporate the idea of phonological recoding. In addition there is the possibility that such effects reflect processing after access.

In the case of ambiguous words it appears that all the meanings of an ambiguous word are accessed when it is first encountered, but that, in an appropriate context, all but the relevant one can be discounted very quickly. This view is initially counter-intuitive, but it provides a framework in which the effects of context can be explained fairly easily. The experiments that appear to favour other theories of accessing ambiguous words do not use on-line measures, and, therefore reflect the ease of making judgements about the unambiguous representation that has been constructed by the end of a sentence containing an ambiguous word.

4

Parsing – the computation of syntactic structure

When the words in a sentence have been recognized and their syntactic categories retrieved from the mental lexicon, the language understanding system must compute the structural relations between those words, so that it can go on to determine the message that the sentence conveys. It should be stressed once again, however, that this sketch of the temporal relations between these processes is not meant to suggest that they operate in a strictly serial order. This point will be made clearer in chapter 8, where the question of interaction between subprocessors will be discussed in detail.

Before describing how structural information is computed it is necessary to consider when and why it is needed in comprehension. It has been suggested (e.g. Schank, 1972; Small and Rieger, 1982) that syntactic analysis can be bypassed, and sentence meaning derived directly from word meanings. In fact, it is not *in general* possible to forgo a structural analysis, though it may sometimes be. This point can be illustrated by considering one of the methods suggested for eliminating a full parse – the use of *case-frames*. In a number of theories of word meaning (for example, Schank's) every verb has one or more case-frames linked to it, which specify (i) the case-roles, such as AGENT, PATIENT and INSTRUMENT, that are associated with the action it denotes, and (ii) which of these case-roles are obligatory and which optional in sentences containing the verb. As an illustration of how a case-frame analysis is supposed to eliminate the need for a complete parse, consider the sentence:

The boy watered the flower.

The analysis proceeds as follows. First *watered* is identified as the main verb of the sentence. Its associated case-frame is then retrieved from semantic memory. This case-frame states that the verb requires two case fillers, an AGENT and a PATIENT, and it also imposes *selectional restrictions* on those case fillers, which delimit the kind of things that can take the case roles. For example, the AGENT that does the watering must be either animate or a natural agency such as rain. From the semantic information in the lexical entries for *boy* and *flower* the referents of the noun phrases in which these nouns occur can be assigned to the appropriate case roles, since, of the two noun phrases, only *the boy* refers to something animate. The boy is therefore the AGENT and the flower the PATIENT, and the meaning of the sentence is given by:

ACTION:	water	
TENSE:	past	
AGENT:	boy1	(some particular boy)
PATIENT:	flower1	(some particular flower)

However, even this derivation of the sentence's meaning assumes some syntactic analysis. For example, the two occurrences of the word *the* have been implicitly grouped with the nouns following them to form noun phrases.

There are many simple sentences that this kind of case-frame analysis cannot interpret, because they contain no semantic cues to the case-roles played by the NPs in them. Two sentences that such an analysis could not distinguish between are:

The boy saw the girl.
The boy was seen by the girl.

The most obvious way to derive the correct interpretation of such sentences is to use structural information.

Every other strategy for bypassing structural analysis that has been proposed also fails on some simple sentences. Furthermore, Forster (1979) has argued that the function of syntax is to allow implausible meanings to be conveyed. It follows that allowing semantic interpretation to bypass syntax would defeat the purpose of a structural analysis. Given this fact and the fact that natural languages contain many complex sentence types in which the same NPs have different relations to the same verb, it is probable that the language understanding system is able to, and often does, compute all the structural relations between the words in a sentence.

Chapter 2 outlined the way in which generative grammarians describe the syntactic structure of English sentences. Psycholinguists view syntax from a somewhat different perspective. There are two main questions that they ask. How is syntactic knowledge mentally represented, and how is that knowledge used in understanding and producing sentences? Although linguistic theory may impose certain restrictions on the correct answers to these questions, it cannot give detailed answers to them. As was stressed in chapter 2, a generative grammar is *not* a theory of sentence production or perception. In this context, the word *generative* has the abstract meaning explained in that chapter.

Early psycholinguistic research

The syntactic theory of Chomsky's *Syntactic Structures* was introduced into psychology by George Miller. Since Chomsky had stressed the central place of syntax in linguistic theory, the earliest psycholinguistic experiments investigated its role in sentence comprehension. The first studies established that syntax does influence sentence comprehension. Epstein (1961) had shown that nonsense syllables were easier to learn if they were put into a sentence frame than if they were presented as a list, suggesting a role for sentence structure in memory:

> The yigs wur vumly rixing hum in jigest miv.
> vs   The yig wur vum rix hum in jig miv.

Miller demonstrated the importance of syntactic structure in comprehension by asking subjects to listen to strings of words in noise, and then to report as many of the words as they could. Miller and Isard (1963) used three kinds of word strings: (a) ordinary sentences, (b) semantically anomalous sentences, constructed by swapping words between sentences. These strings had normal syntactic structure, but made no sense, (c) strings produced by jumbling up the words in type (b). Examples of the three kinds of strings are:

(a) Bears steal honey from the hive.
(b) Accidents carry honey between the house.
(c) On trains hive elephants the simplify.

Subjects reported more words from strings of type (a) than from strings of type (b), and more from type (b) than type (c). This pattern of results demonstrates that syntactic structure aids understanding, even when the words make no sense. In an extended version of this experiment Marks and Miller (1964) included a further kind of word string, which they called anagram strings. These were jumbled versions of type (a), and had no syntactic cues to aid comprehension, but did have semantic cues, for example:

(d) Deter drivers accidents fatal careful.

Such strings were about as easy to hear as strings of type (b), suggesting that both structure and meaning could enhance comprehension in the absence of the other.

The experiments reported so far show that syntax aids comprehension independently of any meaning carried by a string of words, although it is possible that subjects in Epstein's experiment remembered the sentence-like strings by imposing an interpretation on them. Many other experiments were also taken to demonstrate that syntactic structure affects the way sentences are understood, but in almost all of them syntactic and semantic variables were confounded – sentences that differed in structure also differed in meaning. The results of these experiments therefore had two possible explanations – one in terms of structure and one in terms of meaning. One typical experiment illustrates this point. Clifton, Kurtz and Jenkins (1965) taught subjects a series of sentences, and then gave them a yes/no recognition test. In this test the subjects generalized from the sentences they had learned, and recognized sentences that were syntactically related but which had not been presented. This experiment, unlike Miller's, cannot be interpreted unequivocally as demonstrating the effects of syntax on comprehension. The sentences to which the subjects generalized were semantically as well as syntactically related to the sentences they had learned, so their generalization could have been based either on structure or on meaning.

The understandable preoccupation with transformations, and a concomitant failure to consider all the factors that contribute to sentence comprehension, were the main reasons for the spate of uninterpretable results. Miller accepted that a generative grammar was not a theory of language use, and that a psycholinguistic theory must specify how grammatical rules are used in producing and understanding sentences. However, his initial hypothesis – the sensible one to adopt – was that the language understanding system uses the grammar in a straightforward way. Unfortunately, he focused his attention on one kind of grammatical rule – the transformation – at the expense of others.

The theory Miller put forward was intended to explain the 'perceptual complexity' of sentences – how difficult they are to understand. It was later dubbed the 'Derivational Theory of Complexity', because Miller hypothesized that the difficulty of understanding a sentence was primarily determined by the length of the derivation from its underlying kernel to its surface phrase marker in the grammar of *Syntactic Structures*. Miller's theory was, in outline, as follows. When a sentence is heard or read its surface phrase marker is computed – though Miller did not say how. From this phrase marker the phrase markers of the underlying kernel strings are recovered by reversing the transformations that apply in the derivation of the sentence. Thus, for example, if the phrase marker matches the *output* of the passive rule, as defined by the grammar, then the corresponding active is derived by reversing the transformation. Miller made the strong assumption that transformations were reversed serially and independently, and that each transformation took a fixed amount of time to reverse. He also implicitly assumed that transformations *could* be reversed. However, it was later shown (Peters and Ritchie, 1973) that there was no guarantee that underlying structure could be recovered from surface structure.

One further assumption of Miller's theory was that each time a transformation was reversed, a tag was attached to the resulting phrase marker, so that the final representation of a sentence was a kernel plus a set of tags that indicated the transformations needed to regenerate the sentence. This aspect of Miller's theory is referred to as the *kernel-plus-tags hypothesis* of the representation of sentences in memory. The tags indicate not only the surface form of the remembered sentence which, as chapter 7 will show, people are not very good at retaining, but also part of its meaning. In *Syntactic Structures*, Chomsky assumed that transformations could change meaning, so the kernel alone does not determine the meaning of a sentence (compare the 1965 theory in which deep structure contained all the information required for semantic interpretation). However, just as deep structure is a level of *syntactic* representation, not of meaning, the kernel and tags are not the meaning of a sentence. Therefore Miller's theory presupposed another component of the understanding system – one that computes the meaning of sentences from a canonical syntactic representation – kernel and tags.

The Derivational Theory has been described not because it is correct, but because it illustrates a number of pitfalls for theories of comprehension. First, any theory of language understanding must describe how several kinds of linguistic knowledge are used in the comprehension of sentences. The Derivational Theory only partly fulfils this requirement, and this fact gives rise to its principal weakness – untestability. Although numerous experimental tests of the theory were attempted – some apparently favouring it, others not – it was not amenable to experimental refutation. The experiments will not be described in detail, because they are of historical interest only, and they are covered more than adequately in such texts as Slobin (1971), Greene (1972), and particularly Fodor, Bever and Garrett (1974). Not only did the experiments fail to test the theory, it can be seen with hindsight that some of them would have been irrelevant, even if it had been testable. For example, Bever, Fodor, Garrett and Mehler (reported in Fodor, Bever and Garrett, 1974) found that:

John phoned the girl up.

was no more difficult to understand than:

John phoned up the girl.

though the former was, according to the then current syntactic theory, derivationally more complex – it had undergone the transformation of particle movement. More recent accounts of the relation between these two sentences are non-transformational, and hence the original experiment was irrelevant for this reason alone. However, it cannot be concluded that the Derivational Theory should be resurrected in a form consistent with current linguistic theory (see Garnham, 1983a). Even if the sentences had been related by a transformation, the experiment would not have been a test of the theory.

The reason why the Derivational Theory is untestable is as follows. In order to understand a sentence at least three sets of operations are required, according to what is explicit and implicit in the Derivational Theory. First, surface syntactic structure is computed. Second, an underlying syntactic representation is derived by reversing transformations. Third, the underlying representation is semantically interpreted to produce the meaning of the sentence. If it is found that, for example, passive sentences are more difficult to understand than actives, then the additional difficulty could lie in one or more of these three stages in comprehension. It cannot be concluded that the additional processing occurs only at the transformational stage.

By the late 1960s it was widely recognized that experiments that apparently supported the Derivational Theory had alternative semantic explanations (cf. Johnson-Laird, 1974), although the fact that they could often be explained in terms of surface structure differences was less widely noted. Psycholinguists began to lose interest in syntax, and embarked upon the experiments described in chapter 7 on semantic and pragmatic influences on the interpretation of sentences.

Perceptual Strategies

In the late 1960s and early 1970s there was comparatively little psycholinguistic work on syntax. The one important line of research was the attempt by Fodor, Bever, Garrett and their colleagues at MIT to develop an alternative to the Derivational Theory. However, their approach rested on two questionable assumptions. First, they assumed the Derivational Theory was false. This supposition was based on the fact that not all transformations increased the perceptual complexity of sentences – particle movement, for example, had no effect on comprehension. The conclusion that Fodor, Bever and Garrett drew from these experiments was that transformations are not used in understanding sentences.

Second, Fodor, Bever and Garrett thought that they had demonstrated the *psychological reality* of syntactic deep structures in a series of *click location* experiments (Fodor and Bever, 1965; Garrett, Bever and Fodor, 1966; Bever, Lackner and Kirk, 1969; see Fodor, Bever and Garrett, 1974, 329 – 42, for a discussion). In these experiments subjects listened to sentences, and in the course of each sentence they heard a click. They then had to indicate at what point in the sentence the click had occurred. The results were that subjects reported hearing the clicks closer to major syntactic boundaries than they actually were. Furthermore, where deep structure boundaries could be distinguished from surface structure boundaries, there was evidence that the apparent displacement of the clicks was towards the *deep* structure boundaries. However, since deep structure boundaries inevitably coincide with semantic boundaries, these findings, like most other early psycholinguistic results, could have either a syntactic or a semantic explanation.

Fodor, Bever and Garrett developed a theory in which deep structure relations were computed – but not by reversing transformations. They proposed that people employ *heuristic strategies* that compute deep structural relations from cues in surface structure together with information stored in the mental lexicon. These cues were assumed to be, in some sense, perceptual, and hence the strategies were referred to as perceptual strategies.

The new theory had to explain why some sentences are more difficult to understand than others. As a first step towards accounting for these differences, Fodor, Garrett and Bever (1968) proposed the *Verb Complexity Hypothesis.* This hypothesis is based on the observation that some verbs appear in more kinds of verb phrase than others. For example, the verb *meet* can be either intransitive, as in *we met,* or it can take a simple NP as its direct object. *Know,* on the other hand, as well as having an intransitive use, *we know,* can take either an NP object or a sentential complement. Thus, if a sentence begins:

Bill met John...

it is already clear that John is the person who was met. However, in the corresponding:

Bill knew John...

John could be either Bill's acquaintance, or the subject of a sentential complement such as *(Bill knew) John was rich.* Therefore, other things being equal, there should be more perceptual difficulty in processing a sentence with *know* as its main verb than one with *meet.*

Holmes and Forster (1972) tested the Verb Complexity Hypothesis in an experiment using the *Rapid Serial Visual Presentation* (RSVP) technique. In RSVP words are presented on a screen one at a time in rapid succession and, after the last word, subjects are asked to report all the words they can remember. Holmes and Forster found that more words were remembered from sentences with simple verbs (such as *meet*) than from sentences with complex verbs (such as *know*). As the sentences were matched in other respects, this finding was taken as evidence in favour of the hypothesis.

A better test of the Verb Complexity Hypothesis is one in which an on-line measure of processing difficulty – phoneme-monitoring time – is taken as the verb in a sentence is read. Hakes (1971) presented subjects with sentences such as:

The manager { suspended   (SIMPLE VERB) } the book-keeper when
            { suspected (COMPLEX VERB) }
he discovered that five thousand dollars was missing.

(examples from Foss and Hakes, 1978). Although there was no difference in monitoring times for the target phoneme /b/ in book-keeper, whether it followed the simple or the complex verb, there was evidence from the accuracy of paraphrases that sentences with complex verbs were more difficult to understand – the paraphrases were less accurate for these sentences. In some ways it was unfortunate that the on-line measure did not support the Verb Complexity Hypothesis. However, the results are consistent with another claim made by Fodor, Bever and Garrett, namely that major syntactic and semantic processing is delayed until clause boundaries.

The ambiguity in the role of a noun phrase following a complex verb can be resolved by the presence of an explicit sentential complementizer, such as *that* in the sentence:

Bill knew that John was rich.

For Fodor, Bever and Garrett the complementizer was a surface structure cue to a deep structure relation, and could be used by a perceptual strategy. Hakes (1972) provided support for this idea by showing that phoneme-monitoring was quicker in the presence of a sentential complementizer than in its absence. He presented subjects with sentences such as the following, in which the target phoneme was /o/ (at the beginning of a word):

The world famous physicist forgot (that) his old professor had been the first to suggest the crucial experiment to him.

Fodor and Garrett (1967) had pointed out that the word *that* also provides a surface cue to deep structure relations when it is used as a relative pronoun introducing a relative clause. For example, in:

The boy (that) the girl saw left.

the presence of *that* resolves a potential ambiguity between a reading of the sentence in which *the girl* is the subject of the relative clause, and a reading in which that noun phrase is part of a conjoined subject of the main clause:

The boy the girl and the dog walked in the park.

Hakes and Foss (1970) showed that the presence of relative pronouns reduced phoneme-monitoring times in sentences with relative clauses, such as:

The puzzle (that) the youngster (who) the tutor taught devised bewildered the mathematicians. (target /b/)

Bever's strategies

The most elaborate set of non-transformational strategies for interpreting sentences was devised by Bever (1970). Bever intended that his strategies should explain not only why some sentences take longer than others to understand, but also the mistakes people make in interpreting sentences. Bever formulated over a dozen strategies. Some of the most important are shown in Table 4.1. However, Bever's theory was far from adequate as a

Table 4.1 Examples of Bever's strategies

(a) In any sentence, the first clause with a . . . Noun. . . Verb. . . (Noun). . . sequence is the main clause, unless it is marked as subordinate by a subordinating conjunction.
(b) Any Noun Verb Noun sequence is to be interpreted as actor-action-object.
(c) After a DET(erminer), which signals the beginning of a Noun Phrase, the end of the NP is indicated by one of the following: (i) a plural morpheme, such as -s, (ii) a morpheme that indicates the beginning of a new phrase, such as *the*, *that*, *will*, *may*, or *should*, (iii) a word that is probably not a noun, for example, a verb that is only rarely used as a noun.

---

theory of comprehension. He did not produce a complete set of strategies; he failed to explain how conflicts between strategies would be resolved – what would happen if two strategies could both be applied to interpret a sentence; and he did not explain how the limitations of the strategies could be overcome. In cases where the strategies initially lead to an error – for example in garden path sentences – some explanation is needed of how a correct interpretation is eventually derived. For example, strategy (a) in Table 4.1 produces the wrong interpretation for:

The editor authors the newspaper hired liked laughed.

It analyses *authors* as a verb with *the newspaper* as its direct object. The correct reading requires that *authors* be reanalysed as a noun – the direct object of *hired*.

Models of parsing

No one ever worked out what proportion of English sentences Bever's strategies could analyse correctly. Most psycholinguists did not care. Their attention had shifted from syntax to meaning. However, some of the facts that Fodor, Bever and Garrett attempted to explain, for example the difficulty of understanding *centre-embedded* sentences, were, for reasons connected with syntactic theory, also of interest to linguists. In a centre-embedded sentence one clause interrupts another, with perhaps another clause interrupting it. For example, a relative clause may be inside another relative clause, as in:

The rat that the cat that the dog chased bit ran away.

Chomsky (1965, 11–12) argued that no principle of English grammar could sensibly limit the number of centre-embeddings in one sentence. He therefore proposed that the difficulty of understanding centre-embedded sentences should be explained by a theory of performance, rather than by claiming that such sentences were ungrammatical. In the early 1970s one linguist in particular – John Kimball – began to consider, from a linguistic viewpoint, how a model of parsing could account for performance limitations. If the operation of the parser could explain why centre-embedded sentences are hard to understand, then Chomsky's claim that this difficulty need not be explained by the grammar would be vindicated.

Kimball's seven principles

Kimball (1973) effectively proposed a theory of *surface structure parsing* – a theory of how the language understanding system computes the surface structure of sentences. Although his model is a two-stage model, in which the second stage computes deep structure relations, the focus of attention is, as the title of his paper suggests, on surface structure.

Kimball's approach differs from Bever's in two main ways. First, he assumes that the parser uses grammatical rules. Hence it has the potential to interpret every sentence that the grammar generates. Whether it successfully parses all these sentences depends on the principles by which it applies the rules. Second, unlike Bever and most other psycholinguists, Kimball attempted to explain the way in which *surface structure* is computed, and to explain some difficulties in sentence comprehension with reference to how that computation is carried out. Kimball's work is not important for its specific proposals – they are probably wrong – but because it brought to the attention of psycholinguists the need, in a theory of language comprehension, for an account of the way surface syntactic structure is computed. Many psycholinguists still neglect this topic.

Although Kimball's theory is not the final word on parsing, it will be presented in detail as an illustration of the form that a theory of surface structure parsing might take. Kimball's starting point is the assumption that surface syntactic structure is described by a set of phrase-structure rules. In the context of transformational generative grammar, in which Kimball was working, these rules are not necessarily the same as the phrase-structure rules of the base component that generates deep structures. It is the rules of surface phrase structure and the lexical categories of words that Kimball assumes the parser has access to. His parser follows seven principles in attempting to construct phrase markers, which group words into phrases and sentences. By proposing these seven principles Kimball hoped to explain a number of facts about language understanding.

Kimball's general aim was to explain why sentences are assigned the phrase markers that they are. He did not assume that by the end of a sentence its phrase marker is stored in memory, simply that the syntactic relations expressed in the phrase marker have been computed. Once these relations have been used, they may be discarded. If they are used before the end of the sentence, then a complete phrase marker may never be constructed. Kimball's theory is supposed to explain not only how phrase markers are computed, but also why people have difficulty in parsing some sentences, and why they miss some interpretations of potentially ambiguous sentences. His parser, therefore, has difficulty in analysing the following sentences, all of which are assigned phrase markers by widely accepted phrase-structure rules:

That that that $2+2=4$ surprised John astonished Mary bothered Sue.
The boat floated down the river sank.
The girl the man the boy saw kissed left.

And it finds only one interpretation for the following sentences, both of which are assigned two phrase markers by uncontroversial rules.

John believes that Susan left to be interesting.
The woman got the job that was attractive.

The 'difficult' interpretations are, in the first case, that what John believes to be interesting is the fact that Susan left, and, in the second case, that the woman, not the job, was attractive.

In order to explain these facts, Kimball proposed the following seven principles.

(1) *Parsing is top-down, except when a conjunction is encountered.* Parsers may work in either a *top-down* or a *bottom-up* manner. A top-down parser constructs a phrase marker from the top down, starting at the S node. To operate in this way, it must predict, on the basis of surface phrase-structure rules, what constituents the sentence will contain. A top-down parser begins its operations by using a rule that expands S (for example, S → NP VP), to predict the major phrasal constituents of the sentence, in this case an NP followed by a VP. Then it uses a rule for expanding NP to predict, say, a DET followed by an N. These last predictions are of words from specified syntactic classes, so the parser can check to see if the first two words in the sentence belong to these categories. If they do, it attempts to find the VP, if they do not, it must backtrack to its last decision point – a point at which it decided to try one of a number of possible rules for expanding the same node – and try a different one. A bottom-up parser, on the other hand, starts by looking up the categories of the words in the input, and then builds higher-level nodes above them, again by making reference to phrase structure rules. It therefore constructs the phrase marker from the bottom upwards. Kimball's claim is that parsing is top-down. He makes an exception of conjunctions because almost any node can be made up of conjoined constituents. For example, an NP such as *the boys* could equally well be *the boys and the girls*. It would therefore be very wasteful to predict every possible conjunction.

If a grammar contains many alternative expansions for its phrasal categories, a top-down parser will frequently have to backtrack, undoing analyses that it has already performed. Kimball thought that people did not backtrack very much (see Principle 6 below). He therefore proposed a facility of *limited lookahead,* to avoid the necessity of backtracking. Lookahead is also used to disambiguate words that belong to several syntactic categories. Such words, particularly at the beginnings of sentences, are difficult to interpret correctly. One example of such a word is *that,* which can be, among other things, a noun, an adjective or a complementizer:

That is a nice flower.
That boy is her brother.
That the boy left astounded us.

Kimball thought that the ability to look ahead to the next one or two words would be sufficient in a model of the human sentence parsing mechanism.

(2) *The Principle of Right Association* states that words are preferentially attached to the lowest possible non-terminal node in the partial phrase marker so far constructed. This principle ensures that phrase markers have the right-branching structure that is typical of English sentences – nodes on the right-hand side of a tree tend to be further expanded rather than those on the left-hand side. The principle of Right Association explains why the pre-ferred interpretation of the following sentence is *take out* rather than *figure out*, though both would be permitted by English grammar.

John figured that Susan wanted to take the cat out.

In the favoured interpretation *out* is attached under the lowest VP node, the one that dominates *take the cat,* whereas in the other reading it would be attached under the highest VP, *figured that Susan wanted to take the cat.* In the phrase marker below, as in some of those following, dashed lines indicate alternative attachments.

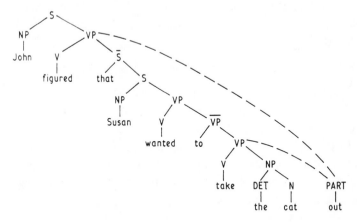

Right Association also explains why:

John figured that Susan wanted to take the train to New York out.

is difficult to interpret. The only reasonable interpretation of this sentence is *figure out,* with the particle *out* attached high in the tree.

There are apparent exceptions to Right Association, for example:

Joe drove down the street in the car.

Kimball assumed that semantic factors rule out the favoured syntactic interpretation (the street is in the car) and force a reanalysis in which the prepositional phrase *in the car* is attached to the comparatively high VP *drove down the street* rather than under a lower NP dominating *the street in the car*. This NP is not present in the correct analysis of the sentence. Kimball, therefore, predicts (see Principle 6) that such sentences are comparatively difficult to understand.

(3) *The Principle of New Nodes* states that a *grammatical function word*, such as a preposition, a determiner or a complementizer signals that a new phrasal node, for example a PP, NP or S̄ (a sentential complement) in the cases just mentioned, should be constructed. It is for this reason, according to Kimball's theory, that the deletion of complementizers can make sentences difficult to understand.

(4) *The Principle of Two Sentences* restricts the parser to analysing daughters of (that is nodes immediately dominated by) just two S nodes at a time. This principle explains the difficulty of understanding centre-embedded sentences, since centre-embedding splits up the daughter NPs and VPs of the outer S nodes. When there are two embedded clauses, daughters of three S nodes, including the one dominating the outermost clause, will all be incomplete. Right branching paraphrases of centre-embedded sentences do not cause problems:

The boy fed the dog that chased the cat that bit the rat. . . .

In such sentences, although none of the Ss are complete until the end, it is not the *daughters* of the earlier S nodes that remain to be found, but constituents at a lower level in the tree.

(5) *The Principle of Closure* states that a phrasal node is assumed to be complete as soon as possible – that is to say unless the next node is a possible daughter of it. Bever's N...V...N strategy (Table 4.1, strategy a) is a special case of the principle of closure, in which a clause is taken to be complete as soon as possible.

(6) *The Principle of Fixed Structure* states that when a phrase has been closed it is computationally costly to reorganize its constituents, and hence reorganization is avoided if possible. This principle explains the difficulty that people have in interpreting garden path sentences, such as:

The horse raced past the barn fell.

In this sentence, the verb *raced* is initially interpreted as the main verb of the sentence. The correct analysis requires a reorganization in which it becomes the verb of a reduced relative clause qualifying *horse.*

(7) The Final Principle is called '*Processing*'. It states that when a phrase is closed it exits from short-term memory into a second syntactic/semantic processing stage where deep structure relations are computed. The reason why phrases must exit from STM is that it has a limited capacity.

The seven principles are not independent. Kimball argues that (3), (4), (5) and (6) all follow from (7), except that (7) does not constrain (4) to be a principle of *two* sentences, rather than some other number.

Although Kimball shared some of the goals of Derivational Theorists – for example explaining why some sentences are harder than others to understand – his approach is completely different from theirs. It is not incompatible with the idea that reverse transformations are applied in the Processing Unit, but it explains the perceptual complexity of sentences not in terms of what happens in that unit, but in terms of how difficult their surface structure trees are to compute. Unlike the data that were supposed to support the Derivational Theory, Kimball's observations cannot for the most part be explained semantically, because the readings of sentences that are difficult to compute are not semantically anomalous or complex. It could be that their meanings are difficult to derive from their phrase markers but, on the assumptions about the relation of syntax and semantics that will be introduced in chapter 5, it is difficult to argue this case convincingly. Since Kimball's principles are primarily concerned with the computation of surface structure, they do not assume the existence of transformations, and are compatible with a Generalized Phrase-Structure account of natural language syntax (see chapter 2). Furthermore, in GPSG the rules of the grammar *are* the rules describing surface phrase markers – there can be no mismatch between the two sets of rules.

The sausage machine

Frazier and Fodor (1978), working in the same general framework as Kimball, proposed a rather simpler account of the human sentence parsing mechanism. In their model, surface structure phrase markers are derived in two stages, as they are in Kimball's model – the Processing Unit assembles phrases as well as deriving underlying relations. The first stage of Frazier and Fodor's parser is called the Preliminary Phrase Packager (PPP or sausage machine). It has a viewing window of about six words. It can, therefore, attach words to structures that contain the previous five words, but cannot make attachments that reflect dependencies over longer distances. The second stage is the Sentence Structure Supervisor (SSS). It assembles the packages produced by the PPP into an overall phrase marker for the sentence, but it does not undo the work of the PPP. The limited capacity of human short-term memory is therefore reflected in different ways in Kimball's model and in Frazier and Fodor's. Kimball restricts the number of clauses that can be analysed simultaneously, Frazier and Fodor restrict the number of words that can be considered at any time. In the original version of their model Frazier and Fodor imposed only one additional condition, other than the *short-sightedness* of the PPP, on the operation of their parser. Both the PPP and the SSS were governed by the principle of *Minimal Attachment*. This principle says that, of two possible ways of attaching a node to a partial phrase marker, the simpler will be preferred. The simpler attachment is the one with fewer nodes intervening between the new node and the existing phrase marker. Because of the limited viewing capacity of the PPP the attachment that it makes can only be minimal in a local context, and may not be in the complete phrase marker for the sentence. For this reason Fodor and Frazier (1980) renamed the principle *Local Attachment*.

Frazier and Fodor claim that the facts subsumed under the principle of Right Association by Kimball are explained by their parsing principles, without the need for a principle of Right Association to be explicitly stated. Furthermore, they argue that when certain additional facts are taken into consideration, their account is preferable to Kimball's. These additional facts suggest that words are only Right Associated in sentences that are too long to fit into the window of the PPP. Thus, in:

John bought the book for Susan.

there is no tendency to favour the *book for Susan* interpretation rather than the *bought for Susan* interpretation. In fact the reverse is true, although Kimball's principle would predict that the former reading should be chosen. However, in longer sentences a low right attachment *is* preferred, according to Frazier and Fodor. For example, the sentence:

John bought the book that I had been trying to obtain for Susan.

is most naturally interpreted as meaning *obtain for Susan* rather than *bought for Susan*. Frazier and Fodor explain the favoured *bought for Susan* interpretation in the shorter sentence by the principle of Minimal Attachment, as can be seen by counting the nodes in the phrase markers below. However, in the longer sentence, the PPP cannot see the possibility of the high attachment that gives the *bought for Susan* interpretation and it has no option but to

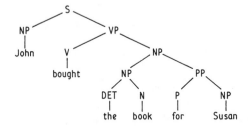

make the low attachment. Thus Frazier and Fodor's parser apparently obeys the principle of Right Association in longer sentences, but there is no explicit statement of that principle in their theory.

The limited window of the PPP also explains why centre-embedded sentences are difficult to understand. As the PPP parses:

The rat the cat the dog bit chased ran away.

it cannot see the verbs and the nouns together. The principle of Minimal Attachment predicts that the nouns will be analysed as a conjoined structure, and passed on to the SSS as such. Counting the nodes in the trees on page 86 shows why the conjoined structure is favoured.

However, if appropriate phrases in centre-embedded sentences are lengthened, then those sentences should be easier to understand as their constituents will be passed on to the SSS in such a way that they can be correctly assembled – there is no limit on the amount of material that the SSS can handle. For example, the vertical lines in the following sentence indicate the way in which it will be split up by the PPP, on the assumption that the PPP starts a new package when it can complete a phrase with five or six words in it.

The very beautiful young woman | the man the girl loved | met on a cruise ship in Maine | died of cholera in 1962.

Often a grammatical function word provides a clue as to where a package should be started. The packages marked in the sentence above are structurally

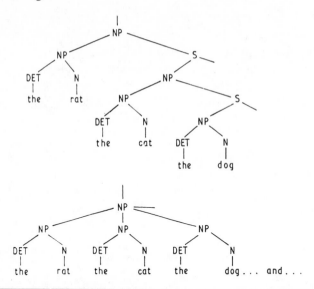

unambiguous, and can be assembled by the SSS to produce the correct phrase marker for the whole sentence. Frazier and Fodor claim that the sentence is relatively easy to understand.

That sentence should be contrasted with one in which different constituents have been lengthened, and which cannot be split up into packages that the PPP analyses correctly. It is very hard to understand.

> The woman the sad and lonely old man the pretty little schoolgirl loved with all her heart met died.

Frazier and Fodor's parser is more satisfactory than Kimball's in two ways. First, it uses fewer principles, and the principles are independent. Second, it accounts for a wider range of data. However, Wanner (1980) pointed out some problems for the model. These problems arise in short (six-word) sentences that ought to be parsed entirely by the PPP. Wanner identified two classes of sentences that do not behave as Frazier and Fodor's theory predicts.

> (1) There are some triply centre-embedded sentences with only six words in them, and they are just as difficult to interpret as longer sentences of the same kind, despite the fact that they fit into the window of the PPP.
>
> Women men girls love meet die.
>
> It cannot be argued that the PPP should analyse the initial NPs as

the beginning of a long conjunction, because it can see that there are three verbs to be analysed as well, and their presence is not consistent with the NPs being a conjunction. Frazier and Fodor imply that the PPP can analyse any six-word sentence.

(2) There are some six-word sentences in which Right Association operates, for example:

Tom said that Bill died yesterday.

The natural interpretation of this sentence is *died yesterday*, as predicted by Right Association, and not *said yesterday*. Frazier and Fodor cannot explain why one reading is preferred to the other, since both attachments require the same number of nodes, and Minimal Attachment cannot choose between them.

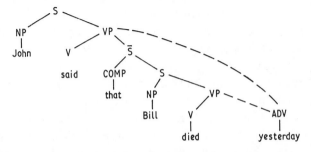

These cases led Fodor and Frazier (1980) to propose a revised version of their theory with an additional principle of Right Association, which operates only when Minimal Attachment cannot determine where a constituent should be attached to a phrase marker. An alternative suggestion (Milsark, 1983) is that the window of the PPP should not be limited to six words, but to a single clause.

Parsers in artificial intelligence

Although there has been comparatively little work on parsing in psychology, in AI, where people have tried to devise computer programs for understanding natural language, the problems of assigning structural analyses to strings of words could not be ignored. Many different approaches have been taken. In some projects, such as those of Schank and his colleagues (e.g. Schank, 1975), contemporary linguistic theory was rejected, and the structural categories employed by the parser defined semantically, violating Chomsky's principle of the autonomy of syntax. In others (e.g. Winograd, 1972) transformational grammar was rejected in favour of one of its rivals – in this case Halliday's (1970) systemic grammar. Many AI programs use a kind of parser called an *augmented transition network* (ATN), devised by Woods (1970, but anticipated in the work of Thorne, Bratley and Dewar, 1968), and capable of operating with many kinds of grammar, including transformational grammars. ATNs are powerful devices – as powerful as transformational grammars – and they have also been used in models of the human sentence parsing mechanism. However, there is little empirical content to the claim that the human parser is an ATN – about as little as there is in the claim that the grammar of English is transformational. A *theory* of parsing must make much more specific claims than that.

Before considering theories of parsing based on ATNs, it is necessary to describe ATNs in more detail. Chapter 2 outlined Chomsky's arguments that natural languages do not have finite-state grammars, and that the language understanding system is not a finite-state automaton. Chomsky's reaction was to develop more adequate kinds of *grammars* for natural languages. An alternative ploy would have been to develop automata better suited to describing language understanding. This is the route that leads to ATNs, which correspond to transformational grammars in the way that finite-state automata correspond to finite-state grammars.

An ATN comprises a set of transition networks, each one like the finite-state automaton described in chapter 2, except that changes of state in the transition networks can occur not only when a word is analysed, but also

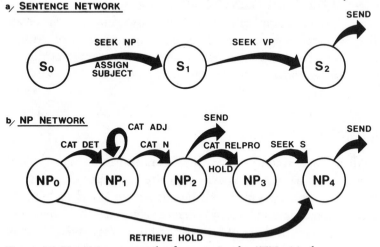

Figure 4.1 Transition networks from a simple ATN: (a) the sentence network (b) the noun phrase network.
(*Source* Wanner and Maratsos, 1978)

when a phrase is analysed. The top level network – the one that searches for sentences – might require that an NP be found first then a VP (see Figure 4.1a). A realistic sentence network would be more complex, so that it could cope with a wider variety of sentence structures. In the simple network of Figure 4.1a the first arc can be crossed when an NP is found. This NP is sought by a lower-level network (see Figure 4.1b). The set of networks is recursive, since the net that is trying to find, for example, an NP might at some stage call itself to find another NP embedded within the first one. Similarly other phrases, and also sentences, can be embedded inside other constituents of the same kind. When a net calls another net, a record must be kept of where the call came from, so that, for example, once an NP has been found, control can be passed back to the sentence level net and a VP sought, following the NP.

A recursive set of transition networks is equivalent to a context-free phrase-structure grammar of the kind discussed in chapter 2. Such networks can be *augmented* by conditions on the arcs and actions to be performed when the arcs are traversed. It is these actions that perform the work of transformations. For example, the first NP in a sentence will initially be labelled SUBJECT (action performed on traversing an arc). However, if a passive verb form is later encountered a further action will have to be performed, namely the relabelling of the current SUBJECT as OBJECT.

There are four main classes of arcs in ATNs: CAT, SEEK, JUMP and SEND. A CAT arc is traversed when an item from a specified lexical category, such as N or V, is found. SEEK is the corresponding arc for phrasal categories, such as NP or VP. JUMP allows a movement between two states without any constituent being found. It is used to omit optional constituents, such as the initial determiner in the NP in Figure 4.1b. SEND returns control to the higher-level network once a lower-level constituent has been analysed. Occasionally a fifth kind of arc, the WORD arc, is introduced. This kind of arc can be traversed when a specified word is discovered in the input.

Two things should be apparent from the above description of ATNs. First, an ATN is a top-down parser. It starts with control in the sentence network – it is searching for a predicted sentence in the input. Control then passes to the NP network – an NP is predicted, and so on. Second, the ATN, unlike Kimball's parser and the sausage machine, is a one-stage parser. It comprises a set of transition networks together with a schedule that determines the order in which it attempts to traverse the arcs in parsing a sentence. Scheduling principles can be used to explain facts about human parsing.

ATNs were introduced into psycholinguistic research by Ron Kaplan (1972) and Eric Wanner. For many years their research, though widely known, remained unpublished. A summary can be found in Wanner and Maratsos (1978). Wanner's main interest was in relative clauses, and in particular in the difference in difficulty between *subject-relative* and *object-relative* clauses – subject-relatives are easier to understand. The terms *subject-* and *object-* in these phrases refer to whether the head noun of the relative clause is interpreted as the subject or object of that clause. For example, the first sentence below is a subject-relative, because it is the witch who did the despising (she is the subject of *despised*). The second is an object-relative, because the witch is the object of *despised*.

The witch who *t* despised sorcerers frightens little children.
The witch whom sorcerers despised *t* frightens little children.

The *t* indicates where material is missing in the relative clause, if it is compared with a corresponding main clause. For example, in the second sentence *the witch* is missing after *despised,* because the corresponding main clause is *sorcerers despised the witch.*

Wanner devised a technique for measuring the transient processing load at various points in a sentence, by interrupting it and presenting a set of unrelated words to be recalled after it has been completed. He found that object-relatives produced more difficulty than subject-relatives when they were interrupted within the relative clause, but not otherwise. In order to explain this finding Wanner and Maratsos proposed the HOLD hypothesis for the interpretation of relative clauses. This hypothesis claims that a relative pronoun, such as *who*, causes the preceding NP (the head NP of the relative clause), *the witch* in the above example, to be entered in a special HOLD register. The relative clause is then interpreted by the normal set of transition networks, except that at some point within the relative clause one of the NPs is analysed by the RETRIEVE HOLD arc (see Figure 4.1b). No lexical material is required to traverse this arc, but information about the underlying subject (in subject-relatives) or object (in object-relatives) of the verb in the relative clause is available from the NP in the HOLD register. The clause can therefore be interpreted correctly. It is further assumed that HOLDing an NP produces a memory load. Therefore, in the middle of an object-relative, before the point at which the object is missing, processing is comparatively difficult, because the head NP is still in the HOLD register, but at the same point in the subject-relative processing is easier, because the item in the HOLD register has already been retrieved at subject position.

Wanner (1980) showed that, contrary to a claim by Frazier and Fodor

(1978), an ATN model of parsing could incorporate the principles of Minimal Attachment and Right Association. These principles correspond to simple scheduling rules in the ATN. Right Association is achieved by attempting to traverse CAT and SEEK arcs before SEND and JUMP arcs. The effect of this rule is that a constituent will be analysed as part of a lower constituent if it can be, before control is passed back to a higher level. JUMPing over an optional constituent and then SENDing could have the effect that, say, a PP that might have been incorporated into the lower constituent has to be analysed as part of the higher constituent that is SENT to. This possibility is avoided by scheduling CAT and SEEK before JUMP. Minimal Attachments are made by attempting to traverse CAT (and WORD) arcs before SEEK arcs. Thus, if a word can be incorporated directly into a phrase marker it will be. Extra intervening nodes will be constructed only if they are necessary.

ATN parsers have been successfully employed in a number of applied AI projects, such as the BBN LUNAR system (Woods, 1977), which was used to store information and answer questions about rocks brought back from the moon. They can also, as in Wanner and Maratsos's work, be used to model the human sentence parsing mechanism. However, a top-down algorithm is in some ways inappropriate in a model of the human parser. For a language such as English, with many different rules for expanding its phrasal categories, a top-down parser, even with a good set of scheduling principles, is likely to make many incorrect predictions, and spend much of its time backtracking. Much of this wasted effort can be avoided by using a parsing algorithm that is either partly or completely bottom-up. Almost every parser identifies words bottom-up. It would be foolish, whenever a noun is predicted, to check each noun of the language in turn, top-down. A further problem for top-down parsers is that they can enter a loop from which they never exit, if the grammar contains *recursive* rules of the form $X \rightarrow X \ldots$, in which the symbol on the left-hand side is also the first symbol on the right-hand side. In such cases one network (NP in the example below) keeps calling itself. Such rules are required for English constructions such as:

John's mother's brother's umbrella.

```
                              |
                              NP
                           DET    \
                        NP          N
                     DET   \        |
                  NP         N    umbrella
               DET  \        |
            NP        N    brother  's
            |       mother  's
            N
          DET  \
        NP       N
        |      mother   's
        N
      John    's
```

A recent alternative to ATN parsers is Marcus's (1980) PARSIFAL. This parser uses a mixture of bottom-up and top-down principles. An important feature of Marcus's project was his decision to build a *deterministic* parser – one that avoids backtracking by the use of limited lookahead similar to that proposed by Kimball. However, Marcus limits the amount of lookahead to a certain number of *constituents* (three), rather than a certain number of words. These constituents are already partly analysed, but their final place in the parse tree has not been determined. He claims that PARSIFAL, equipped with this limited look-ahead will make parsing errors only on sentences that produce genuine garden paths when people read them, for example:

> The balled rolled across the grass burst.

Although PARSIFAL has proved fairly successful in parsing the kinds of sentences that people have no conscious difficulty with, Johnson-Laird (1983, 314) has shown that there are sentences with syntactic ambiguities that cannot be resolved within three constituents. For example, in many topicalized sentences, it is not possible to tell from the first three constituents where the topicalized word or phrase comes from. A sentence beginning *Tom, I like. . .* could end in a number of ways, in particular:

> Tom, I like *t* to tell jokes.
> OR Tom, I like to tell jokes to *t*.

In each case the *t* indicates the position in an untopicalized sentence in which *Tom* would appear. PARSIFAL would have difficulty in analysing these sentences, but people do not.

Another way to avoid backtracking, one that is especially useful for phrase-structure languages, is to maintain a record of all possible analyses. For context-free languages it can be shown that once a sequence of words has been analysed as, say, a noun phrase it need never be reanalysed. To put this more technically, any *well-formed substring* of a sentence will be analysed the same way in all parses of the sentence. A model of the human sentence parsing mechanism based on the idea of well-formed substring tables has been developed by Johnson-Laird (1983). Johnson-Laird's parser uses the *left-corner* parsing algorithm, so-called because construction of a phrase marker for any constituent begins at its bottom left-hand corner. This algorithm analyses right-branching structures – the most typical kind in English – in a top-down manner. Such structures are usually found inside major constituents, and have a predictable structure of the kind that lends itself to top-down analysis. The algorithm analyses left-branching structures and the beginnings of constituents bottom-up. Left-branching structures, as mentioned above, pose problems for top-down analysis, and it is much more difficult to predict which constituent will come next, than to predict how the current constituent will end. Hence top-down analysis is an inefficient way of determining what the next constituent is. The combination of top-down and bottom-up processing in the left-corner algorithm has the further advantage that it allows the parser to build up a phrase marker word by word, in a more or less left to right fashion. Subjective reports, though not necessarily reliable, suggest that people think that they understand sentences in this way.

Summary

In the process of understanding sentences, after the words have been recognized, the structural relations between them must be computed. The job of the parser is to compute these relations, though its operations may sometimes be bypassed. The nature of its task depends on the kind of language that it is analysing. If it is a phrase-structure language, then the parser's work is comparatively straightforward, since there is just one set of phrase-structure rules that define the phrase markers. However, if the language is transformational, the parser's computations are more complex. One possible sequence of operations is that the parser first computes surface phrase structure. To perform this task it uses a special set of surface phrase-structure rules, which may differ considerably from the phrase-structure rules of the base component of the grammar. Then it computes deep structure from surface structure by reversing transformations. However, other parsing procedures for transformational languages can be envisaged, and may be more compatible with recent transformational grammars (e.g. Chomsky, 1981).

Early psycholinguistic research was based on the assumption that sentences are understood by reversing the transformations that generate them from an underlying representation (kernel strings or deep structures). However, almost all of the results of these early experiments are impossible to interpret, because the sentences used – for example actives and passives – differed not only in transformational complexity, but also in surface structure and in meaning. A further problem for this theory was that deep structure cannot always be recovered from surface structure – not every set of forward transformations has a corresponding set of reverse transformations.

At the end of the 1960s psycholinguists, with a few exceptions, lost interest in syntax and focused their attention on 'semantics'. The main exception was Bever, who developed an alternative to the earlier Derivational Theory of Complexity, and proposed that deep structure relations are computed from surface cues by using perceptual strategies rather than reverse transformations. He also attempted to explain comprehension difficulties in terms of these strategies.

Since the mid 1970s interest in parsing has begun to revive. Linguists interested in performance have proposed parsing strategies that predict the difficulties people have in understanding certain sentences, and in appreciating some readings of ambiguous sentences.

In artificial intelligence, parsing has been taken more seriously, and some ideas from AI have been used in models of the human parser – notably in Wanner's ATN-based model. In producing an AI parser a number of design issues have to be addressed, such as whether the parser is to operate top-down, bottom-up, or in some mixed mode, and whether backtracking is allowed to rectify mistakes, or whether errors are avoided by lookahead or by parallel processing. These considerations are also relevant to models of the human parser, but there is little firm evidence about how that parser operates. However, the availability of precisely formulated theories of parsing will allow empirical tests, both in the form of experiments and of model programs, to proceed in future years.

5

Introduction to the concept of meaning

The last two chapters have discussed how people recognize words and how they group those words into phrases and sentences. However, neither word recognition nor the computation of syntactic structure is the final goal of the language understanding system. Its goal, as was emphasized in chapter 1, is to construct a mental representation of the information that is conveyed by a sequence of sentences. It has to work out the *meaning*, in a rather general sense, of what is seen or heard.

In chapter 2 the three major components of linguistic grammars were introduced: phonology, syntax and semantics. According to Chomsky the central part of a grammar is its syntactic component, and most research in generative grammar has investigated sentence structure. Having a formal syntactic theory, or rather a framework within which such theories can be constructed, is useful to the psycholinguist, who must provide an account of how and when syntactic structure is computed. Even if a linguistic grammar does not reflect the way that syntactic information is represented in the mind, the syntactic relations computed during comprehension must be identical to, or at least very similar to, those specified by linguists.

However, syntax is not meaning, and to compute syntactic structure is not to understand. In both REST and GPSG the semantic representation of a sentence is obtained from its syntactic structure by semantic interpretation rules. To understand a sentence it is therefore necessary to compute meaning from structural relations, and a psycholinguistic theory of how these computations are performed benefits from the existence a formal theory of meaning, just as a theory of parsing benefits from syntactic theory. Because of Chomsky's emphasis on syntax, generative grammarians have done comparatively little work on semantics, and most of it has spread rather than alleviated confusion. Generative semantics is a case in point. Despite its name, it was not a theory of meaning, but a theory of sentence structure. Those linguists who have recently become interested in semantic issues have had to look to mathematics and formal logic for ideas. In those disciplines the semantics of formal languages has been studied.

Meanings of 'meaning'

Although people experience no conscious difficulty in working out the meaning of most of the utterances that they hear, and feel they have a good grasp of what meaning is, the concept of meaning is one of the most tricky that will be encountered in this book. The ability to understand is not the same as being able to explicate the concept of meaning, and it is not commonly realized that *meaning* is used in many different ways. Philosophers distinguish a number of senses of the word. Ogden and Richards (1923), for example, in their classic study *The Meaning of 'Meaning'*, identified sixteen. Psycholinguists need not be concerned with all of these niceties, but there are some distinctions that they must be aware of. One is that between *sense* and *reference* (or *denotation*), originally formulated by the founder of modern formal logic, Gottlob Frege. This distinction is one of Frege's two major contributions to semantic theory. The other, his principle of compositionality, will be discussed later in this chapter. The denotation of an expression (the term *reference* will be used more informally) is the thing that it stands for. Different kinds of expression have different kinds of denotation. For example, proper names, at least on the most straightforward view, have objects (including people) as their denotations, and one-place predicates, such as ...*sleeps*, and ...*is red*, have sets of objects as their denotations. For example, the denotation of ...*is red* is the set of things that are red. The *sense* of an expression is more closely connected with its meaning, in the everyday sense. It is, roughly speaking, the content of the expression, and specifies, for any potential denotation, whether the expression has that object as its denotation. Thus the sense of an expression determines which things it can denote.

Another important distinction is to be found in the way in which *meaning* is applied to words and to sentences. Questions about the meaning of words have a different import from those about the meaning of sentences. The question 'what does *monkey* mean?' asks what sort of thing a monkey is, not about a specific monkey. A partial answer would be that a monkey is an animal. This answer can be thought of as a statement about the relation between the meaning of two concepts, or about the relation between two sets of objects. These sets of objects (monkeys and animals) are the respective *denotations* of *monkey* and *animal*. Lyons (1977, vol. 1, ch. 7) contrasts the denotation of a common noun with the *referent* of a phrase containing that noun, which might be an individual monkey in the case of the simple NP *the monkey*. Since nouns, and most other words, do not have referents in this sense, questions about word meaning are not usually questions about specific people or things, but about classes of things.

In contrast, questions about the meanings of sentences and phrases almost always have a more specific interpretation. Consider the question: whom did she mean by *the man she saw last night*? Such questions can be answered only with reference to specific facts about the world. However, it should not be concluded that all questions about the meanings of complex expressions are of this nature. It simply happens that native speakers are rarely in doubt about the way complex expressions of their language are to be interpreted, as opposed to being in doubt about who or what they denote – which they often are. Consider a revised version of the question above: what does *the man she saw last night* mean? It is not immediately apparent what is being asked. Perhaps the force of *the* is unclear, or perhaps the questioner is not sure who saw whom (imagine that the question has been asked by someone learning English as a foreign language). There are many other possibilities. A *semantic theory* must specify, for each expression in the language, what semantic information that expression conveys. For the definite description *the man she saw last night* it states, among other things, that the denotation of the description is a unique male adult, and that that person was seen by whoever *she* denotes on the night previous to that on which the expression was used. The semantics of an expression, therefore, determines what it *can* refer to. To take another example, an explanation of the meaning, in this sense, of the sentence:

The man with the martini spoke to the hostess.

specifies the range of situations of which this sentence is an appropriate description.

The point of this discussion is not that native speakers are ever likely to ask such questions about the language that they speak, but rather to demonstrate that sentences and other complex expressions, such as definite descriptions, do have senses as well as denotations, and to suggest that the language understanding system may have to compute those senses in the course of comprehension. A theory of such computations should draw on a principled account of the semantics of English sentences, which assigns one or more senses to each. A native speaker of English asking the question what was meant by the sentence above is likely, in the case of such a simple sentence, to be looking for some hidden significance. However, this observation should not obscure the fact that just as a word serves as potential label for a number of different objects – monkeys, for example – a sentence is potentially a description of a range of situations. A semantic theory for a language should specify which situations each (descriptive) sentence of that language can describe.

The domain of semantics

In chapter 2 there were no real problems in deciding what a theory of syntax should be about – it describes structural relations between words in sentences. There may be some dispute about which facts are syntactic facts, but the domain of syntactic theory is agreed upon. In the study of meaning the question arises as to whether all aspects of meaning should be studied together in a unified subdiscipline of semantics, or whether a division of labour would be more profitable. Traditionally semantics is said to be the theory of meaning, but at least one additional distinction, between semantics and *pragmatics,* has frequently been made. Morris (1938) proposed a threefold division of semiotics, the theory of signs, into syntactics (i.e. syntax), semantics and pragmatics. He defined semantics as the theory of the relation between signs and objects, and pragmatics as the study of the relation between signs and their users. An example of an aspect of meaning that would be studied in pragmatics on this definition is the assignment of reference to the personal pronouns *I* and *you*. The referent of *I*, for example, depends on who is speaking (i.e. the user of the sign), and hence is properly studied in pragmatics.

It is difficult to make a clear distinction between semantics and pragmatics using Morris's informal definitions, and therefore a number of more specific suggestions have been made. Montague (1968, 1970) proposed that formal pragmatics should be defined as the study of the meaning of words such as *I, you, here, there, now, then*, which philosophers call *indexical terms,* and whose reference depends upon the context in which they are used. If Montague's definition of pragmatics is accepted then, on his theory, semantic and pragmatic aspects of meaning are accounted for in a similar fashion. However, there are many aspects of the meaning of sentences that are not covered by either Montague's semantics or his pragmatics, and at least one further subdivision of the study of meaning will have to be introduced.

Gazdar (1979) made a proposal that has proved more acceptable to both linguists and psychologists. He suggested that the term *semantics* be used to cover the study of those aspects of meaning that contribute to the *truth conditions* of sentences. The truth conditions of a (descriptive) sentence are a specification of the circumstances in which it would be true. That is to say they determine the set of situations of which the sentence could be a correct description. Montague's theory of meaning is a theory of truth conditions so, if Gazdar's proposal is accepted the term semantics covers both semantics and formal pragmatics, in Montague's sense. Gazdar reserves the term pragmatics for the study of certain non-truth conditional aspects of meaning that have been studied in linguistics in the past decade or so – presupposition, implicature and general principles governing conversation, all of which will be discussed later in this chapter.

One other aspect of meaning should be mentioned before formal theories of semantics are discussed. In their semantic theories both linguists and philosophers have focused their attention on sentences, or their equivalent in logical languages – well-formed formulae, rather than on larger meaning-bearing units, which do not exist in most logical languages. But paragraphs, texts and stories, and monologues and discourses are more than just sets of sentences, and they convey more meaning than their sentences would in isolation. In the past few years workers in many disciplines have begun to study questions about text meaning, and some of the results of their research will be reported in chapter 7.

Lexical and structural semantics

It is customary to divide semantic theory into two parts – lexical semantics and structural semantics. Lexical semantics studies the meaning of words and, perhaps, morphemes. Structural semantics studies the way in which the meanings of complex expressions depend on the meanings of their parts, and on the way in which those parts are put together. There is little agreement on the form that a theory of lexical semantics should take. In the next chapter five proposals will be described – all with different conceptual bases – that psycholinguists have put forward since the early 1970s. Within linguistics perhaps the most important idea in lexical semantics is that of a *semantic field* of related words (see for example Lyons, 1977, vol. 1, ch. 8), though this concept has never been adequately formalized.

For two reasons the primary concern of this chapter will be with structural semantics. First, the way in which the meaning of a complex expression is derived from those of its parts has been studied intensively. Second, many people find it difficult to grasp the point of theories of structural semantics, though they can see the necessity for a theory of word meaning.

Formal semantic theories have their origin in formal logic. Aristotle, the father of formal logic, produced a theory of one kind of reasoning, called syllogistic reasoning. This theory comprised virtually the whole of formal logic up to the end of the nineteenth century. Aristotle's theory is correct as far as it goes, but comparatively little of our everyday use of language takes the form of arguments from two premises of one of the four forms: *all A are B, no A are B, some A are B, some A are not B*. It was Frege who suggested that, if languages had been devised rationally – he thought that all natural languages left much to be desired – then every thought could be expressed in a logical formula, and every argument could be evaluated by the standards of logical precision. Frege (1879/1972) devised his own language, called *conceptual notation*, which was supposed to overcome the limitations of natural languages, such as English and Frege's own language, German. Conceptual notation is *predicate calculus*, albeit with rather arcane symbols.

Unlike Frege, a number of later logicians, and in particular Richard Montague (see Thomason, 1974, especially chapters 3, 4, 6, 7, 8, and, for an introduction to Montague's work, Dowty, Peters and Wall, 1981), have claimed that ordinary languages can be satisfactorily translated into (a somewhat extended version of) predicate calculus, and that this translation provides the basis of a semantic theory for those languages. Montague's method is not simply to state, as is done in elementary logic textbooks, that a certain formula of predicate calculus is the translation of an English sentence, but to provide a precise method of translation into predicate calculus, that can be carried out mechanically.

How can translation into predicate calculus provide a semantic theory for English? A number of steps in the argument are still missing. The first step was taken by Tarski (1931/1956), who set himself the task of defining the semantic notion of *truth* for a formalized language such as predicate calculus. He noted that semantic paradoxes inevitably arise in languages that contain semantic predicates, such as *is true*, that can be applied to their own sentences. In English, for example, it is impossible to use the sentence *this sentence is false* in a sensible way, if the phrase *this sentence* is intended to refer to the sentence in which it occurs, and not, for example, some other sentence that the speaker is pointing to. When the sentence is used in a *self-referential* way, it follows that if the sentence is true, then it is false, and if it is false, it is true.

To overcome this problem Tarski distinguished between an *object language* for which a theory of truth is required, and a separate *metalanguage* in which the theory can be stated. A metalanguage is a higher order language in which things can be said about expressions in the object language. The theory of truth specifies in the metalanguage the conditions under which each sentence of the object language is true. Because the object language has indefinitely many well-formed sentences, the theory of truth cannot be a mere listing of true sentences, just as the specification of the grammatical sentences of English cannot be a list. Indeed, in Tarski's view, in order to state a theory of truth it is necessary to provide a complete syntax and semantics for the object language. In practice only a structural semantics is given. It is assumed that appropriate meanings have been assigned to words, and that those meanings can enter into the combinatorial process that produces the meanings of complex expressions. To produce an interpretation for each sentence of the language, a structure called a *model* is required. A model is a set of objects that sentences of the language are about. A function called the *interpretation function* is then defined, which specifies what each word of the language denotes. Thus a name might denote one of the objects, a common noun, such as *dog*, a set of the objects (that is the set of dogs), and a transitive verb, such as *see*, a set of pairs of objects, such that the first object of each pair stands in a certain perceptual relation – that of seeing – to the second object. It is usually assumed that sentences denote the truth values, true and false (only recently has this assumption been challenged within the formal tradition, by Barwise and Perry, 1984, who claim that sentences denote *situations*).

The job of structural semantics is to show how sentences come to have the truth values that they do, given the meanings of the words in the language – as assigned by the interpretation function – and the way in which the syntax puts those words together. The principle embodied in this last statement is usually called Frege's *principle of compositionality*, though it was never explicitly formulated by him. It states that the meaning of a complex expression is determined by the meanings of its component parts and the way in which those parts are combined. The simplest way of satisfying the principle is to assume that corresponding to each syntactic rule, such as S → NP VP, there is a semantic rule that specifies the meaning of the constituent on the left-hand side, as a function of the meaning of the constituents on the right hand side. For example, corresponding to the syntactic rule S → NP VP is the semantic rule: the sentence is true if the entity denoted by its subject NP is a member of the set of objects denoted by its VP. Thus:

John sleeps.

is true if the person called John is one of the things that sleep.

Tarski, like Frege, was sceptical about the application of his ideas to natural languages. However, two developments have, in the opinion of many contemporary logicians, bridged the gap between formal and natural languages. The first is a series of advances in formal logic, notably in the branch of logic known as modal logic, and the second is the distinction between semantics and pragmatics, with its precise delimitation of what a semantic theory should explain. Modal logics are used in the analysis of such concepts as possibility and necessity, knowledge, belief, obligation and permission. The most important device introduced to explicate the semantics of these concepts is that of a set of *possible worlds* (Kripke, 1963). Each possible world is described by a set of sentences – sentences are said to be true or false *at* possible worlds. Possible worlds are added to the models used to interpret languages, so sentences are no longer simply true or false, but true or false at each possible world. Furthermore, possible worlds can be either accessible or inaccessible from other possible worlds. To take two simple examples, the sentence:

It is possible that Fred is kind.

is true if and only if there is at least one possible world at which the sentence:

Fred is kind.

is true, and the sentence:

Madge hopes that Fred is kind.

is true if and only if, in a world corresponding to Madge's hopes, Fred is kind.

To logicians, a theory of truth is a semantic theory. The principal goals of a formal semantic theory are, therefore, to specify the conditions under which the sentences of a language are true, and to specify their entailments. This latter specification follows directly from the truth conditions, since a sentence S is entailed by a set of sentences A, B, C, D, . . . if there are no circumstances in which all of A, B, C, D, . . . are true, and S is false.

Semantics, like syntax, is an empirical science. Syntactic facts about English, for example facts about which sentences are grammatical, and facts about how the words in sentences are structurally grouped, can falsify a proposed grammar. Similarly semantic facts about English can be used to test semantic theories. For example, the sentence:

John found a unicorn.

entails the sentence:

There is a unicorn.

but the sentence:

John is looking for a unicorn.

does not. The correct semantic theory for English must predict these entailments.

In logical calculi there are well-formed formulae corresponding roughly to sentences of natural languages, but no larger units that carry additional meaning. In applying formal semantics to natural languages, logicians have usually restricted themselves to the semantics of sentences. However, it might be asked – even given the rather rarefied concept of meaning in formal seman- tic theories – whether the sentence is the appropriate unit of semantic analysis for natural language. The answer to this question is most probably no. A consideration of some of the failures of standard formal semantic theories as applied to natural languages suggests that it is necessary to consider larger units.

In standard versions of *model-theoretic semantics*, as the kind of semantics under discussion is called, every sentence of a given language is interpreted with respect to the same model, regardless of its textual context. The only account of the truth of texts in such a framework is, therefore, that a text is true if and only if all of the sentences in it are true. Given the usual inter- pretation of the past tense in model-theoretic semantics, it can be shown that the two (short) texts below have the same truth conditions.

John and Mary got married.
Mary became pregnant.

Mary became pregnant.
John and Mary got married.

However, these texts are so misleading if the events occurred in the opposite order to that in which they are related, that they are correctly considered to be false in such circumstances. A theory of semantics (that is a theory of truth conditions) should therefore explain how the structure of a text, and not just the truth values of the sentences in it, determines whether it is true.

The formal logician Hans Kamp (1979) noted another set of facts about the use of tenses in natural languages that is difficult to accommodate within standard model-theoretic semantics. The simple past tense is used to describe events that, *from the point of view of the story of which they are part*, occur at a single moment of time. However, in a broader context, for example, that of a text describing the same events in more detail, those events can be treated as temporally divisible. An appropriate model of the temporal structure of the events in the shorter text is not therefore appropriate for the longer text. This fact suggested to Kamp that discourses and stories are initially interpreted with respect to their own mini-model, which is a partial submodel of the world that the language as a whole can be used to describe. A partial submodel is a representation of just that bit of the real or imaginary world that the text is about. The idea of a single model with respect to which all sentences of a given language are interpreted is incorrect.

The idea of a partial submodel also explains how expressions such as *the man* can be correctly interpreted in the context of a discourse. The real world, and hence any model of it, contains many men, any one of whom could be referred to by *the man*. However, if the partial submodel that represents a text contains only one man, which it may well do, then there will be no difficulty in interpreting *the man*, as referring to that one person.

Kamp (1981) proposed that texts are understood in two stages. First a *discourse representation* is constructed that contains tokens standing for just those items mentioned in the text, and that indicates only those relations between them described in the text. He formulated a set of rules for constructing such representations for simple texts. To assess the truth of a text, its discourse representation is compared with a model of the real world. The details of the relation between the two that determine whether the text is true are of no concern here. Kamp's analysis is motivated by linguistic considerations, but it has clear implications for a psychological theory of text comprehension. Indeed, his notion of a discourse representation is closely related to that of a *mental model*, which was introduced in chapter 1. Mental models have been discussed in both the psycholinguistic literature (Johnson-Laird, 1980, 1983; Johnson-Laird and Garnham, 1980; Stenning, 1977, 1978) and that of AI (Webber, 1981). A mental model is a mental representation of the information conveyed by a text or a discourse. It also contains information about the participants in the linguistic exchange that it represents. This information is required so that, for example, in a conversation one can phrase what one has to say so that it is comprehensible to the other participants. It is no good asking someone to take a message to *the chairman of the residents' committee* unless the message-bearer not only knows the person, but also knows that they chair the committee in question.

Mental models are dynamic rather than static in nature. People do not wait to the end of a book or a conversation before they construct a representation of it. They construct a partial representation from the first sentence (or even the title) and use that representation to interpret the next sentence. The model is then updated, and the cycle is repeated for the next sentence. As Isard (1974b) has pointed out, communications not only receive context-dependent interpretations, but also change the context for the interpretation of other, mainly following, communications.

A theory of comprehension based on the notion of a mental model must include a general account of how the information in sentences is extracted, and of how it is used to update models. The account of how sentences are interpreted should draw on model-theoretic insights into the meaning of sentences, but, just as a syntactic theory is not a theory of parsing, a theory of discourse comprehension must have a processing component as well as specifying what people know about the meaning of sentences. Information is extracted from sentences by identifying the event, state or process denoted by the main verb in the sentence, and its participants and their roles. The participants are usually introduced by NPs and PPs (prepositional phrases), and their roles depend on the syntax of the sentence. Examples of rules for determining these roles are given by Gazdar (1982). Relating the current clause to what has gone before is primarily a matter of establishing which expressions refer back to which items in either the preceding text or the model – both kinds of back references are possible. These *anaphoric links* can sometimes be established on the basis of simple features such as number and gender, for example in:

John and Mary went to the park.
She hired a rowing boat.

the *she* in the second sentence must refer back to Mary. In other cases inferences based on detailed knowledge of the world are required, for example to determine the referent of *she* in the second sentence of:

Kate lent Sally her car.
She thought cycling was healthier.

Pragmatics

The use of knowledge about the world in text comprehension is connected with the question of what further processing the language understanding system must perform in addition to semantic processing. There are many aspects of the meaning of an utterance that are not truth-conditional. For example, a sentence such as:

I do not have any gravy.

is true if and only if the speaker is without a certain foodstuff. Yet when uttered in an appropriate context, the sentence may be a request that the gravy be passed. How does someone who hears such an utterance determine the speaker's intentions? A psycholinguistic theory must answer this question.

The philosopher Paul Grice (1975) first brought to the attention of linguists and psycholinguists the importance of the fact that what people mean very often differs from what they say. He developed an account of how intended meaning can be derived from what is said, and information about the context in which it is said. Such a theory is a *pragmatic theory*, in Gazdar's sense. Grice's ideas, although imprecise in parts, have been widely influential in both linguistics and psychology. One reason why they are popular with linguists is that they complement the idea that a semantic theory should be model-theoretic and should describe only truth-conditional aspects of meaning.

Frege and Tarski, among others, were sceptical about the application of formal logic to natural language semantics. One of the main reasons for such scepticism was that the fundamental *logical connectives*- those logical terms that are roughly equivalent to *not, and, or, if. . .then* – do not appear to be sufficiently similar in meaning to their natural language counterparts to make the comparison between natural languages and logical calculi illuminating. Grice proposed that many apparent deviations of the meanings of English words from their putative logical equivalents could be explained by pragmatic principles. He claimed that what is *said* by a sentence containing, for example, *and* is adequately captured by translating *and* as the corresponding logical connective, and that what is *meant* by the sentence follows from this translation plus general principles governing contributions to text and discourse. If the workings of the language processor reflect this division of linguistic labour, it will have one component that computes the semantic interpretation of sentences, and a further component that uses the semantic interpretation to compute the intended message.

Grice's theory

The central tenet of Grice's pragmatic theory is that conversation is usually a co-operative activity, and that it is therefore governed by the same kinds of consideration as any other co-operative activity. Grice claimed that, at any point in a conversation, a speaker should be guided by the following Co-operative Principle (CP), in formulating what to say next:

> make your conversational contribution such as is required, at the stage at which it occurs, by the accepted purpose or direction of the talk exchange in which you are engaged (1975, 45)

This principle is very general, and Grice therefore gives a number of sub-maxims that he considers to follow from it. The submaxims are grouped under four heads (see Table 5.1), though Grice chose this number primarily

Table 5.1 Submaxims of Grice's Co-operative Principle

(1) Quality – say only what is true and what you know to be true.
(2) Quantity – say no more and no less than is required.
(3) Relation – be relevant.
(4) Manner – be perspicuous (be brief and orderly; avoid obscurity and ambiguity)

to mirror a set of distinctions in Kant's *Critique of Pure Reason* (1787/1929), and it has no real significance in the theory. These maxims are not scientific laws that govern the operation of the language processor. They are *norms* that can be deliberately *violated* in order to mislead, just as any other norm can be violated. Someone who lies, for example, is violating a sub-maxim of quality. When Grice says that conversation is *usually* a co-operative activity, he is recognizing that adherence to the maxims may conflict with a speaker's other goals, such as being polite or creating a good social impression. As well as being violated, maxims can also be deliberately and blatantly *flouted*. In such cases the hearer can recognize an apparent failure to conform to the CP. For example:

What lovely weather we're having.

said on a dreadful day quite obviously violates a maxim of quality. In such cases the hearer can assume a general intention to conform to the CP, and use a *conversational implicature* to work out what was meant from what was said, and hence to discover its ironic intent. However, irony is a special case, and it is not usual to flout maxims of quality, though they are often deliberately violated.

What is conversationally implicated is not logically entailed by what is said, and therefore conversational implicatures cannot be explained by a semantic theory whose principal concerns are entailment and truth conditions. Such implicatures have two defining features. First, they are *cancellable*. For example, adding an extra clause to the above sentence can, in some contexts, change its import:

What lovely weather we're having, I really like rain.

Second, they are *non-detachable*. They do not change when the same thing is said in different words. For example,

It's very pleasant to-day, isn't it?

carries the same implicature as the first sentence, if uttered in the same circumstances.

Does formal semantics plus Gricean pragmatics provide an adequate theory of meaning for natural languages? If it does, there can only be a narrow level of (semantic) meaning and a set of implied (pragmatic) meanings, and *no residue* – no other kinds of meanings. The two theories working in tandem solve a wide range of problems that were previously without a solution. Nevertheless there *are* some phenomena that appear to be residual. Grice himself identified what he called a second kind of implicature (conventional implicature), but conventional implicatures have different properties from conversational implicatures, and cannot be accounted for by general pragmatic principles. Conventional implicatures, are carried by particular lexical items. For example, the use of *but*, rather than *and*, suggests that what is stated in the *but* clause is surprising given the fact in the other clause. However, such implicatures have the opposite properties from conversational implicatures. They are non-cancellable but, as they attach to specific lexical items they are detachable. Their non-cancellability is illustrated by the fact that the following sentence does not make sense:

Even John likes Mary, but no one else does.

The last clause cannot cancel the conventional implicature carried by *even* – that people other than John also like Mary.

Presupposition

So far this discussion of pragmatic aspects of meaning has been about the message conveyed by the actual words spoken. A further topic that linguists and philosophers have studied under the head of pragmatics is what is taken for granted, or to use the technical term, what is *presupposed* by what is said. Like implicature, presupposition cannot be defined in terms of the semantic relation of entailment. The simplest reason for not identifying presuppositions with entailments is that the presuppositions of a sentence, unlike its entailments, do not change when the sentence is negated. For example, both:

The King of France is bald.
AND The King of France is not bald.

presuppose that there is a King of France. The first sentence arguably also *entails* that there is a King of France (Wilson, 1975; Gazdar, 1979). However, although:

John saw a unicorn.

entails that there is a unicorn,

John did not see a unicorn.

does not. Presuppositions were first discussed in the philosophical literature (Strawson, 1950), but only those of definite descriptions, such as *the King of France*, were considered. Since that time, linguists have identified other presuppositional phenomena, and described more of their properties. In particular they have attempted to solve the *projection problem* – what happens to the presuppositions of a simple sentence when it becomes one clause of a complex sentence – and to determine whether there are different kinds of presupposition. Wilson (1975) and Kempson (1975) argued that all presuppositional phenomena are pragmatic rather than semantic, and this position is now widely accepted, though Karttunen and Peters (1979) have shown how a formal extension of Montague's semantic theory can accommodate Grice's conventional implicatures, which are sometimes regarded as a kind of presupposition.

Speech acts

A further set of questions about the meaning of an utterance is addressed by the theory of *speech acts*. Speech act theory is based on the observation by the Ordinary Language Philosopher J.L. Austin (1962) that, contrary to an implicit assumption of many semanticists, describing the world is not the only function of utterances. It is one function among many – one kind of *act* that can be performed by making an utterance. Others include promising, naming and marrying, as the following sentences illustrate.

I promise to come to the meeting.
I name this ship the *Queen Elizabeth the Second*.
With this ring I thee wed.

Austin called such utterances *performatives*, but they are more frequently referred to by the name given to them by John Searle (1969), *speech acts*. Some verbs, such as *promise*, are performative verbs and are associated with specific speech acts, in this case promising. However, not every speech act requires a performative verb. For example, although there are performative verbs for asking questions (e.g. *question* and *ask*), and for demanding things (e.g. *command* and *order*), comparatively few questions and commands contain these verbs. Speech act theory, like Grice's theory, assumes that each sentence has a meaning, in the narrow sense, assigned to it by a 'Fregean' semantic theory. Austin, who had a penchant for arcane terminology, called the semantic meaning of a sentence its *locutionary meaning*, and the speech act performed by uttering the sentence its *illocutionary force*. Austin pointed out that utterances also have what he called *perlocutionary effects* – intended effects that are not part of its meaning. For example, the illocutionary force of

Smarten yourself up or you'll be on report!

is a combination of a command and a threat. Its perlocutionary effect may be to scare the living daylights out of a raw recruit.

In the theory of language understanding outlined in chapter 1, the locutionary meaning of an utterance or set of utterances will be represented in a mental model. For example, utterances of the two sentences:

John went to the pictures.
Did John go to the pictures?

will lead to the construction of very similar, if not identical, representations of an event. However, this model will have a different status, for both speaker and hearer, in the two cases. In the first case the speaker makes the utterance on the basis of a representation of how the world is, and intends the hearer to construct a similar representation, to be construed similarly – as a representation of part of the world. In the second case the utterance is derived from a hypothesis about how the world might be, and the hearer is expected to ascertain if the model constructed from the sentence matches his or her model of the world. The speaker assumes that, in the relevant respect, the hearer has more detailed knowledge of the world.

Searle's (1969) major contribution to the theory of speech acts is his attempt to formulate the conditions under which they are appropriate, or *felicitous*. For example, the felicity conditions for issuing a command include the following: (i) the hearer must be able to hear the speaker, (ii) the hearer must be able to understand the language that the speaker is speaking, (iii) if the hearer is about to do what is commanded independently of the command, that fact must not be obvious to the speaker, (iv) the speaker must have some authority over the hearer. The first two of these conditions are general conditions for the felicity of any speech act. The others are specific to commands. If a psycholinguistic theory is to explain when and why people perform speech acts, and how they are interpreted, it must postulate an internal representation of knowledge of these felicity conditions, and a mechanism for recognizing when they are satisfied.

This section on pragmatics began with an example in which what was apparently a statement was intended as a request. Such an utterance is called an *indirect* speech act. The existence of indirect speech acts depends on two facts. First, certain sentence forms are *typically* associated with certain illocutionary forces, for example interrogatives with questions. Second, in some contexts those forms may have different illocutionary forces. In these latter cases the speech act is said to be indirect. A combination of speech act theory and Grice's maxims explains how such indirect speech acts are interpreted. An utterance expresses an indirect speech act when the usual illocutionary force of its sentence form makes the utterance unnecessary, or irrelevant. By assuming adherence to the Co-operative Principle, the intended illocutionary force of the utterance can be recovered by a conversational implicature.

Some apparently indirect speech acts may not require conversational implicatures for their interpretation. Just as metaphors can become dead metaphors, and be incorporated into the language as new literal meanings of words, some very common indirect speech acts, such as *can you pass* – meaning *please pass* – are probably interpreted as having their intended meaning without any implicature being required.

Knowledge of the world

So far this chapter has outlined a semantic theory that defines what information is encoded into text representations, and a pragmatic theory that specifies the import of that information when it is derived from a particular utterance in a particular context. The information in a semantic representation reflects fairly directly the actual words used. Experiments to be reported in chapter 7 show that people can go beyond this information, though they do not always do so. This elaboration of text representations is achieved using both specific and general knowledge about the world. By general knowledge is meant, not what is generally known, but knowledge of general facts, such as that reindeer have antlers. By contrast, a piece of specific knowledge would be that Rudolph has a red nose, since that is knowledge about a particular reindeer. General knowledge is typically knowledge of empirical regularities – of probabilities rather than the possibilities that possible-worlds semantics accounts for. For example, most (male) reindeer have antlers, so a randomly chosen male reindeer probably has them. But sometimes antlers get broken off, and a reindeer that has lost its antlers is no less a reindeer for its mishap.

To see how knowledge of empirical regularities can influence the way in which language is understood, consider the sentence:

The animal ran towards the kennel.

uttered in an appropriate context. The animal will most probably be a dog, although there is no entailment between running towards a kennel and being a dog. In a different context the animal might be a cat, for example. However, many people know about the connection between dogs and kennels. Not only do they know that a kennel is a house for a dog, they also know how dogs and kennels fit into a pattern of life in which dogs frequently run towards kennels (cf. Wittgenstein, 1953, on forms of life). This knowledge influences the way they interpret the sentence.

If semantics is defined as that part of a theory of meaning that explains truth conditions, semantics cannot concern itself with the probabilities with which events occur. It simply determines which events a sentence can describe, regardless of how likely they are. However, probabilistic knowledge is used to elaborate mental models, and a psycholinguistic theory must, therefore, explain how our knowledge of the world is organized in memory, and how it is accessed by cues in texts and discourse. In the next two chapters a number of ideas about the use of world knowledge in comprehension will be discussed, but formulating testable theories of this ability has proved very difficult, and an adequate theory has never been worked out.

Summary

Linguists produce theories of syntax, which specify what the human parser has to compute. Psycholinguists produce theories of parsing. Similarly semanticists and pragmaticists from a number of disciplines have formulated theories of meaning, on which psycholinguists can base theories of how those meanings are computed.

There are many aspects of meaning. The most useful approach in studying them is to define the domain of semantics rather narrowly, so that semantics is the theory of truth conditions of descriptive sentences, and corresponding conditions for non-descriptive sentences. For example, the semantics of commands should state the conditions under which they have been obeyed. Other aspects of meaning are accounted for by a pragmatic theory, with three main components. Speech act theory defines the functions that utterances can have. The theory of presupposition describes what is taken for granted in what is said, and the theory of implicature, how the intended message can be computed from the literal meaning, using a set of general principles governing linguistic interchanges.

In language understanding, the semantic processor computes the basic content of the mental representation of a text, and the pragmatic processor determines how that content is related to what is already known, and its intended import (for example, a description of the world, or a query). The representation is fleshed out into a mental model by knowledge of the world, which enables inferences to be made about details that are not actually mentioned, but which are probably true.

6

Word meaning

The previous chapter introduced the concept of meaning, but included comparatively little discussion of the meaning of words. Psycholinguists do study word meaning, about which they ask two principal questions. (1) How is knowledge about word meanings stored in the mind? (2) How are meanings brought out of storage in the course of understanding or producing discourse? The first question is a question about representations, the second a question about processes.

Chapter 3 described an internal store of knowledge about words – the mental lexicon. Information about the meaning of words is one aspect of this knowledge. However, as was indicated in that chapter, our knowledge about word meanings is complex, and the most appropriate model of the mental lexicon is one in which its entries contain no semantic information, but merely pointers to locations in another store in which meanings are held. This second store is called *semantic memory*. There have been several proposals about the kinds of information in semantic memory, but they all agree that it includes word meanings. In the context of the present chapter it is therefore unnecessary to enter into a debate about what other information it contains.

The psycholinguistic question about the representation of word meanings can be formulated as follows. What in semantic memory corresponds to the definitions of words in an ordinary dictionary? In answering this question it must be remembered that dictionary-makers can take many things for granted about the way their definitions will be interpreted. These assumptions do not carry over to semantic memory.

Dictionaries define one word in terms of others, and semantic memory must represent relations among word meanings too. However, dictionaries and semantic memories have different purposes and make different uses of the interconnections between words. Dictionaries are consulted to ascertain the meaning of unknown words. Their entries assume that the meanings of other words are known, and use known words to explain the meaning of new words. If there are any unknown words in a definition, they in turn must be looked up. Dictionary-makers assume that users of dictionaries have some linguistic sophistication. Their definitions of the most common words are not particularly useful, and are included for completeness rather than for consultation. Furthermore, although an explanation of meaning should relate language to the world, dictionaries perform this function only implicitly. Someone who wants to know the meaning of *tamarack* wants to know what kinds of things tamaracks are. A dictionary gives this information by assuming that its users are familiar with the things mentioned in the definition.

Semantic memories cannot work in the same way as dictionaries since, in comprehension, the meaning of every word in a discourse or text must be made available. Frequent words are, by definition, often encountered and their meanings must be both correctly and usefully represented. Semantic memories cannot rely on knowledgeable users to relate the information in them to the world, since they themselves are partly responsible for performing that function.

In the last chapter it was argued that a semantic theory should provide a principled account of (i) the truth conditions of descriptive sentences, and the corresponding conditions for non-descriptive sentences, and (ii) the entailments of sentences. Truth conditions are assigned to sentences by relating words to the world – via a model and an interpretation function – and by showing how the meanings of sentences are built up from word meanings and structural relations between words. In formal semantic theories, such as Montague's, relations between words and the world are stipulated (*dog* denotes the set of dogs in each possible world). However, a theory of semantic memory cannot incorporate such stipulations. It must *explain* how words relate to the world. Furthermore, people perceive the same things that they talk and write about, and classify the things they perceive in much the same way that they describe them. Therefore a theory of semantic memory must be compatible with a theory of (high-level) perceptual processes. More ambitiously the theory might help to *explain* how conceptual and perceptual processes interact. In this way a theory of word meanings could contribute to an explanation of how language relates to the world.

What other facts should a theory of word meaning explain? Many suggestions can be found in the literature, but explanations of most of them follow directly from an account of the contribution of word meanings to the truth conditions and entailments of sentences. For example, a theory of word meaning should account for lexical ambiguity, but to say, for example, that *bank* is ambiguous is to say that sentences in which it occurs have two different meanings (sets of truth conditions). Similarly relations between word meanings such as set inclusion (dogs are animals), and antonymy (long is the opposite of short), will follow from a theory that can explain the following kinds of entailments:

Fido is a dog.
so, Fido is an animal.

The plank is long.
so, The plank is not short.

The philosopher Hilary Putnam (1970, 1975) has drawn attention to a second kind of fact that theories of semantic memory should explain. Putnam points out that, although many people know that the words *beech* and *larch* denote different kinds of trees, they cannot tell a beech from a larch. However, since the two words have different meanings, there must be some difference in how they are used, and it is therefore crucial that there are 'experts' who can distinguish the two kinds of tree. Putnam concludes that the meaning of a word is not something in the mind of an individual language user. Nevertheless, non-experts make some use of words like *beech* and *larch*, and a theory of semantic memory must explain how people can use words of whose meanings they have, and know they have, only partial knowledge. None of the theories discussed in this chapter specifically addresses this question, though this omission can only be regarded as a defect in them.

Finally, a theory of semantic memory should be compatible with the wide range of psycholinguistic data on word meaning. As well as the studies of adults, discussed in this chapter, there are also data on the acquisition of concepts that may have implications for theories of semantic memory (see for example, Clark and Clark, 1977, 509–13), but these studies fall outside the scope of this book.

Psychological theories of word meaning

The distinction between competence and performance can be drawn in the domain of lexical semantics as it can in any other branch of psycholinguistics. Linguistic theories about word meaning are therefore potentially relevant in psychology. However, there is no generally accepted framework for studying word meaning in linguistics and in practice its influence has been limited. Psycholinguists have borrowed ideas from AI in formulating theories of word meaning, and have produced some ideas of their own. In the past fifteen years or so five different theories of the organization of semantic memory have been proposed. They have been developed from different underlying assumptions but, as will become apparent in the ensuing discussion, it is difficult to distinguish between them. Before any experimental work is described, the representational aspects of the five theories will be outlined.

Feature theories

The earliest psycholinguistic research was inspired by transformational grammar (see chapter 4). In *Aspects* (1965) Chomsky endorsed a version of the semantic theory developed by Katz and Fodor (1963) that was compatible with Katz and Postal's (1964) proposal that transformations should preserve meaning. It was therefore natural that psycholinguists looked to this source for a theory of meaning.

In their theory of word meaning, Katz and Fodor (1963) proposed that a dictionary entry took the form of a hierarchical tree, and that each path from the root of the tree to a 'leaf' corresponded to a different meaning of the word. Chomsky showed that word meanings are more accurately described by sets of bivalent features, which he called *semantic markers* and which are not fully ordered into a hierarchy. For example, the distinction MALE/FEMALE is neither subordinate nor superordinate to the distinction HUMAN/NON-HUMAN. A bivalent feature is one that can take only two values, represented as + <feature> and - <feature>. Examples of semantic markers are MALE, ANIMATE and HUMAN. Those hierarchical relations that do exist are captured by *redundancy rules*, for example, if a word meaning has the feature +HUMAN, then it also has the feature +ANIMATE. Semantic markers *decompose* the meanings of words into more primitive elements.

Katz and Fodor assumed that most, if not all, words are ambiguous. On Chomsky's version of their theory a dictionary entry therefore usually comprises several different sets of markers. Each of these *readings* of the word has an associated *distinguisher.* The semantic markers capture the systematic aspects of meaning, and the distinguishers the non-systematic aspects. The inclusion of a marker in the theory is therefore justified if it enters into the definitions of many words, and provides systematic contrasts between word meanings. For example, the following pairs of words – and many others – differ only in the value of the feature MALE/FEMALE: *man/woman, boy/girl, uncle/aunt, nephew/niece.* Katz and Fodor proposed that there was a universal set of markers which could represent the meaning of words from every possible language. Knowledge of this set of features would be part of what Chomsky called Universal Grammar.

Feature theories were introduced into psycholinguistics by Schaeffer and Wallace (1969), and developed in more detail by Smith, Shoben and Rips (1974). Smith *et al.* elaborated the theory by distinguishing between *defining* and *characteristic* features. Defining features are those that an object must have to fall under a concept. For example, among the defining features of *bird* (the ordinary language concept, not the scientific one) are *has a beak* and *has wings*. Characteristic features of birds that most but not all birds have include *can fly* and *builds nests*. Smith *et al.* did not intend their distinction to be all-or-none. They proposed a continuum of features from the truly defining to the merely characteristic.

Semantic networks

Semantic networks became known in psychology through the collaboration of Collins and Quillian (1969). Quillian (1968) had used semantic networks to represent word meanings in his computer program TLC, the Teachable Language Comprehender. In a semantic network, concepts, which correspond to word meanings, are represented by *nodes*. The nodes are joined together by a network of *links* that represent relations between concepts, such as set membership (Fido is a dog), set inclusion (dogs are animals), part-whole (a seat is part of a chair) and property attribution (canaries are yellow). The meaning of a word is determined by the place of the node representing it in the network as a whole. The most important aspect of semantic networks is the hierarchical organization of the set inclusion links (usually called ISA links). Such hierarchies are easiest to find among concrete nouns. For example, *collie, boxer, terrier, setter* are joined by ISA links to *dog*. On the next level up *dog* together with *cat, bird, fish*, and so on are linked to *animal* (again this is the hierarchy of the non-expert, not the biologist), and so on.

Hollan (1975) showed that the simple semantic networks of Collins and Quillian are equivalent to feature representations, in the sense that any information that can be represented in one can be represented in the other. However, as Rips, Smith and Shoben (1975) point out in reply to Hollan, this formal equivalence does not imply psychological equivalence. A psychological theory must account not only for how knowledge is represented, but also for how it is used. The processing assumptions that go naturally with one theory might lead to an adequate performance theory, while those that go with the other may not.

Prototypes

The theory of prototypes (Rosch, 1973, and many later papers – see Rosch, 1978, for a summary) derives partly from Wittgenstein's (1953) ideas about word meaning. Wittgenstein argued that most words could *not* be defined by stating sets of necessary and sufficient conditions for membership of the classes that they stood for. His best known example of a word that cannot be so defined is *game.* Wittgenstein argued that there is no set of characteristics that all games have in common – not all games are played for amusement's sake, not all games have an element of skill or of chance, the concepts of winning and losing are not always applicable, and so on. Instead there are overlapping sets of similarities between games – what Wittgenstein called *family resemblances.*

On their simplest interpretations both feature theories and network theories assume that words can be defined in terms of necessary and sufficient conditions. For example, a featural representation of the meaning of *dog* can be interpreted as stating that if something has a certain set of features (if it is +ANIMATE, -HUMAN, and so on) then it is a dog, and if it does not have those features then it is not a dog. Such theories of meaning, referred to by Fillmore (1975) as 'checklist theories of meaning', fail to explain two important facts: (a) sometimes the correct classification of an object is in doubt, even if its features are not; (b) some exemplars of a concept are more typical than others, and come to mind more readily.

The essence of the theory of prototypes is that an entry in the mental dictionary is centred around a representation of the prototypical member of the class that the word denotes. There are two different accounts of prototypes. Consider the meaning of the word *bird.* American college students (the subjects from whom most data have been collected) rate robins as the most typical birds. On one interpretation, the prototypical bird is therefore a robin. However, although the robin is the most typical real bird, there are 'possible' birds that would be even more typical if they existed. The most typical of these possible birds represents a more abstract bird prototype.

A prototype itself is not the meaning of a word. Ostriches are birds, however atypical they may be. To give the meaning of a word in prototype theory it is also necessary to say how far something can differ from the prototype and still be, say, a bird. A prototype is located in a multidimensional space with dimensions corresponding to characteristics on which exemplars of the concept can vary – in the case of *bird* these dimensions will represent such things as length, wingspan, clutch size, lifespan and colour. A boundary in the space around the prototypical bird defines which things are birds.

For some concepts the boundary is not sharp. This fuzziness explains why judgements about set membership are not always easy to make. Rosch and Mervis (1975) suggested that such fuzzy boundaries could be formally characterized using the concepts of fuzzy set theory (Zadeh, 1965), but the fuzzy set notion of membership-to-a-degree has undesirable consequences for semantic theory (Johnson-Laird, 1982a; Jones, 1982). Jones suggests a more satisfactory way of representing fuzzy boundaries.

An alternative way of formalizing the notion of prototypes uses Minsky's (1975) concepts of a *frame* and a *frame-system*, which he developed to describe the structure of knowledge in long-term memory. It is difficult to find a precise formulation of frame-system theory, but only three facts about frames are crucial to the present discussion. First, each concept in semantic memory has a frame associated with it. Second, frames have *terminals* or *slots* that are filled differently in frames representing different instances of the same category – one cat frame may have the TABBY filler in its COLOUR slot, another the BLACK filler. Third, some slots have *default values* for their fillers. A default value is a typical value, which may be assumed if there is no evidence to the contrary. For example, the default value for the NUMBER-OF-LEGS slot in the CAT frame is four. A prototype can be defined as a frame in which all the slots that have default values are filled with them, and all the others are empty (Johnson-Laird and Wason, 1977, 342). The boundaries of a concept on this view are implicit in the structure of its frame, and in any constraints on the values of slot fillers.

One further aspect of Rosch's theory deserves mention – the notion of a *basic level category* (Rosch, Mervis, Gray, Johnson and Boyes-Braen, 1976). It is via this notion that prototype theory attempts to link theories of perception and semantic memory. As network theories make explicit, many noun meanings are hierarchically related. Rosch claims that some parts of the hierarchy are more fundamental than others. Consider the part of semantic memory that represents edible things. Its basic level includes such concepts as *apple, orange, potato, carrot, and honey.* Exemplars of these categories are perceptually distinct, but within any one category all the exemplars share perceptually salient features. These features have a high *cue validity* for distinguishing members of one category from those of another. At higher levels in the hierarchy different exemplars of a category such as *fruit,* or *vegetable,* or *condiment* do not share many salient perceptual features. At lower levels different categories share too many perceptual features for discrimination to be easy. *Winesap, Red Delicious* and *Jonathan* apples are comparatively difficult to tell apart. Basic level concepts are therefore the first to be learned, and the easiest to make judgements about.

Meaning postulates

Meaning postulates are a device introduced into formal semantics by Carnap (1952) to capture relations between the meanings of words. The standard example of this kind of relation is that between *bachelor* on the one hand, and *unmarried* and *male* on the other. In a quasi-formal notation the meaning postulate that expresses this relation could be written:

for any x (if bachelor(x) then unmarried(x) and male(x))

Meaning postulates restrict the range of possible situations that need to be considered. For example, the meaning postulate above rules out worlds in which some bachelors are not male, and worlds in which some bachelors are not married.

Bar-Hillel (1967) argued that meaning postulates are superior to semantic markers, because markers cannot represent *arguments* of lexical items, such as the x, y and z in *x sells y to z* and *z buys y from x*. These arguments are essential for expressing the relation between the meanings of *buy* and *sell.*

for any x, y, z (x sells y to z if and only if z buys y from x)

Meaning postulates readily capture such relations, since they are expressed in a predicate-calculus-like notation in which predicates of any number of arguments are permitted.

Semantic marker theory was quickly reformulated to meet Bar-Hillel's criticisms. However, the idea of representing semantic relations by meaning postulates has been adopted by some psychologists (Kintsch, 1974; Fodor, Fodor and Garrett, 1975). Fodor *et al.* connect a meaning postulate representation of relations between word meanings with the idea of a mental language that is virtually a one–one mapping of natural language – Fodor's (1976) *Language of Thought* or *mentalese.* Fodor *et al.* propose a two-stage process of language understanding. The first stage is the relatively trivial translation of, say, English into the mentalese of English speakers. At the second stage meaning postulates defined over mentalese representations are used to draw inferences from the initial encoding.

In formal semantics, meaning postulates were introduced as a relatively minor part of a more general semantic theory. In psycholinguistics they have been proposed as a semantic theory in themselves. In this capacity they have met with less than total success, and compared with the other theories they have inspired little empirical research.

Procedural semantics

Procedural semantics (e.g. Johnson-Laird, 1977a) is part of an approach to the study of cognitive functions that takes computer programs as a metaphor for mental processes. This metaphor gains credence from the fact that any general purpose computer can in principle run any program, except where it is prevented by such theoretically uninteresting factors as limitations on the size of its memory. Furthermore, Turing (1950), who did as much as anyone to formalize the theory of computability, conjectured that any computation that the mind can perform can also be carried out by a computer.

The contribution of procedural semantics to the theory of word meaning is the claim that meanings can be represented as functions or procedures in a high-level list-processing language akin to POP11 or LISP. For many words such procedures are similar to sets of features or sets of meaning postulates – to determine if an object falls under a certain concept the appropriate procedure determines whether it possesses a number of features. However, procedures have certain advantages over these other kinds of representation. They share with meaning postulates the ability to link parts of a definition with connectives other than 'and', whereas a featural representation is naturally interpreted as stating that in order to belong to some category it is necessary to have property P *and* property Q, *and* property R, *and*. . . . Procedures can specify more complex combinations of properties. They can include conditional tests using *if. . .then*, and disjunctive tests using *or*. For example, there is no difficulty in giving a procedural definition of a concept such as *sister-in-law* (a sister-in-law is either one's brother's wife *or* one's spouse's sister). Such concepts are difficult to define using sets of features. The advantage of procedures over meaning postulates is that the elements in a procedural definition need not correspond to lexical items, whereas meaning postulates by definition state relations between words. Most features that have been proposed also correspond to words, although there is no reason why they should. Procedures may contain specifications for manipulating mental models that are easier to describe using the mathematical language of matrices and arrays, than using natural language.

A second claim made for procedural semantics is that it provides a theory of word meaning that is compatible with a computational account of high-level perceptual processes, because both theories draw on the same set of conceptual primitives.

Experimental investigations of word meaning

Most of the experiments to be described below were carried out in the late 1960s and early 1970s. They were designed primarily to test between feature and network theories – the only two that had been developed at that time. In the mid 1970s interest in word meaning began to decline as it became apparent that the two theories could not be distinguished experimentally. The reason why no distinction could be made was that auxiliary assumptions had to be introduced to produce theories of processing from theories of representation. Initially, fairly simple assumptions were made, but as more findings had to be explained, more complex processing assumptions were required by both kinds of theory. It therefore became difficult to tell whether subsequent experimental findings reflected underlying assumptions about representation or auxiliary assumptions about processing. Furthermore, neither theory was able to provide independent motivation for either its assumptions about representation or its assumptions about processing. In this respect, research on word meaning contrasts unfavourably with work on parsing. Linguists provide independent evidence about the syntactic structures that the human parser has to compute. Although there is no final agreement among linguists about the structure of, say, English sentences, the agreements they have reached are independent of the results of psycholinguistic experiments. Psychological data therefore bear only on the way the parser computes phrase structure, not on what structures sentences have.

The experimental paradigm most frequently used in semantic memory research is the *sentence verification task*. Subjects are presented with sentences expressing simple facts that are represented either directly or indirectly in semantic memory, or with falsehoods of comparable complexity, and have to decide whether they are true or false. Two kinds of sentences are typically used – set inclusion sentences such as:

A robin is a bird.
A whale is a fruit.

and property-attributing sentences such as:

A robin has feathers.
A whale has seeds.

It might be asked why word meaning has been studied using a *sentence* comprehension task. The reason is that psycholinguists wish to study normal comprehension, and in normal comprehension word meanings are processed in sentential contexts. To avoid contaminating the results of these experiments with effects of sentence-level processing, the words are put into simple sentence frames, so that syntactic processing is straightforward and is the same in all experimental conditions.

Tests of the network model

Collins and Quillian (1969, 1972) tested the hierarchical aspect of network representations by asking people to verify sentences about items 0, 1 and 2 levels apart in the hierarchy. True set inclusion sentences of these three kinds are:

> A canary is a canary.
> A canary is a bird.
> A canary is an animal.

Property-attributing statements for these three distances were constructed on the assumption that, in some cases at least, properties are stored only at the highest appropriate level in the hierarchy. This principle of *cognitive economy* holds that, for example, it is not necessary to store the information that a robin has feathers, that a sparrow has feathers and that a blackbird has feathers. The property of having feathers can be stored just once at the *bird* node. The fact that the various species of bird have feathers will follow from the fact that they are linked by ISA links to *bird*. Examples of true property attributions at the three distances used in the experiments are:

> A canary is yellow.
> A canary has feathers.
> A canary eats.

The results of the experiments were promising. For both kinds of sentence, verification times increased with increasing distance apart in the hierarchy. However, two kinds of difficulties for the network model quickly emerged – alternative explanations for Collins and Quillian's results, and data that their model could not explain. On the first of these counts, Landauer and Freedman (1968) had already suggested that set inclusion verification times could be explained in terms of set size. The set of animals is larger than the set of birds, and therefore takes longer to search for the included set of canaries. Conrad (1972) questioned Collins and Quillian's explanation of their property verification results. She noticed that Collins and Quillian had failed to control for the fact that there is a stronger association between *canary* and *yellow* than between *canary* and *feathers*, which might have speeded verification. She used sentences in which the features varied in both distance from the node in the hierarchy and in associative strength to the concept represented by the node. Conrad found that verification time varied with associative strength, but not with distance. However, explaining away Collins and Quillian's results is not the same as proposing an alternative theory of semantic memory. For example, simple associations may explain property verification times, but they do not contain the same information as links in a network and cannot explain the entailments that follow from the semantic relation between a concept and its properties.

The second problem for the network model was created by data that it could not explain, particularly some of the findings on negative judgements (decisions that sentences are false). In their early papers Collins and Quillian gave no account of such judgements. However, there is an obvious extension of their account of positive judgements that fills this gap in their theory. Collins and Quillian had proposed that positive judgements were made by searching for a path through the network from the two relevant nodes (for example, *canary* and *bird*), and then checking whether it was the right sort of path to support the relation described by the sentence. A negative judgement should therefore be made if no path of the right kind can be found, or perhaps if no such path can be found within some time limit. This hypothesis predicts that variability in times for negative judgements should be low, but Collins and Quillian (1972) found that it was higher than for true judgements. They proposed an alternative account of negative judgements according to which subjects searched the net for information contradictory to a presented statement. This idea predicted that negative judgements should be easier to make for items closer together in the network. However, Collins and Quillian's experimental results showed that closeness in the network slowed down negative judgements.

A canary is an ostrich.

is more difficult to judge false than:

A canary is a salmon.

Two further problems beset the early versions of network theory. First, it could not explain the within-category typicality effects that motivated prototype theory. It is easier to verify that a robin is a bird than that an ostrich is but, because both are one level removed from bird in the hierarchy, the simple network theory predicts that the judgements should take the same time. Second, Rips, Shoben, and Smith (1973) showed that it is easier to verify that a dog is an animal than that it is a mammal, contrary to predictions based on a dog-mammal-animal hierarchy. Network theorists were forced to claim that uncommon or specialized concepts in the hierarchy could be bypassed by additional ISA links going directly from, say, dog to animal.

The last major revision of Collins and Quillian's network theory of semantic memory was that of Collins and Loftus (1975). At about the same time Glass and Holyoak (1975) proposed an alternative, but equally complex, network-based theory. Collins and Loftus described a more detailed mechanism for searching a network, based on the idea of *spreading activation* from the nodes accessed by the concepts in a sentence. To account for typicality effects they proposed links of different strengths, along which it was more or less difficult for activation to spread. The major problem with Collins and Loftus's model – as with Glass and Holyoak's – was the proliferation of the auxiliary assumptions about the way in which information is accessed from the network. It is impossible to design an experiment that tests the underlying theory of representation rather than the auxiliary assumptions.

Although semantic networks have encountered problems as psychological theories of semantic memory, in AI there has been a continuing interest in them, and important advances have been made in two areas. First, in projects in which networks have been regarded as general information stores rather than specifically as repositories of information about word meaning, the retrieval of information from them has been made more efficient (e.g. Brachman, 1979; Fahlman, 1979). Second, the representational adequacy of semantic networks has been improved (e.g. Hendrix, 1979), for example to allow them to handle the meaning of quantifiers. This second advance is more relevant to the use of semantic networks to represent the meanings of sentences and texts, which will be discussed in the next chapter.

Tests of the feature model

Schaeffer and Wallace (1970) proposed an early version of the feature theory, which explained the effect of semantic similarity on negative judgements about the relatedness of two nouns. In their model, criteria for affirmative and negative judgements are respectively lowered and raised as featural overlap of the two nouns increase. Schaeffer and Wallace argued that the experimental results explained by their model did not reflect the organization of concepts in semantic memory, but only a comparison process that took place after retrieval. However, their theory assumes, at the very least, that word meanings are represented in such a way that the amount of overlap between two concepts can be computed.

The most influential processing model based on feature theory is the two-stage model of Smith, Shoben and Rips (1974), which incorporates their distinction between defining and characteristic features, and which was designed to account for the results of sentence verification experiments. In the first stage of this model the complete feature sets of the two nouns (subject and predicate) are compared, and an overall similarity measure is computed. If this measure has a very high value a fast 'yes' response can be given, and if it has a very low value a fast 'no' response can be given (Smith *et al*. do not consider sentences such as *a bird is a robin*). This stage uses a kind of rule, called a *heuristic*, that might give the wrong answer. For example, a very atypical member of a category (for example, ostrich as a member of the category of birds) may share only a few defining features with the category prototype. Hence, their feature sets – containing both defining and characteristic features – have comparatively few items in common. To avoid errors, the high and low criteria for the quick responses must be well separated. The second stage of the model is required only if the overall similarity measure takes an intermediate value. At this stage the defining features of the two concepts are compared. A match leads to a 'yes' response and a mismatch to a 'no' response. Whichever response is made, it will be relatively slow. The second stage uses an *algorithmic* procedure. The discovery of a match or mismatch between the two sets of defining features guarantees that a correct decision will be made – though there can, of course, be no guarantee against computational error.

Like Schaeffer and Wallace's model, this model explains typicality and similarity effects. A typical category member has not only the defining features of its category, but also many of the characteristic features. Therefore overall similarity is high, and a quick 'yes' response can be made. Atypical category members have few characteristic features, therefore overall similarity is lower, and the response must be based on a second stage comparison. Similarity slows down negative judgements because it produces a fairly high similarity measure at the first stage, and a comparison of the defining features is required. Smith *et al*.'s model is wider in scope than that of Schaeffer and Wallace, and unlike the latter model it is specifically addressed to the question of how information in semantic memory is organized.

One problem for Smith *et al*.'s model is that similarity does not always increase falsification time for untrue sentences. For example, as Holyoak and Glass (1975) showed, sentences of the following kinds are easy to reject:

All cats are dogs.
All animals are birds.

However, these sentences are semantically more complex than the set inclusion and property attribution sentences typically used in semantic memory experiments. A theory of how they are understood has to take into account the contribution of the meaning of *all* as well the meaning of the nouns. Therefore, no definite conclusions about *word* meanings can be drawn from these findings.

When does decomposition occur?   In both Schaeffer and Wallace's model and Smith *et al.*'s, word meanings, or at least those of common nouns, are *decomposed* into sets of features every time the words are processed. Intuitively it is implausible that comprehension always requires semantic decomposition. Consider, for example, the way people respond to a question such as:

   What is your name?

As Johnson-Laird (1981) points out, it is unlikely that *name* is decomposed into a set of features in order to answer this question. A feature theory of word meaning need not claim that decomposition always occurs. It may be required only in certain circumstances, for example to verify set inclusion sentences. Smith *et al.*'s model may not therefore reflect the way in which meanings are processed in normal comprehension.

A number of experiments have attempted to find evidence for the analysis of words into more basic elements of meaning in other circumstances. Clark (1974) used the sentence-picture verification task, in which subjects have to say whether a sentence correctly describes a picture, to investigate the comprehension of words such as *absent* and *present*. It has been suggested (see Clark, 1974) that *absent* is an implicitly negative lexical item, whose semantic representation is NOT(PRESENT). Clark found that sentences containing such negative items were responded to more slowly than corresponding sentences with positive lexical items, such as *present*.

Despite Clark's apparent success in demonstrating decomposition into elements of meaning, if not into semantic markers, many other attempts to provide evidence for decomposition have failed (see for example, Kintsch, 1974). One null result may indicate an insensitive experimental technique, but repeated failures with different techniques suggest that decomposition does not always occur, but is a strategy that is used only when it is required by the experimental task. Johnson-Laird, Gibbs and de Mowbray (1978) devised a task in which decomposition was essential. They asked subjects to mark all instances of natural consumable solids (e.g. apple) in a list of words. Immediately afterwards the subjects were given an unexpected recall test for all of the words in the list. Words in the target category were the best recalled, but the main interest of the experiment was in how well subjects remembered the other words. Recall of these words depended on the amount of featural overlap between them and the target category. For example, coal shares two features with the target category – it is natural and solid. It was comparatively well remembered. Paraffin, on the other hand is a man-made non-consumable liquid with no features of the target words. Very few subjects remembered it.

The explanation of this result appeals to the amount of processing needed to accept or reject the words as members of the target category. Any featural mismatch is sufficient for rejection, but a match on each of the three features is required if a word is to be accepted as a member of the target category. The average number of checks required to make a decision therefore increases with the amount of featural overlap, and the more processing that has been performed on a word, the better it is recalled.

It might be objected that the Johnson-Laird *et al.* experiment bears even less relation to ordinary language processing than sentence verification experiments. Tabossi and Johnson-Laird (1980) therefore attempted to demonstrate selective priming of components of a word's meaning in sentential contexts. Subjects read sentences and were asked a question immediately after each one. For example,

> The goldsmith cut the glass with the diamond.
> Are diamonds hard?
> OR Are diamonds valuable?

The results were that the first question was answered more quickly, and the second question more slowly, than when those questions followed a sentence that did not prime either component – hardness or value – of the meaning of *diamond*, for example:

> The film showed the person with the diamond.

These experiments show that some aspects of a word's meaning may, if the task demands it, be processed separately from others. However, these aspects need not be identified with semantic features, they could, for example, be sets of relations to other concepts in a semantic network.

Tests of prototype theory

Rosch's prototype theory was motivated by typicality effects, and Rosch herself performed many experiments to investigate them (see Rosch, 1978, for a summary). This work arose from her earlier cross-cultural studies on colour terms and geometric shapes (Heider, 1972 – Rosch was formerly known as Heider). Even people whose languages have only two colour words (corresponding roughly to *light* and *dark* or *black* and *white*), and no words for geometrical shapes (for example, the Dani of New Guinea), find focal reds, blues, yellows and greens (that is the best examples of those colours), and squares, circles, and equilateral triangles, easier to re-identify than non-focal colours or distorted versions of those shapes. Rosch used a variety of techniques, including priming and rating, but all her experiments point to the single conclusion that some exemplars of a concept are more typical than others, and are for this reason easier to relate to that concept. However, a recent finding by Armstrong, Gleitman and Gleitman (1983) casts doubt on whether these findings reflect the mental representation of word *meanings*. Armstrong *et al.* found typicality effects for what they call *well-defined* categories, for example that of even numbers, whose meanings should not be represented by prototypes. The number 2 is rated a more typical even number than 106, though both are equally good even numbers according to the mathematical definition. These results suggest that typicality judgements may reflect familiarity or degree of association rather than semantic relations.

Rosch has also provided experimental support for her idea of basic level categories. Rosch *et al.* (1976) showed that such categories develop earlier and are processed more easily than categories at other levels.

Since both feature and network theories have been modified to account for typicality effects, there is no longer a need for a separate prototype theory of word meaning. In any case, prototype theory has difficulty in explaining some aspects of word meaning, including complex semantic relations, such as that between *buy* and *sell*. If prototype theory were to be modified to account for these facts, some additional apparatus would be required. This apparatus would probably be borrowed from one of the other theories, and the resulting hybrid theory would be similar to more recent versions of network or feature theory.

Procedural semantics

Procedural semantics has not directly inspired any experiments on the mental representation of word meaning, but procedural accounts of word meaning have been incorporated into many AI programs from Winograd (1972) onwards. The most detailed procedural analysis of word meanings is that of Miller and Johnson-Laird (1976), but perhaps the most interesting is Johnson-Laird's account of spatial terms (reported in Johnson-Laird, 1982b). Although Johnson-Laird's theory is decompositional, in the sense that the meanings of the spatial terms *on the left of, on the right of, in front of* and *behind* are built up from more primitive elements, those elements do not correspond to vocabulary items, as semantic markers typically do. They are procedures for manipulating arrays that represent spatial layouts.

A further advantage of procedural semantics is that it is not only a theory of word meaning, but also an account of sentential and text meaning. A procedural account of the meaning of a word should therefore be formulated in such a way as to capture its contribution to the truth-conditions of sentences in which it occurs.

Unresolved problems about word meaning

The five theories of word meaning outlined at the beginning of this chapter have more in common than their conceptual bases suggest. For this reason aspects of meaning that are problematic for one theory tend to be problematic for the others. Their major problem is that, apart from meaning postulates which are in any case inadequate, and procedural semantics, the theories were formulated to express the meanings of concrete nouns, and they do not easily generalize to other kinds of words. The following questions pinpoint some of the difficulties. What features should be used to analyse the meanings of abstract nouns? (or: What is a prototype for an abstract noun?). How should grammatical function words be analysed? And what about verbs, adjectives and adverbs? The feature theory fares worst of all the theories, since verbs, adjectives and function words all present immediate problems for featural analysis.

Procedural semantics fares best, largely because its practitioners have been semantically sophisticated, and have considered how to express meanings of words other than concrete nouns. Miller and Johnson-Laird (1976), for example, devoted many pages to the analysis of verbs, and Johnson-Laird has more recently produced procedural accounts of spatial terms (1982b) and quantifiers (see 1983, ch. 5). The meaning of a function word in procedural semantics is its contribution to the (procedural) meaning of a sentence. However, procedural semantics is not entirely without its problems. For example, the theory attempts to relate language and perception, and it is here that abstract, as opposed to concrete, nouns pose a problem for procedural semantics.

The success of procedural semantics in describing the meaning of many kinds of words suggests that as a framework for studying word meaning it does have adequate representational power. Johnson-Laird, Herrmann and Chaffin (1984) have argued that the same is true of semantic networks. They are equivalent to Turing machines, and hence can perform any well-specified computation. However, there are two major obstacles to providing a fully adequate psychological theory of word meanings, both of which can be related to points made by Wittgenstein (1953) in *Philosophical Investigations*. First, the real difficulty of the task is far from apparent. Our facility as language users prevents us from recognizing the complexity of the representations and processes that underlie our mastery of word meanings. For example, as Wittgenstein and others since (e.g. Dreyfus, 1979) have pointed out, the use of words takes for granted knowledge of the way things usually happen in both the physical and the social worlds. It presupposes what Wittgenstein called a *form of life*. There may therefore be some truth in the structuralists' claim that a complete theory of meaning is impossible, because it requires a prior formalization of all our knowledge about the world. Second, words have many different kinds of meanings – those meanings must not all be forced into a single mould. The existence of general notations for expressing word meanings does not guarantee that those notations will be used as flexibly as they need to be. It is easy to get into the habit of always using a formalism in the same way. These observations suggest the need for more sophisticated psychological theories of word meaning. Psycholinguists should also bear in mind Putnam's remarks about partial knowledge of meanings, and formulate theories that are compatible with them.

Summary

In this chapter two questions have been discussed. How is the mental equivalent of the set of definitions in a dictionary organized? How is information extracted from that store? The answers to these questions must take into account a number of facts about word meaning – facts about ambiguity, semantic relations, the use of words without full knowledge of the things that they refer to, and the relation of language to the world via perception. In psycholinguistics, five accounts of word meaning have been proposed – feature theories, network theories, prototypes, meaning postulates and procedural semantics. The earliest research was inspired by models of the first two kinds, and led to elaborations of two aspects of both models: the underlying representational systems – in particular to include information about typicality, and the procedures that retrieve knowledge of word meanings from semantic memory. This work ceased when it was realized that the large number of processing assumptions, which had no independent motivation, prevented any test of the underlying theories of representation.

Research into lexical decomposition – implied both by feature theories and by some versions of procedural semantics, which propose underlying semantic primitives – has continued. This work suggests that decomposition occurs only when it is required by the experimental task.

Most of the theories were developed primarily to represent the meanings of concrete nouns. In the case of feature theories, an extension to other kinds of word meanings, say those of grammatical function words, would change their nature considerably. In this respect procedural semantics offers the best hope for a psychologically plausible and semantically sophisticated account of our knowledge and use of word meanings.

7

Understanding discourse and text

The previous chapters have described processes, such as word recognition and parsing, that are important to the language *user* only in so far as they contribute to the understanding of discourse and text. This chapter discusses how that understanding is achieved.

To understand a text it is necessary to understand the sentences in it. The meaning of a sentence depends on, among other things, the meanings of its words, and on the structural relations between them. Similarly, the meaning of a discourse or text depends on that of its component sentences, though additional information may be required to produce a full interpretation. This additional information includes both knowledge about language – in particular pragmatic knowledge about both sentences and discourse, and knowledge about the world.

The distinction between sentence meaning and text meaning has rarely been drawn by psychologists, since psycholinguistics is the study of language use, and when a sentence is *used* it assumes the properties of a monologue or text. Psycholinguistic experiments with single sentences are therefore experiments on *discourse* comprehension. There are questions, both linguistic and psycholinguistic, about sentence meaning as opposed to text meaning, some of which will be briefly touched on in this chapter, but all the experiments investigate text comprehension.

The two principal psycholinguistic questions about the interpretation of discourse concern, first, the information that is encoded from a text (by a particular person on a particular occasion) and, second, how the mental representation of that information is constructed. Since the early 1970s there have been hundreds of studies of the interpretation of sentences and texts. However, it is not always easy to relate their results to these two questions. In the case of the first question, the problem is that psychology and AI, like linguistics, suffered, in the late 1960s and early 1970s, from a lack of clarity about meaning, semantics and the kinds of information that a text could convey. In the case of the second question, psycholinguists for a long time failed to recognize the problems that have to be solved.

Only a small proportion of the many studies on text comprehension can be discussed in this chapter. The ones that have been selected are those that produced results of lasting interest, and those that illustrate particular pitfalls. The chapter starts by considering how the explicit content of sentences is encoded, and then investigates the way in which information from different sentences is integrated. Next the use of knowledge about the world to go beyond what is explicit is discussed, and a distinction is drawn between inferences necessary for comprehension and those that are merely elaborative. In the second half of the chapter, global aspects of text comprehension are considered. The influence of context on the interpretation of expressions in a text is discussed first. Then the possibility is mooted that texts, like sentences, have a syntactic structure. It is concluded that the structure of texts is not specific to them, but mirrors the structure of their subject matter. Finally factors that determine the import or significance of a text are described.

The shift of interest from syntax to 'semantics'

When the Derivational Theory of Complexity was shown to be untenable (see chapter 4), many psycholinguists lost interest in the effects of syntactic factors on comprehension. Findings that had been attributed to syntactic processing were re-explained in terms of meaning, so it was natural that experiments started to focus on what were labelled 'semantic' factors. In fact, the term *semantic* covered all aspects of the information carried by a sentence, and mental representations of this information were misleadingly referred to as *semantic representations*. This early research proceeded in two overlapping phases. In the first it was shown that people remember the 'semantics' of what they hear or read, rather than its syntax or other details of its surface form. In the second it was argued that information not explicit in a text is incorporated into its representation, and that that representation cannot be characterized by any *linguistic* description of the text. However, psycholinguists investigating sentence comprehension, like their colleagues, had initially looked to neighbouring disciplines for accounts of the competence underlying the skill they were studying.

There were two potential sources of ideas. The first was linguistic theory. Following the suggestion of Katz and Fodor (1963), a transformational grammar in Standard Theory (Chomsky, 1965) had a component that assigned semantic interpretations to the sentences generated by its syntactic rules. On Chomsky's view that linguistics is part of cognitive psychology, these semantic interpretations corresponded to mental representations of (the semantic content) of sentences. The second source of ideas was AI. A number of programs had been written that responded to questions by generating representations of their content and computing answers from those representations. Psychological theories of meaning were based on these computer programs.

Katz and Fodor's sentential semantics

Katz and Fodor (1963) attempted to provide a framework within which semantic descriptions for particular languages could be constructed, just as Chomsky had provided the transformational framework for syntactic descriptions. In fact Katz and Fodor's work did not inspire much linguistic research of this kind. Neither did it directly influence psycholinguistic experiments, though it did provoke more general controversies. Nevertheless, it is of interest because it raises questions about the construction of mental representations of meaning that psycholinguists have never properly addressed.

A semantic theory specifies how the truth-conditional part of the meaning of a sentence or text depends on the meanings of its parts and on the structural relations between them (see chapter 5). The corresponding psychological theory of text comprehension should explain how mental representations of word meanings are put together to produce text representations. However, it is not immediately apparent how the representations described in chapter 6 should be combined, and the problem is particularly acute for feature theories, which derive from the work of Katz and Fodor.

Katz and Fodor themselves attempted to solve this problem in the sentential part of their semantic theory. They proposed that the meanings of sentences are assembled by a set of *projection rules* that amalgamate sets of features. The amalgamation takes place according to the syntactic structure of the sentence, and works upwards from the bottom of the phrase marker to the top. Katz and Fodor did not state clearly which phrase marker, underlying or surface, was semantically interpreted. Chomsky (1965) argued for deep structure, though more recently (for example, Chomsky, 1981) he has favoured a different kind of semantic theory that interprets slighly elaborated surface structures, called S-structures.

The larger sets of features that result from amalgamation represent the meaning of higher nodes in the phrase-structure tree. For example, the meanings of a DET (e.g. *the*) and an N (e.g. *book*) combine to give the meaning of the NP (e.g. *the book*) of which they are constituents. The NP meaning might then combine with a VP meaning to produce a sentence meaning. Unfortunately Katz and Fodor's account of amalgamation is not perspicuous. In some cases, including many adjective-noun pairs (for example, *red car*), a simple combination of features produces approximately the correct meaning for a phrase – a red car has the features of a car plus the feature red. However, summation of features is incorrect as an account of how, say, the meaning of a direct object combines with that of a transitive verb. Katz and Fodor employ *selectional restrictions* to ensure that verbs have objects (and subjects) of the right kind, but their account of the relation between a main verb's meaning and that of its direct object is inadequate.

The principal achievement of Katz and Fodor's sentential semantics was to provide a partial explanation of why a sentence with, say, two words each with two meanings need not have four different interpretations. Consider the sentence:

The princess threw the ball.

Both *throw* and *ball* have two common meanings, but the sentence can be interpreted in only two ways. The reason it does not have four meanings is that two of the four combinations of word meanings are incompatible. For example, if *threw* means projected, its grammatical object (as defined by Chomsky, 1965, see chapter 2) must be a physical object. A selectional restriction prevents *ball* in the sense of social occasion from filling this grammatical role.

The immediate heirs to Katz and Fodor's theory – Generative Semantics and the interpretive semantics of Extended Standard Theory – shared many of its defects. Their concern with structural aspects of meaning arose primarily from the failure of Standard Theory to assign the correct meaning to transformed sentences containing quantifiers, such as *all, some, most, many* and *few* – the case of passive sentences with quantifiers was discussed in chapter 2. Both theories tried to solve the problem by ensuring that the quantifiers were in the 'right position' in the structure that was semantically interpreted, though they made radically different proposals about this structure. However, neither gave a detailed account of how the meaning of a quantified sentence is computed, once the quantifiers are correctly placed. This question was not addressed until model theory was applied to natural languages.

Model-theoretic semantics differs in many ways from Katz and Fodor's theory, but they share the idea of a set of rules (Katz and Fodor's projection rules) for combining word meanings to produce the meanings of larger expressions. Model-theoretic semantics is more rigorous than Katz and Fodor's theory, and its semantic interpretation rules are better specified.

Among the questions to which it provides clearer answers are (i) what are the projection rules for different syntactic constructions? (ii) what must *word* meanings be like if they are to be combined by projection rules? (iii) what sorts of meanings do phrases (NPs, VPs, PPs, and so on) have? (iv) what aspects of meaning can this kind of *compositional* semantic theory explain?

Many linguists now accept model-theoretic semantics, together with its delimitation of the domain of semantics (see chapter 5). On this view, the semantic representation of a (descriptive) sentence determines the conditions under which the sentence is true. That is to say it defines the set of situations that the sentence could correctly describe. However, the goal of comprehension cannot be to construct a semantic representation in this narrow sense. The language understanding system must produce a representation of the *particular* situation described in a text. Nevertheless, semantic processing contributes to the construction of this representation, and a theory of text comprehension must draw on a clearly formulated account of sentential semantics, such as that of model theory. The fact that it has not done so to date merely shows that many details of the comprehension process have not been adequately modelled.

What is remembered – syntax or 'semantics'?

Although Katz and Fodor's work did not directly inspire any psycholinguistic experiments, it helped to create the climate in which interest switched from syntax to meaning, and it suggested that the mental representation of a sentence might be 'semantic', rather than syntactic. Because of Chomsky's emphasis on syntax, the first psycholinguistic proposal about the representation of sentences – Miller's kernel-plus-tags theory, described in chapter 4 – held that sentences are remembered in terms of their syntactic structure. Once this assumption was questioned, it became necessary to determine empirically what aspects of sentences people actually remember, and it transpired that they cannot remember syntactic details very well. To someone unfamiliar with the history of generative grammar and psycholinguistics this finding will not be surprising. When people talk to each other and when they read books, newspapers and magazines they are primarily interested in the content of what they hear or read (its meaning) not the way it is said (its form or syntax).

Several factors hasten the rapid loss of memory for the *surface form* of sentences, which has been reported in many studies. Auditory as opposed to visual presentation of the to-be-remembered texts is one such factor –

it is more difficult to remember the form of spoken sentences than that of written ones (Flagg and Reynolds, 1977). Another is the time between presentation and testing – surface form is remembered well only for a short time (Bartlett, 1932; Dooling and Christiaansen, 1977). Third, people who are expecting a memory test on surface form can remember it, when others, who have seen or heard the same material, cannot (Johnson-Laird and Stevenson, 1970). Finally, if the surface form of a sentence has been specifically chosen to convey information it may be comparatively well remembered (Keenan, MacWhinney and Mayhew, 1977).

What people remember has been characterized in several ways: gist rather than verbatim detail, content as opposed to form, 'semantics' and not syntax. These rather general contrasts should not be taken too literally. The experimental findings give a clearer indication of how texts are encoded.

Sachs (1967) showed that people rapidly forget surface syntax. Her subjects listened to passages containing sentences such as:

He sent a letter about it to Galileo, the great Italian scientist.

After a further 0, 80, or 160 syllables a test sentence was unexpectedly presented, and subjects had to say if it was the same as a previous sentence in the passage. Four kinds of test sentence were used: the original, a passivized version of it, a version with the phrases switched round, such as:

He sent Galileo, the great Italian scientist, a letter about it.

and a version in which the roles of the characters were reversed:

Galileo, the great Italian scientist, sent him a letter about it.

When the test was immediate the subjects were good at detecting all three kinds of changes. However, after 80 or 160 syllables they could only guess if there had been any alteration, except in the last case, the only one in which the meaning was different: 80 per cent of such changes were still detected. Wanner (1974) demonstrated similar forgetting of verbatim detail at even shorter delays. He asked subjects to remember the wording of what were ostensibly instructions for a different experiment immediately after they had read them, and found that they were unable to.

The sentences that Sachs's subjects failed to distinguish had the same meaning, but they also had the same underlying syntactic structure. Therefore, although her experiment shows that people rapidly forget details of surface structure, it does not resolve the issue of whether they remember deep structure or meaning. Johnson-Laird and Stevenson (1970) addressed this question by testing memory for sentences with different deep structures, but the same content, for example:

> John liked the painting and he bought it from the duchess.
> John liked the painting and the duchess sold it to him.
> The painting pleased John and he bought it from the duchess.
> The painting pleased John and the duchess sold it to him.

John is the deep structure subject of *liked*, in the first two sentences, but the deep structure object of *pleased* in the second two. The other NPs also have different deep structure roles in the two pairs of sentences. In a broad sense the four sentences have the same meaning, though on some theories they would have different semantic representations, and the relations between them would be captured by meaning postulates linking *like* and *please*, and *buy* and *sell*.

Johnson-Laird and Stevenson presented subjects with a passage that included the first of these sentences. Less than a minute after they had heard it, they were given a recognition memory test and had to say which one of eight sentences had been in the passage. The eight items were the four sentences above, and four others derived from them by interchanging *John* and *the duchess*. Although those subjects who had not been warned of the test rarely chose sentences in which the roles of the characters were reversed, they could not remember which one of the four sentences was compatible with the passage they had heard. This result shows that people do not remember deep structure.

In a similar experiment Johnson-Laird, Robins and Velicogna (1974) found that people forgot what kind of lexical item, noun or verb, had been used to express particular concepts. They confused:

> The owner of the magic staff dispatched the ship.
> AND The dispatcher of the ship owned the magic staff.

Garnham (1981a) demonstrated that people confuse sentences that are *semantically*, as well as syntactically, different. Two sentences differ semantically if the range of situations that they could describe are distinct. Such sentences may be mistaken for one another if, in the context of a passage, they describe the same event. For example, in a passage that starts:

> By the window was a man with a martini.

the noun phrases *the man by the window* and *the man with the martini* are coreferential, though in other passages they are unlikely to be. Subjects who heard a passage beginning with the sentence above could not remember whether they had later heard:

The man with the martini waved to the hostess.
OR The man by the window waved to the hostess.

Thus people remember neither the syntax nor the semantics of what they hear, but rather its content, in a more general sense. They produce a representation of what the *world* would be like if the passage were true – a representation that is not closely related to any linguistic description of the text, and which should not be called a semantic representation. A more appropriate name for it is a *mental model* of a situation in the real or an imaginary world.

Semantic networks – an AI representation of the content of sentences

In AI the term *semantic representation* has been (ab)used in much the same way as in psycholinguistics with similar consequences. However, there is one important difference between research on the representation of meaning in AI and that in psychology. Programs that 'understand' natural language must generate representations of content, and the question of how these representations are constructed cannot be ignored. In the early 1970s AI had a greater influence than linguistics on the psychological study of sentence meaning. The most popular approach (e.g. Anderson and Bower, 1973; Rumelhart, Lindsay and Norman, 1972; Schank, 1972) was to use semantic networks, which had previously been used to encode word meanings (see chapter 6), to represent the meanings of sentences.

Semantic networks are made up of nodes and links. To represent sentence meanings it is necessary to introduce new types of both of these components – new kinds of nodes to represent the things that sentences are about, and new kinds of links to represent the relations between them that sentences express. The set of nodes must be expanded to include nodes standing for *individuals* (i.e. people, things, places, and so on). Individual nodes are connected to nodes in semantic memory – the ones described in the last chapter – by set membership links. For example, a node standing for Florence Nightingale would be linked to, among others, the NURSE node. A further requirement is nodes standing for propositions – the meanings of simple sentences.

In expanding the set of links, several approaches have been taken. Anderson and Bower (1973; Anderson, 1976) assume that each proposition comprises a SUBJECT and a PREDICATE, though philosophers have long argued that this analysis is inappropriate for sentences with quantifiers. For example, *no man is an island* has no subject in any straightforward sense.

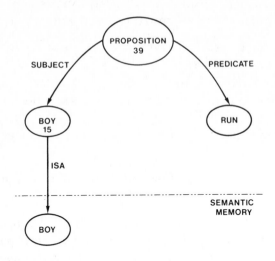

Figure 7.1 Semantic network, with subject-predicate links, representing 'the boy runs'

On Anderson and Bower's theory, the simple sentence *the boy runs* is represented by the network shown in Figure 7.1. For more complex sentences, nodes representing predicates are introduced, and each predicate is analysed as a RELATION and an OBJECT. The network corresponding to *the small boy sees the woman* is shown in Figure 7.2. Links to semantic

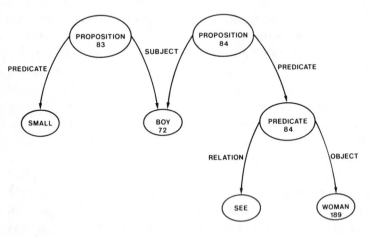

Figure 7.2 Semantic network, with subject-predicate links, representing 'the small boy sees the woman'

memory have been omitted. This network illustrates the fact that a single sentence may express more than one proposition. All network theories postulate one such node for each clause in a complex sentence, and in some, including Anderson and Bower's, adjectives and adverbs also introduce separate propositions. On this view a sentence such as *The small boy walks* expresses propositions corresponding to the sentences *The boy walks* and *The boy is small*. The numbers on the propositional and predicate nodes are arbitrary labels to keep different propositions and predicates distinct in memory.

An alternative way of representing relations between individuals is to introduce links standing for case relations (see chapter 2). On this account, a sentence such as *John sells the book to Mary* can be represented by the network in Figure 7.3. Case relations have been used by Rumelhart *et al.* (1972),

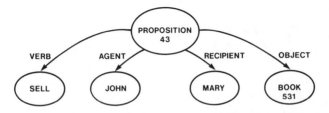

Figure 7.3 Semantic network, with case relation links, representing 'John sells the book to Mary'

Simmons (1973) and, in a modified form, by Schank (1972).

All versions of network theory assume that there is more to understanding discourse than translating sentences into pieces of network. Most importantly, networks that share nodes are combined so that all the information about a person, object, place or event is linked to the single node representing it. However, although a single node can enter into many different relations, network theory does not itself explain how the language understanding system recognizes that two expressions, say *the man* and *he*, refer to the same individual. The theory may specify how information is represented in memory, but it says nothing about the construction of memory representations in the course of comprehension.

Early versions of network theory suffered from two further defects. First, their expressive power was limited. They were incapable, for example, of representing quantified sentences correctly. Second, new kinds of nodes and links were introduced without any specification of what they represented, and hence it was impossible to determine if a piece of network correctly captured the meaning of a sentence (see Woods, 1975, for a cogent critique of this early work). Both of these problems have been solved in more recent network models (e.g. Anderson, 1976; Hendrix, 1979). For example, Hendrix has introduced a technique called *partitioning* to represent quantifiers, and he provides a formal specification of what each component of his network stands for.

Once the question of what nodes and links represent is taken seriously, it becomes apparent that semantic networks are a *language* in which the meaning of sentences can be expressed – a language in need of its own semantic theory. Semantic networks cannot by themselves provide a semantic description of English or any other natural language, since translation is not semantic interpretation, though it may make such interpretation easier. The advantage of semantic networks over natural language is that they are computationally tractable. It may therefore be appropriate for the language understanding system to translate sentences in natural language into a network-like representation.

Psychologists often express sentence meanings using a modified version of semantic networks, known as *propositional representations*. As was mentioned above, semantic networks contain propositional nodes, which represent the meanings of simple sentences. If there are no quantifiers, the information in a network can be written out as a set of propositions. Trivially, the network in Figure 7.1 corresponds to the single proposition:

(TALL JOHN)

The slightly more complex sentence, *The small boy walks*, contains two propositions:

(SMALL BOY785)
(WALKS BOY785)

In a set of propositions the arbitrary label on a node in a semantic network, such as the 785 on the BOY785 node, may be repeated several times. It is this device that allows networks to be 'linearized' into sets of propositions without losing the information that several predicates apply to the same person or thing. Propositional representations suffer from the same problems as the early network theories – inability to handle quantification, lack of a clear semantics and lack of an account of how two expressions in a text are recognized as referring to the same individual. Nevertheless, they are frequently encountered in the psycholinguistic literature, though often only as informal specifications of meaning (see especially Kintsch, 1974). In a more recent version of Kintsch's theory (e.g. van Dijk and Kintsch, 1983) a propositional representation is one of three memory representations of a text – surface form, textbase (or set of propositions), and situation model (similar to the mental models described below).

Experiments based on network theory

Network theory inspired a number of experiments that demonstrated how information about an individual is clustered around a single node in memory. The most important prediction was that facts about, say, a person are stored in a way that is independent of how he or she was described when those facts were encoded.

Anderson and Bower (1973, ch. 9) showed that people could not remember whether they had heard:

> George Washington had good health.
> OR The first president of the United States had good health.

What they knew about George Washington did not reflect how he had been described on a particular occasion.

In a related experiment Anderson and Hastie (1974) taught people the occupations of fictitious characters, for example:

> James Bartlett is the lawyer.

The subjects then learned additional facts, such as:

> James Bartlett rescued the kitten.
> The lawyer caused the accident.

Finally they were given a sentence verification task that included sentences they had seen, and others in which coreferential names and noun phrases were swapped around, for example:

> The lawyer rescued the kitten.

The two kinds of sentence were verified equally quickly – the way a person was described did not matter. However, a second group of subjects, who learned the occupations after they learned the additional facts, were quicker to verify the sentences they had actually seen. When it is discovered that two expressions refer to the same person, memory must be reorganized, and this experiment suggests that reorganization is not immediate.

It should not be concluded from these results that names and definite noun phrases can be indiscriminately substituted for one another *in text*. Ortony and Anderson (1977) point out that names are more appropriate in some contexts, and noun phrases in others. However, these *textual* constraints are not necessarily reflected in memory.

The propositional variant of network theory suggests that the content of a text may be remembered as a set of propositions, and attempts have been made to provide experimental support for this idea. Goetz, Anderson and Schallert (1981) showed that simple propositions are either recalled completely or not at all, which is consistent with the idea that propositions form units in memory. Ratcliff and McKoon (1978) presented subjects with a series of sentences, and then asked them to decide which of a list of words were in the sentences. Decisions were faster when a word was preceded by another from the same sentence, and the effect was greater when the words came from the same proposition than when they came from different propositions. Ratcliff and McKoon argue that these findings suggest a propositional memory representation. However, while it is easy to ensure that the results of such experiments cannot be explained in terms of surface features, such as distance between words, it is difficult to show that they must be explained in terms of propositional representations rather than some other representation of content, for example a situation model. All such representations group information in a similar way.

Integrating information from different parts of a text

The 'semantic network' experiments show that different facts about a single individual are stored together in memory, regardless of how they are acquired. However, network theory does not explain how the language understanding system recognizes that different expressions in a text (e.g. 'Wuthering Heights', Emily Bronte's novel, the book, it) refer to the same individual. The theory gives no account of how the understanding system treats a discourse or text as a related whole, and not as merely a string of sentences. A psycholinguistic theory, by contrast, must describe the processes that bring together information, and integrate it into a representation of the overall message conveyed by the text. Since the early 1970s Bransford and his colleagues (see Bransford and McCarrell, 1975, for a review) have stressed the integrative aspects of text comprehension, but they have never put forward a detailed account of how integration is effected.

The sentences of a text are related to one another by a variety of linguistic and non-linguistic devices. Although some linguistic devices, such as those that come under the head of style, are global, the ones that have most interested psycholinguists are those that establish local or cohesive (Halliday and Hasan, 1976) links. Non-linguistic links, which will be discussed later in this chapter, depend largely upon knowledge about the world.

Halliday and Hasan distinguish five kinds of cohesive tie. One is conjunction; the other four, coreference, substitution, ellipsis and lexical cohesion, are usually grouped together under the head of *anaphora*, though Halliday and Hasan themselves use this term in a more restricted sense. An anaphoric expression, or anaphor, in the sense that the term will be used in this chapter, is one that takes its meaning from some other, usually preceding, part of the text, or from context. Examples of anaphoric expressions are definite pronouns (*he, she, they, it*), indefinite pronouns (*one*), elliptical verb phrases and some definite noun phrases.

Interpreting anaphoric expressions

When considered in isolation, most anaphors have little or no semantic content. Before the information in a sentence containing an anaphor can be integrated into a memory representation of a text, the language processing system must determine which other part of the text it takes its meaning from, and assign it a meaning. To take a simple example, in the passage:

Mary and John went into the room.
He took off his coat.

the anaphoric pronoun *he* has to be recognized as coreferential with *John*, and not *Mary* or *the room*, before the information in the second sentence can be combined with that in the first.

Anaphors can take their meanings in two ways from their *antecedents*. Some anaphors are *identity of reference* anaphors. Definite pronouns, for example, typically *refer* to the same person or thing as some previous expression in the text, as in the example above. Other anaphors, for example indefinite pronouns, are *identity of sense* anaphors. They refer to a different example of the same *kind* of thing as a previous phrase. The passage:

Mary baked a cake.
John baked one, too.

is about two separate cakes.

To interpret, or *resolve*, an anaphor it is necessary to know what kind of thing the anaphor can refer to – pronouns refer to individuals, elliptical verb phrases to predicates, and so on – and what things of that kind have been made available for anaphoric reference by linguistic and non-linguistic context. Some anaphors are easily resolved, either because there is only one possible antecedent, or because the semantic content of the anaphor itself – in the case of a definite pronoun its number and gender – reduces the set of possible antecedents to one. For example, in the sentence:

John sold Sue his car because he hated it.

if *he* is unstressed, it must refer to John. However, if *Sue* is replaced by
Bill, it is not immediately clear to whom the pronoun refers, and knowledge about buying, selling and whether a buyer or a seller is likely to take
part in the transaction because they hate the object of transfer becomes relevant
to its resolution. Note that a minor change to the second clause of the sentence
can alter the assignment:

John sold Bill his car because he needed it.

Examples of this sort show that simple syntactic strategies for the resolution of pronouns do not work. More sophisticated structural strategies, such
as the one proposed by Winograd (1972) for his SHRDLU program, are
also unsuccessful. For example, SHRDLU takes the first *it* in:

I put the pencil in my pocket but because it had a hole it fell out.

to refer to the pencil. However, there are some syntactic constraints on the
relations between an anaphor and its antecedent particularly if the anaphor
comes first. Compare, for example:

Before he went into the meeting, John straightened his tie.
He went into the meeting, before John straightened his tie.

Only in the first case can *he* and *John* refer to the same person. The exact
nature of these constraints has been much debated in the linguistic literature
(see Reinhart, 1983, for a recent discussion).

People make few mistakes in resolving anaphoric expressions. A
psychological account of anaphor resolution must therefore describe how
the correct antecedent is chosen in the most general cases. However, it must
also allow for the fact that some anaphors may be easier to understand than
others. For example, although simple syntactic strategies for pronoun assignment do not always produce the correct antecedent, some syntactic locations may be more probable than others, and it would make sense to give
these priority.

General principles for resolving anaphoric noun phrases

The kinds of general principles needed to resolve anaphors will be illustrated
by detailed discussion of one type of anaphor – the definite noun phrase.
Consider a noun phrase, such as *the man* in the following passage:

A man walked up the garden path and stopped just before the front door. It was standing slightly ajar. I had seen the man somewhere before.

Unlike many anaphors, no general knowledge, except for knowledge about language, is needed to work out the referent of this noun phrase. Its resolution depends chiefly on the semantics of *the* and *man*. Nevertheless, explaining how such anaphors are resolved is not a trivial problem, though it is a more tractable one than describing how knowledge is deployed in comprehension.

The semantics of singular definite noun phrases specifies that they refer to one thing of the kind denoted by the content of the noun phrase. Only one man is mentioned in the passage, the one introduced in the first sentence. Hence he is the one that *the man* refers back to.

These observations form the basis of an algorithmic account of how one aspect of text meaning is computed. As each sentence (or perhaps clause) of a text is heard or read, it is analysed syntactically and semantically, and a representation of the kind of situation it describes is constructed. For simple sentences this representation will be similar to one of Kintsch's propositions, though for sentences with quantifiers it will be more complex. In principle, there is no problem in specifying how such representations are computed. Montague's (1973) algorithm for composing sentence meanings can be adapted. Kintsch's propositional theory was unsatisfactory because he never availed himself of such a device. Furthermore, contrary to Kintsch's supposition, extracting propositions is not sufficient for anaphor resolution. Further work is required.

In order to convert a set of propositions into a model of a particular situation, the referents of the noun phrases must be identified. At the beginning of a text, noun phrases inevitably refer to people and things not previously mentioned. The identification of their referents is achieved in one of two ways. The text may be about people, places and things already known to the reader, and identifiable by their names or from the context provided by, say, the title of a book. Alternatively, for example when a reader begins a novel, representations of the people, places and events have to be created as they are introduced. Very quickly, however, some noun phrases refer back to things that have already been mentioned. The anaphor resolution system must determine which noun phrases do refer back, and what they refer back to.

One cue to whether a noun phrase is anaphoric is the use of the definite as opposed to the indefinite article (cf. Vendler, 1967, ch. 2). An indefinite noun phrase, as at the beginning of the passage above, usually introduces a new referent, whereas a definite noun phrase typically, but not always, refers back.

The introduction of new referents into a model   A singular indefinite noun phrase signals that a new token should be set up in the representation of a text. The token stands for an individual and it must be distinguished from other individuals of the same type. For example, the noun phrase *a tree* might introduce the thirty-fifth tree mentioned in a text. This tree could be represented in the mental model of the text by the token TREE35. There are a number of other linguistic devices that can be used to introduce new referents (for example, the word *another*). Providing that they can be exhaustively listed, the items that should be introduced into the representation of a text can be computed. For a given text, this set of items will be comparatively small, particularly when compared with the set of all items that can be mentioned in texts, and it will determine what items can be referred to anaphorically in the subsequent text. Thus, the existence of a mental model corresponding to each text goes part of the way to explaining how potentially ambiguous noun phrases, such as *the man* can have, in the context of a passage, unambiguous referents.

Interpreting definite noun phrases   A procedure for interpreting definite noun phrases can now be outlined. When a definite noun phrase is encountered, semantic analysis provides the information that (i) it refers to one individual, and (ii) it refers to the kind of individual denoted by the content of the noun phrase. On the basis of this analysis a search can be made through the representation of the text so far to see if there is an appropriate antecedent. If more than one is found, then the text is ill-formed and cannot be uniquely interpreted. In a conversation, it may be possible to ask for further clarification, thus allowing the speaker to make a *repair* (cf. Ringle and Bruce, 1982). If there *is* one item of the appropriate kind in the representation then it is the referent of the noun phrase, and the information in the current sentence can be integrated with what has gone before. However, in some cases there will be no appropriate antecedent. Under these circumstances the understanding system tries to infer one. For example, to understand the passage:

> John went walking at noon.
> The park was beautiful.

it is necessary to assume that the location of John's walk was a beautiful park. If such *bridging inferences* (Clark, 1977) fail, the definite noun phrase is taken to introduce a new referent, as if the noun phrase had been indefinite. The use of a definite noun phrase to introduce a new referent is often used as a literary device at the beginning a text. Once a definite noun phrase has been interpreted, then information from its clause can be incorporated into the representation of the text so far. The updated model then becomes the context for the next clause of the text.

This account of the resolution of one kind of anaphor explains some aspects of the integration of information from text that do not depend on knowledge about the world. Although such knowledge is sometimes needed to resolve anaphoric definite noun phrases – its chief use is in the construction of bridging inferences, the account does not explain *how* it is used. This aspect of comprehension will be discussed below. World knowledge is used in different ways in the comprehension of other kinds of anaphor. For example, in resolving definite pronouns it is used to compare the plausibilities of the situations that would be described on different assignments of antecedent to the pronoun.

Deciding between potential referents for an anaphoric expression

The processes described above are essential for determining the meaning of anaphoric expressions. However, they leave open many questions about how the anaphor resolution system works, and in particular about how sets of potential antecedents are searched – whether, for example, they are checked serially or in parallel, and what factors determine the order of any serial search. The fact that people rarely misunderstand anaphoric expressions shows that the search process does not usually lead to errors of assignment. Any ordering can determine only which antecedents are preferred. As was noted above, simple syntactic strategies for pronoun *resolution* fail on sentences that are not difficult to understand.

Experimental evidence suggests that people do make a principled search through the set of possible antecedents for an anaphoric expression. Grober, Beardsley and Caramazza (1978) demonstrated the use of parallel function (Sheldon, 1974) in pronoun comprehension. Parallel function means that the antecedent of a pronoun plays the same role in its clause (e.g. subject or object) as the pronoun in its. Thus, the sentence:

John sold Bill his car because he hated it.

is correctly interpreted by the parallel function strategy – both *John* and *he* are subjects, but the version in which *hated* is replaced by *needed* is not, and is therefore more difficult to understand.

Several other strategies are used in anaphor resolution. Caramazza, Grober, Garvey and Yates (1977) showed that people use information about the verb in one clause to predict whether its subject or object is likely to be pronominalized in a subsequent clause – for some verbs (e.g. *sell, question*) the subject is more likely, and for others (e.g. *punish, envy*) the object. Yekovich, Walker and Blackman (1979) found that people expect anaphors to occur in the given portion of the current sentence and to have their antecedents in the new part of the previous sentence. Finally, many studies (e.g. Clark and Sengul, 1979) have indicated that antecedents in clauses close to the anaphor are preferred to those in clauses further away.

Experiments on integrating information from text

The best-known demonstration of integration of information from related sentences is an experiment by Bransford and Franks (1971). They took sets of four sentences such as:

> The ants were in the kitchen.
> The ants ate the jelly.
> The jelly was on the table.
> The jelly was sweet.

and combined the sentences to produce new ones containing two or three of the ideas. Subjects listened to lists of these sentences, including some of the original ones expressing a single idea. They were then given an unexpected yes/no recognition test, and asked to rate their confidence in their responses. Of the sentences that were consistent with the information presented, subjects were unable to distinguish those that they had heard from those that they had not. Furthermore, their confidence that they had heard a sentence increased with the number of ideas in it, regardless of whether it had been presented. Indeed, subjects were most confident that they had heard sentences expressing all four ideas, such as:

> The ants in the kitchen ate the sweet jelly that was on the table.

none of which had been read to them.

Bransford and Franks explained this result by assuming that confidence judgements were based on the similarity of the test sentence to an integrated representation of information from the originally presented sentences. A number of alternative explanations of this particular result have been advanced (see especially Reitman and Bower, 1973). Nevertheless, comprehension of continuous prose does require that information from different sentences be combined, and a psycholinguistic theory must explain how this integration is achieved.

The integration of information in Bransford and Franks's experiment depends on only one type of cohesive tie – lexical repetition. The jelly in one sentence must be identified as the same jelly that is mentioned in another, for example. More complex integrative processing is needed to combine information about spatial relations between objects, and work out what *spatial array* is described in a passage. Several experiments have investigated this type of processing, and have shown that *relations* between objects, as well as the objects themselves, are encoded in a way that does not resemble the linguistic form of discourse and text.

Barclay (1973) used one-dimensional arrays with five members, such as:

lion   bear   moose   giraffe   cow

with the relation between the members being *on the right (left) of*. He presented sentences describing such arrays, and asked half of his subjects to memorize the sentences, and half to try and figure out the array. Later all subjects were given an unexpected recognition test. Subjects who were asked to memorize the sentences performed fairly well, whereas those told to figure out the array tended to sort the sentences into those that were true of the array and those that were false, regardless of which sentences they had heard. The subjects who had to extract the content of the sentences had derived a representation that was compatible with any true description of the array, but which did not contain information about how the array was originally described. Barclay's results can be explained by assuming that people who are told to figure out the array construct a representation analogous to the array – a mental model of it.

A series of studies by Potts (1972, 1973, 1974; Scholtz and Potts, 1974) confirms this conclusion. Most importantly, Potts (1972) showed that subjects were faster to verify sentences describing relations between objects far apart in an array than those describing objects close together – as if it were easier to see in the mind's eye the relation between objects further apart. This result held even when the subjects had seen only sentences about adjacent objects and had to infer relations between distant objects. Moyer and Bayer (1976) demonstrated that models of arrays contain more than just ordinal information. Arrays were easier to learn if they comprised circles of widely differing sizes than if the circles were nearly the same.

More recent work on the representation of spatial relations by Johnson-Laird (Ehrlich and Johnson-Laird, 1982; Mani and Johnson-Laird, 1982) suggests that models of more complex arrays are not always constructed. In these experiments subjects were presented with descriptions of two-dimensional arrays. Constructing a mental representation of such an array was easy if each successive sentence referred back to an object introduced in the previous sentence, but difficult if there was a *referential discontinuity* (Ehrlich and Johnson-Laird, 1982), as there is between the first and second sentences of the following passage:

> The knife is in front of the pot.
> The glass is behind the dish.
> The pot is to the left of the glass.

Model-building is also more difficult if the relations are indeterminate, so that two different arrays are consistent with the description (Mani and Johnson-Laird, 1982). For example, in the following description the bed could be either in front of or behind the chair.

> The bookshelf is to the right of the chair.
> The chair is in front of the table.
> The bed is behind the chair.

Subjects remember the surface form of such descriptions better than that of determinate descriptions. This finding suggests that people do not construct models of indeterminate descriptions, but encode them in a form that is closer to that of the sentences.

Experiments on spatial arrays again suggest that non-linguistic, model-like representations of content are set up when sentences are read. However, caution is required in applying the results of these experiments to normal text comprehension. Subjects may adopt special strategies when they know they will be asked questions about spatial arrays. The times spent examining the spatial descriptions in Johnson-Laird's experiments, for example, are very long (about 6 seconds per sentence), and suggest that subjects are doing more than just reading the sentences.

Further experiments on the resolution of anaphoric NPs will be discussed later in this chapter, since their results have been related to the question of how knowledge about the world is used in text comprehension.

Focus and foregrounding

There was one major omission from the account of interpreting definite noun phrases. It ignored the phenomenon of *focus* or *foregrounding*. Not everything mentioned in a text is equally easy to refer back to. Some things remain in the foreground, others become part of the background. For example, in the following short passage, taken from Tyler and Marslen-Wilson (1982), the puppy remains foregrounded, but the wasp does not.

The little puppy trod on a wasp.
The puppy was very upset.

It is for this reason that an attempt to continue the passage with the sentence:

It started to buzz furiously.

appears awkward. A theory of text comprehension should explain how things go out of focus, and describe the consequences of an item's being focused or defocused for the interpretation of subsequent sentences.

In AI, Grosz (1981) studied the effect of task structure on focusing and reference in dialogues between instructors and apprentices performing tasks such as the disassembly of an air compressor. She found that people use their knowledge of what they are trying to achieve in order to focus on particular items, and to provide unambiguous interpretations for definite noun phrases such as *the screw*, which have a number of potential referents in the scene that they are looking at. However, differences in knowledge between instructors and apprentices sometimes led to misunderstandings.

In psychology, Anderson, Garrod and Sanford (1983) showed that the set of focused items is updated when there is a time change that indicates that the current episode is over. Episode-bound characters become defocused at the end of an episode, and subsequent anaphoric references back to them are difficult to resolve. For example, the entertainer is an episode-bound character in a short story about a birthday party. Anderson *et al.* presented subjects with passages such as:

The children were all enjoying the birthday party.
There was an entertainer to amuse them.
No expense was spared to make the party a success.
One hour/five hours later energies flagged.

After one hour a children's party is likely still to be in progress, but after five hours it is most probably over. The passages continued in one of two ways. In the first kind of continuation there was a reference back to the main characters, the children in this case:

Playing the games had exhausted them.

This sentence was read equally quickly in the two conditions. It did not matter whether one hour or five hours had elapsed. In the second kind of continuation there was a pronominal reference to the episode-bound character:

Organizing the games had exhausted him.

This sentence was read more quickly when the time change did not take the action beyond the bounds of the episode. This result suggests that when episodes finish, episode-bound characters move out of focus. Main characters, however, remain focused throughout several episodes.

Sanford and Garrod (1981) developed a more general account of the memory representation of texts, in which they distinguish between *explicit focus* and *implicit focus*. Items in explicit focus are those that have been explicitly mentioned in the preceding text, and which are currently foregrounded. They can be referred to pronominally. Items in implicit focus are those whose existence is implied by what is in explicit focus. For example, if a house is in explicit focus, then various parts of it, such as its walls, its roof and its chimney, are in implicit focus. Sanford and Garrod are therefore able to explain how people make bridging inferences, to integrate the information in passages such as:

I looked around the house.
The lounge was very spacious.

Items in implicit focus cannot be referred to pronominally. If the second sentence had been:

It was very spacious.

it could not have referred to the lounge, even though the existence of the lounge is implied by mention of the house in the first sentence. Sanford and Garrod also describe the search procedures through explicit and implicit focus that anaphoric expressions of various types trigger. Their theory is an extension of the account of how definite noun phrases are interpreted outlined above.

The use of knowledge about the world in text comprehension

It has already been noted several times that knowledge about the world is important in text comprehension. For example, it is often required to establish cohesive links between sentences. This section discusses in more detail how that knowledge is used.

The realization that computer programs for understanding natural language should be given knowledge about the world was a major conceptual advance in AI, which quickly had an impact in psycholinguistics. A program with detailed information about a limited domain – a *microworld* – can perform impressively, as Winograd's (1972) SHRDLU demonstrated. There are several ways in which knowledge about the world can be used in language understanding. Two of them are particularly important. First, knowledge of the overall context restricts the interpretation of expressions in a text. This aspect of comprehension will be discussed later in this chapter. Second, knowledge of specific facts or about how things usually happen can be used to fill in details that are not explicit in the text. Although *inferences* based on knowledge about the world, like conversational implicatures (see chapter 5), are not usually logical entailments from the sentences in a text, knowledge of how things typically happen allows a reader or listener to elaborate what is explicitly stated and produce a representation of how the world *most probably* is, given that the text is true.

Inferences can be classified in a number of ways. Three of these classifications are pertinent to a theory of text comprehension. First, inferences range from logical entailments (for example, the car is red, so the car is coloured), which depend only on the meanings of words, to those that require detailed world knowledge. Second, some inferences, such as bridging inferences, *must* be made if a text is to be coherently interpreted, whereas others, even though their conclusions are very probably true, are *merely elaborative*, and are not needed to link the sentences in a text. For example, it follows with a high probability from the passage:

The teacher cut the juicy steak.
He was enjoying his meal.

that the teacher used a knife to cut the steak, though it is not necessary to make this inference in order to link the two sentences. Third, there are inferences about the situation described in a text, such as the ones discussed so far, and inferences about the point of a text or the motives of its writer. This second type of inference, of which many conversational implicatures are examples, contributes to the pragmatic interpretation of the text.

There are two main sets of questions that psycholinguists ask about inference making. The first concerns which, if any, inferences are made as a text is read, and whether they are encoded into a representation of its content. The second is about the organization of knowledge in long-term memory, and how cues in a text access that knowledge.

On-line encoding of bridging inferences

A partial answer to the first set of questions is that in normal comprehension bridging inferences are made on-line. This view is supported both by the observation that replies in conversation may depend on such inferences, and by experimental studies of ordinary reading.

To show that inferences are made as texts are read it is necessary to collect data on-line. The most widely used technique is self- or subject-paced reading (SPR). In an SPR experiment subjects read passages one section at a time, usually on a visual display unit. When they have read the current display, they press a button and the next one replaces it.

Haviland and Clark (1974) measured the time that subjects spent reading sentences such as:

The beer was warm.

in two different contexts. In one context beer was explicitly mentioned in the preceding sentence:

We got some beer out of the trunk.

In the other an inference was required to establish that beer was among some picnic supplies:

We checked the picnic supplies.

This inference is plausible because picnic supplies often include beer. The sentence *the beer was warm* was read more slowly in the second of these contexts, suggesting that computation of the inference took time. This result could not be explained by the fact that the word *beer* was repeated in the other passage. A non-specific mention of beer did not help. Subjects spent a comparatively long time reading *the beer was warm* after:

Andrew was especially fond of beer.

When are elaborative inferences made?

Haviland and Clark's experiment showed that inferences necessary to establish the coherence of a text are made as it is read. However, there is some debate about elaborative inferences. A text can support indefinitely many inferences of this kind, and not all of them can be drawn during reading. In the early 1970s it was thought in both psychology and AI that the most probable ones were, although the evidence that suggested this conclusion came from memory experiments and was therefore indirect.

Consider the example of an elaborative inference cited above – an inference about an implicit instrument. The verb *cut* describes an action that requires an instrument, but no instrument need be explicitly mentioned in a sentence describing this action. Someone hearing the passage about the teacher knows that steaks are usually cut with knives. They also know that steaks *can* be cut with scalpels, saws or other more exotic implements, and in some contexts in which no instrument is mentioned, one of these other instruments may have been used. However, in a normal context, or when the sentence is presented out of context, the most likely instrument is a knife, and it is reasonable to assume that one was used. Knife is the *default value* for a steak-cutting instrument, and if a knife has not been used *explicit information to the contrary* might be expected. For this reason the inference that a knife was used is a safe one, which could be made on-line and encoded into a memory representation.

However, it does not follow from the fact that the inference is safe either that it is drawn, or that a knife is subsequently included in the mental encoding of the sentence. The theory that inferences *are* encoded into memory representations as texts are read – the dominant theory of the early 1970s – has been called the *immediate inference* theory by Garnham (1982). An alternative, and in some ways more plausible, theory is the *deferred inference* theory. Its plausibility derives from the fact that indefinitely many inferences can be made from a sentence or set of sentences. If they were all encoded, the mental representation of even a single sentence would become indefinitely large. In any case, most of the inferred facts would not be useful, so it would be inefficient to encode them. The deferred inference theory claims that only necessary inferences are drawn as sentences are encoded – inferences without which the text cannot be coherently interpreted. Elaborative inferences are made only when they are needed, for example to answer questions. If they can be drawn from the text, then they can also be derived from an adequate memory representation of it. On the deferred inference theory, the initial encoding of the sentence about the steak would contain no information about a knife, but if a person who had heard it was later asked:

Did the teacher use a knife?

they would be able to answer 'yes' by making an inference at that time.

Experiments on elaborative inference making

Johnson, Bransford and Solomon (1973) presented short passages containing sentences such as:

He slipped on a wet spot and dropped the delicate glass pitcher on the floor.

In a recognition test subjects claimed that they had heard:

He slipped on a wet spot and broke the delicate glass pitcher when it fell on the floor.

However, if *dropped* was changed to *just missed*, the second sentence was rejected. The first sentence does not explicitly mention that the pitcher broke when it was dropped, but people know that when delicate glass objects fall to the floor they *usually* break. Johnson *et al.* argued that this knowledge of what usually happens affects the way in which sentences are encoded.

Similar conclusions were drawn by Bransford, Barclay and Franks (1972). Their subjects heard sentences such as:

Three turtles rested on a floating log and a fish swam beneath them.

Then, in a recognition test they claimed, falsely, that they had heard:

Three turtles rested on a floating log and a fish swam beneath it.

However, other subjects, who initially heard that the turtles were *beside* a floating log, did not subsequently recognize a sentence with *it* substituted for *them*. Bransford *et al.* argued that this result shows that people use their knowledge of spatial relations and of the relative sizes of turtles, logs and fish when they construct representations of such sentences. These representations, which do not contain irrelevant details about surface form, are used in the recognition test. Subjects say 'yes' if the test sentence is consistent with their representation.

Another result suggesting that inferences are made as text is read was obtained by Paris and Lindauer (1976, Expt 1). They showed that for adults, but not young children, *knife* is an equally good cue for two versions of the sentence:

The teacher cut into the juicy steak (with a knife).

one in which the instrument is explicit, and one in which it is implicit. Paris and Lindauer claimed that implicit instruments are good recall cues because they are incorporated into representations of sentences. Like Bransford and his colleagues, they endorsed the immediate inference theory. However, a number of subsequent findings were inconsistent with this interpretation of the results.

Corbett and Dosher (1978) carried out an experiment that was similar to Paris and Lindauer's, but in which both probable and improbable explicit instruments were presented. Their subjects read sentences such as:

The grocer dug a hole.
The grocer dug a hole with a shovel.
The grocer dug a hole with a pitchfork.

As in Paris and Lindauer's experiment, *shovel* was a good cue for the first and second of these sentences, but it was also a good cue for the third, better than *pitchfork*. However, when subjects remembered the third sentence, they knew which instrument was mentioned in it. This result shows that a good cue for a sentence has not necessarily been encoded into its representation. *Shovel* was a good cue, even when *pitchfork* had been encoded.

Singer (1979, 1980, 1981) produced another set of findings that is difficult to reconcile with the immediate inference theory. For example, Singer (1979) presented subjects with either:

> The sailor swept the floor with the broom.
> OR The sailor swept the floor in the cabin.

and then asked them to verify:

> The sailor used the broom to sweep the floor.

Verification was quicker after the first sentence – the one in which the broom is explicitly mentioned. If the implicit instrument *broom* had been inferred in the other case, then no difference in verification times would have been expected. A minor problem in interpreting these results is that there is more lexical overlap between the first sentence and the to-be-verified sentence in the condition in which verification is quicker. However, Singer argued that the effects he obtained were too large to be explained by lexical repetition.

Both Corbett and Dosher, and Singer agree with Thorndyke (1976) that inferences are made only when they are necessary for comprehension or question answering (the deferred inference theory). In Thorndyke's experiment subjects falsely recognized an inference that was needed to tie a passage together, but failed to recognize other inferences that were independently judged to be equally plausible. For example, the two sentences:

> The hamburger chain owner was afraid his love of french fries would ruin his marriage.

and:

> The hamburger chain owner decided to join weight watchers in order to save his marriage.

can be linked by the inference:

> The hamburger chain owner was very fat.

Subjects who read a story containing the two sentences falsely recognized the inference as a sentence from the passage, but they did not falsely recognize:

The hamburger chain owner's wife didn't like french fries.

which was judged to be an equally plausible inference from the hamburger chain owner's fear. However, Thorndyke's inferences have rather low probabilities. They are not safe in the sense that inferences to highly plausible implicit instruments are – explicit information to the contrary would not be expected if they were incorrect. His results may not, therefore, be relevant to whether highly probable inferences are made when they are unnecessary for comprehension.

Garnham (1982) has shown how findings that support the immediate and deferred inference theories can be reconciled. The immediate inference theory claims that, for example, implicit and highly probable explicit case fillers are treated in the same way – both are encoded. The *omission theory* (Garnham, 1982) suggests that neither are encoded into a representation of content, though explicit case fillers are encoded into a relatively short-lived representation of surface form. Highly probable fillers are reconstructed, for the purposes of answering questions, by a process similar to that required in the immediate inference theory for inferring implicit case fillers at the time of encoding.

The omission theory explains why implicit and highly probable explicit case fillers are confused in long-term memory – neither are encoded. It also explains why, at short delays, explicit case fillers are easy to verify – unlike implicit case fillers, they are present in a representation of surface form. Kintsch (1974, ch. 8) provides further evidence for this interpretation of Singer's results. After 20 minutes, when surface form is no longer available, explicit information takes just as long to verify as inferable information.

Instantiation - a further type of elaborative inference

Another type of inference that depends on knowledge about empirical regularities is *instantiation*. It, too, has been extensively studied in memory experiments, and these experiments illustrate further pitfalls in drawing conclusions about on-line processing from memory data.

Instantiation occurs when a general term, such as *vehicle*, takes on a more specific interpretation from its context. For example, the vehicle mentioned in the sentence:

The vehicle hovered over the crowd.

is probably a helicopter or a balloon, and almost certainly not a car, bus, train, or submarine.

Anderson and Ortony (1975) presented subjects with two different sentences containing the same the general term, for example:

The container held the cola.
The container held the apples.

They found that *bottle* was a better recall cue for the first, and *basket* for the second. The reason is that the container in the first sentence is probably a bottle, and the one in the second a basket. The design of the experiment ensured that the results could not be explained by simple associations between the cues and words in the sentences to be remembered.

In a similar experiment, Barclay, Bransford, Franks, McCarrell and Nitsch (1974) found that *something heavy* was a good cue for:

The man lifted the piano.

whereas *something with a nice sound* was a good cue for:

The man tuned the piano.

Barclay *et al.* suggested that their results should be explained in terms of the properties of the *referents* of the words in the sentences they used, but they did not develop this idea. Anderson and Ortony, on the other hand, claimed that all words are polysemous – in different contexts they have different meanings. This idea is at odds with common sense, and with the principles of lexicography, which assign each word a limited number of senses, often only one. Furthermore, as Johnson-Laird (1981) points out, *bottle* is likely to be a good recall cue for:

It held the cola.

Though *bottle* is not a *meaning* of *it* and *it* cannot be said to be polysemous. Barclay *et al.*'s suggestion is more plausible. Context can be used to elaborate a representation of the object that a particular occurrence of the word *container* stands for, even if *container* has only one meaning. Such elaboration is based on knowledge about the world – about what is usually used to store what – not on lexical semantics. This idea is consistent with the notion that the representation of the content of a sentence – its mental model – is not linguistic in nature. Its components represent objects, not word meanings.

In a later experiment Anderson, Pichert, Goetz, Schallert, Stevens and Trollip (1976) showed that *basket* was a better cue for:

The container held the apples.

than *container*, the general noun in the sentence. Furthermore, they found that when general nouns appeared in different sentence contexts, the best cue varied according to the context. Anderson *et al.* interpret this second finding as refuting a strong interpretation of Rosch's prototype theory – a general noun is not always represented by the one best exemplar of its category.

Garnham (1979) showed that verbs as well as nouns can be instantiated. *Fried* is a better cue than *cooked* for:

The housewife cooked the chips.

He developed Barclay et al.'s suggestion that context restricts the set of possible *referents* of a general term rather than selecting one of a potentially infinite number of meanings.

As with implicit case fillers, memory experiments on instantiation provide only an indirect indication of what happens when sentences are encoded. They do not prove that people instantiate general terms as they hear or read sentences. In a number of respects this *instantiation hypothesis*, espoused by Anderson *et al.* (1976), is implausible. A container holding cola could be a bottle, but it could also be a can or a glass. The claim that one particular instantiation is always chosen is unjustified. Indeed Gumenik (1979) showed that several potential instantiations can cue recall of sentences. More worryingly for the instantiation hypothesis he also showed that 'instantiations' can cue phrases in which there is no general noun for them to instantiate – *architect* is a good cue for the predicate *planned the house*, as well as for the sentence:

The man planned the house.

Furthermore, some words that cannot be instantiations are better cues for sentences than general terms in those sentences. *Arctic*, as well as *Eskimos* is a better cue than *group* for:

The group built their houses out of ice.

Gumenik claims that his results should be explained in terms of retrieval processes rather than encoding. But although his experiments indicate the need for more careful thought about how cue words access memory representations, they do not address the question of whether instantiation occurs at encoding. Furthermore, if psycholinguists had been better informed about memory research, they would have known that a cue need not be encoded into a representation that it retrieves. Retrieval may be mediated by the generation-recognition mechanism discussed by Bahrick (1970) and Kintsch (1970).

Sanford, Garrod and Bell (1979) used the SPR technique to discover whether people instantiate general terms as they read. They argued that if *woman* in:

The woman was outstanding in the theatre.

is instantiated as *actress*, then referring back to this person as *the actress* should be easier than referring back to her as *the woman*. Sanford *et al.*'s findings did not support this prediction. Instead, they showed that the ease with which the second reference was resolved depended on the specificity of the information in the first sentence – being outstanding in the theatre was deemed to be more specific than living near the theatre. However, Garnham (1981b) did produce evidence for on-line instantiation. He found that:

The shark swam rapidly through the water.

was read slowly after:

The fish avoided the swimmer.

since there is nothing in that sentence to indicate that the fish is a shark. However, with a context that cued an instantiation:

The fish attacked the swimmer.

the use of *shark* in the following sentence did not produce any difficulty, suggesting that, when people read that a fish attacked a swimmer, they represent the fish as a shark or something like one.

Organization of memory for inference making

The question of how long-term memory is organized to facilitate inference making has been tackled primarily in AI rather than psychology. Indeed, most AI research on text comprehension has sought to describe ways in which knowledge can be used to construct elaborated representations of the content of texts. In early programs that used semantic networks comparatively little knowledge was stored in memory, and it was organized into the kind of hierarchy described in chapter 6. Inferential question answering was achieved by combining networks representing sentences and relevant information from the memory network. The emphasis in these programs was on elaborative inferences, and attempts to explain how information from different sentences is integrated were crude.

Winograd's (1972) SHRDLU had a more sophisticated mechanism for combining information from different parts of a text. This mechanism and the fact that it knew about only a very simple world – a collection of wooden blocks on a flat surface, enabled SHRDLU to make impressive contributions to dialogue. However, SHRDLU's memory was comparatively simple. For example, it knew nothing about objects with complex structures, let alone the beliefs, wants and goals that are necessary for understanding discourses about human action.

Since the early 1970s attempts have been made to write programs that understand texts about people (for some recent proposals see Schank and Abelson, 1977; Rieger, 1979; Lehnert, 1982; Wilensky, 1982; Dyer, 1983). Many knowledge structures have been proposed for interpreting such stories, in particular by Schank and his co-workers. The best known of these structures is the script. A script contains information about a stereotypical sequence of events, such as a visit to a restaurant. Schank originally proposed that there was a separate script for each such sequence. In recent writings writings (e.g. Schank, 1982) he has recognized that scripts for, say, visiting the doctor and visiting the dentist duplicate information in an inefficient way. He therefore proposes to replace scripts by smaller and more modular Memory Organization Packets (MOPs), from which scripts can be created when they are required.

Schank makes two important claims about text comprehension. First, knowledge structures are used in a *top-down* manner to understand texts. Once a script has been recognized as relevant, it is *imposed* upon the text. Events in the text are, where possible, identified with events in the script, and events in the script but not in the text are inferred to have taken place. Second, the imposition of structure on to a text can bypass the need for a full syntactic analysis of its sentences (see chapter 4).

It cannot be claimed that Schank's work has fully resolved the question of how knowledge is used in text comprehension. One problem is that most AI programs analyse only a limited number of texts – to take an extreme example Rieger (1979) has written a program to understand just one very short story, 'The Magic Grinder'. There can be no guarantee that a program that works for one set of texts will generalize to others. This criticism would be irrelevant if the programs were based on general principles about the organization of memory. However, it is difficult to find any statement of these general principles. More specifically, it is unclear what it means to say that, for example, scripts, as opposed to some other kind of structure, are used in text comprehension.

Current ideas about the organization of memory for text comprehension derive from Bartlett's (1932) concept of a schema, which he describes as 'an active organization of past reactions, or past experiences' (1932, 201).

Unfortunately, Bartlett gave no indication of what properties a memory structure must have in order to count as a schema, and a similar problem affects recent proposals. Minsky's (1975) frame-system theory, Schank and Abelson's (1977) theory of Plans, Scripts and Goals, and Rumelhart and Ortony's (1977) schema theory (which is no more closely related to Bartlett's work than the others) are better specified than Bartlett's ideas in the sense that they have been implemented in computer programs – particular frames, for example, have been described in great detail (e.g. Charniak, 1977). However, as general accounts of the organization of information in memory these new proposals have little more substantive content – it remains unclear in virtue of what properties a frame is a frame. The theories do not say much more than that information in memory has some structure.

Accessing knowledge from memory during comprehension

The question of how information is accessed from memory by cues in text has received little attention from psycholinguists. In AI, language understanding programs that make use of stored knowledge must employ some method for accessing information. Two techniques are commonly used. The first is that a word accesses its corresponding frame or script. The second is the use of *keywords* – the restaurant script, for example, may be activated by *waiter* or *menu*. These simple techniques provide an incomplete account of how information is made available for comprehension. For example, *the five-hour journey from London to New York* suggests a plane flight, but no single word in it should, otherwise the plane flight script would be accessed in many inappropriate contexts. Furthermore, the keyword technique is most useful when a limited number of knowledge structures are stored in memory, and they do not share many keywords. It may work in microworlds or in limited knowledge domains, but it has not been demonstrated that the technique is either efficient or even successful when a long-term memory is more complex. Riesbeck (1982) provides an illuminating example of how the keyword technique can go wrong. A program called FRUMP (de Jong, 1982) analyses news items by looking for keywords, accessing scripts from those keywords and using the scripts to produce summaries. The program summarized an item with the headline:

Pope's death shakes Western World.

as

There was an earthquake in the Western World.
The Pope died.

The use of stored knowledge in anaphor resolution

The results of a number of experiments on inferential processing in the resolution of anaphoric noun phrases have been related to the question of how information from long-term memory is used in text comprehension. Garrod and Sanford (1977) measured reading time for the second sentences in passages of the following types:

> A bird would sometimes wander into the house.
> The robin was attracted by the larder.

> A robin would sometimes wander into the house.
> The bird was attracted by the larder.

In the first passage the anaphoric noun phrase *the robin* is more specific than its antecedent, *the bird*, and therefore carries extra new information about its referent. In the second passage the anaphor is more general and carries no extra information – if something has been described as a robin it is already known to be a bird. Garrod and Sanford showed that the second sentence was read more slowly in the first passage, suggesting that the extra information was taking time to assimilate. Garnham (1981b) supported this interpretation of the results by repeating the experiment with two new conditions in which the general noun or the instance noun was repeated. In both of these conditions the second sentence was read comparatively quickly, as predicted, since in neither case does the anaphor introduce extra information.

Sanford and Garrod (1980) obtained a different result in a similar experiment. They found that the reading time for the second sentence was shorter when the first contained a specific noun (for example, *robin*) than when it contained a general noun (for example, *bird*). Their tentative explanation of these results was that instance nouns are able to access more specific *scenarios* (their term for schemata) from long-term memory. Such scenarios facilitate the assimilation of subsequent text, and hence the second sentence is read more quickly.

The differing results of Garnham and of Sanford and Garrod are puzzling. However, Garnham (1984) replicated his original findings with different materials in which specificity was achieved by adding an adjective to a simple noun phrase, for example *the car* was contrasted with *the blue car*. He found no effects of specificity (*blue car* vs *car*) in the first sentence, even when the anaphoric noun phrase in the second was a pronoun. It is difficult to decide whether *car* and *blue car* should access different scenarios, but this difficulty indicates a weakness in scenario theory. It does not predict when particular scenarios will be accessed from memory.

Garrod and Sanford (1981), in another SPR experiment, obtained a different pattern of results again, but in this case an explanation is readily forthcoming. They showed that:

The clothes were made of pink wool.

took no longer to read in the context:

Mary dressed the baby.

than when it followed:

Mary put the clothes on the baby.

No extra time was required to understand *clothes* when it did not have an explicit antecedent. The reason is that the definition of the verb *dress* makes reference to clothes – to dress means to put clothes on. Therefore, when the meaning of *dress* is retrieved from semantic memory, information about clothes automatically becomes active, and subsequent sentences about clothes are easy to understand. However, this result does not mean that the representation of *Mary dressed the baby* has been elaborated by knowledge about the world, it has simply been built up out of the meanings of the words in the sentence.

The use of context in the interpretation of text

So far it has been established that people can use their knowledge of the world to expand the information explicit in a text, though they only reliably do so when an inference is needed to link parts of the text together or to answer a question. Lack of knowledge may make a text more difficult to understand, particularly if it prevents a bridging inference from being made. A much more serious failure to comprehend may arise from ignorance of the context in which the text is intended to be interpreted. For example, switching on the radio in the middle of a programme may cause bafflement, because it is impossible to tell what simple words and phrases such as *it, the one, then* and *his friend* refer to. Furthermore, if the general topic is not known, then much of the knowledge that could be used to elaborate what is being said cannot be made available. This phenomenon has been investigated in a number of experiments.

Dooling and Lachman (1972) showed that a passage containing sentences such as:

Three sturdy sisters. . . forging along sometimes through vast calmness yet more often over turbulent peaks and valleys.

is difficult to understand unless its title, 'Christopher Columbus Discovering America', is known beforehand. The title clarifies the interpretation of many of its phrases. The 'sisters' are Columbus's ships, the Nina, Pinta and Santa Maria; the peaks and valleys are waves. Dooling and Mullet (1973) showed that being told the title after the passage did not help subjects to remember it. They needed the title to interpret the expressions in the passages as they read it.

Dooling and Lachman's passage contains many figures of speech, but it is not their presence that makes it hard to understand without a title. Bransford and Johnson (1972) produced similar results with a more straightforward passage. It was difficult for subjects to interpret sentences such as:

It is better to do too few things at once than too many.

unless they knew that they were hearing a description of how to wash clothes. Bransford and Johnson also showed that a picture can provide as effective a context for interpreting a passage as a title. This result reflects the fact that a perceptual scene often provides the context for a conversation or a description.

Bransford and McCarrell (1975) point out that language is not alone in being interpreted with respect to context. Parts of pictures may be difficult to recognize if their surroundings cannot be seen, and the function of an object may be obscure, if it is not seen in its typical context of use. Context-dependent interpretation is a general cognitive skill.

Mental models

Several conclusions about mental representations of the content of discourse and text have been reached up to this point. First, such representations are structurally similar to part of the world rather than to any linguistic structure. Neither syntax nor semantics, in the narrow sense, is remembered – individuals and relations between them are represented directly. Second, information not explicit in a text may be included in a representation of its content, particularly if it is required to establish links between parts of the text. Third, the context in which a discourse or text is interpreted determines the meanings of otherwise ambiguous expressions in it. Fourth, representations are built up as the text is read, according to well-defined procedures. Certain kinds of expression in the text signal that new elements must be introduced; others refer back to established elements. Fifth, at any point in a text, the representation constructed up to that point is the context for the interpretation of the next sentence. In particular, it restricts the set of possible referents for anaphoric expressions, and allows such expressions to be interpreted correctly in context.

Johnson-Laird and Garnham (1980) call such representations *mental models of discourse*. They point out that participants in the same discourse may have different models, and each must take into account what they know about the others' models in order to make their contributions interpretable. When talking to someone who does not know about your recent travels, it is unhelpful to refer to *the town I was in last Wednesday*. The notion of a mental model of discourse is closely related to proposals that have appeared recently in the literatures of psychology (Stenning, 1978; van Dijk and Kintsch, 1983), linguistics (Karttunen, 1976; Sag and Hankamer, 1984) and AI (Webber, 1981). This convergence of ideas suggests that mental models are an essential element in a theory of text comprehension.

The theory of mental models was used above to explain how expressions such as pronouns and definite noun phrases are assigned meanings, and hence how the information in sentences containing such expressions is incorporated into an overall representation of a text. A further aspect of text comprehension, to which the theory has not been addressed, is the computation of more global relations between the sentences in a text. For example, one sentence may describe a cause and another its effect, or one sentence may describe the goal of a character in a story, and a later one the attainment of the goal. Such relations are rarely stated explicitly, and need to be computed with reference to knowledge about how things usually happen. This observation raises two questions: are such relations computed as texts are read, and what kind of knowledge is needed to compute them?

Story grammars

The most popular approach to global aspects of text meaning has been to compare texts and sentences, and to suggest that the two should be analysed in the same way. On this view, just as there are sentence grammars that specify which strings of words are sentences of a language, there are text grammars that specify which texts are well formed. This type of analysis has been applied primarily to stories rather than other kinds of text, so the question under discussion is whether *story grammars* (e.g. Mandler and Johnson, 1977; Rumelhart, 1975; Thorndyke, 1977) are useful for analysing stories and explaining how they are generated and understood. The notion of a story grammar was formulated by Lakoff (1972), who proposed that the ideas of Propp (1928/1968) on the 'morphology of the folk-tale' could be recast in the form of a rewrite-rule grammar.

The intuition underlying story grammars is that stories have structure. Most story grammarians have attempted to capture this structure using context-free phrase-structure rules, such as:

STORY → SETTING THEME PLOT RESOLUTION
EPISODE → EVENT REACTION

These structural rules have semantic counterparts, though not all story grammarians have provided interpretation rules for their grammars. An example of a semantic rule is:

INITIATE (EVENT, REACTION)

proposed by Rumelhart (1975), as a counterpart to the second syntactic rule above.

To make the concept of a story grammar more concrete, consider the following simple story (Rumelhart, 1975) and its story grammar analysis.

(1) Margie was holding tightly to the string of her beautiful new balloon. (2) Suddenly a gust of wind caught it, (3) and carried it into a tree. (4) It hit a branch, (5) and burst. (6) Margie cried and cried.

The numbers refer to propositions – the units of story analysis. Propositions correspond to words (or morphemes) in the analysis of sentences. The same numbers appear in the analysis tree in Figure 7.4. Note that the INTERNAL RESPONSE is not explicit in the story, and must be inferred.

Just as a sentence grammar is not a theory of how sentences are processed, neither is a story grammar a theory of how stories are produced and understood. A theory of story comprehension based on a story grammar would have to explain how that grammar was used in the parsing and interpretation of stories. Black and Wilensky (1979) point out that most story grammarians have failed to recognize this fact. Garnham (1983b) discusses in detail why the competence/performance distinction must be made for stories as well as for sentences.

Despite the lack of an adequate processing theory based on story grammars, it is assumed in the story grammar literature that a story grammar account of text comprehension explains a number of empirical findings. First, in both recall and summarization of stories, the less important details

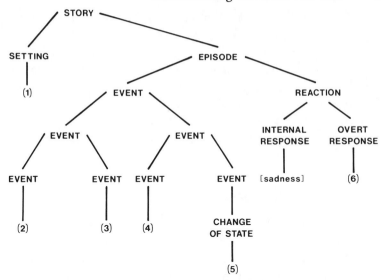

Figure 7.4 Story grammar analysis of Rumelhart's 'Margie' story
(*Source* Rumelhart, 1975)

are omitted. Story grammarians account for this result by claiming that people compute the importance of a sentence in a story – to determine either what should be remembered, or what best conveys the gist of a story – from the hierarchical structure assigned by a story grammar. The details that are omitted correspond to nodes low in the structure (but see Mandler, 1984, 62–73, for some problems with this idea). Rumelhart (1975) formulated explicit rules for generating summaries from the semantic representations assigned by his story grammar.

Second, versions of stories in which the sentences are jumbled are more difficult to understand and remember than the original versions. Story grammarians claim that jumbling the sentences destroys the story structure, and removes an important aid to comprehension. However, randomizing the order of the sentences in a passage also destroys its *referential continuity* (Garnham, Oakhill and Johnson-Laird, 1982). For example, pronouns that are readily interpretable in the original version of a story may have no clear referents in a jumbled version. Garnham *et al.* restored referential continuity to jumbled passages, and showed that this alleviated some, but not all, of the difficulty that subjects had in understanding and remembering them.

A third finding that story grammarians claim to explain comes from a study by Thorndyke (1977). He showed that, when subjects had two stories to remember, they performed better if the two had the same structure, and worse if they had content in common (that is if the same characters appeared in both). The facilitatory effect of repeated structure parallels some results in sentence comprehension (Mehler and Carey, 1967), and Thorndyke argued that it demonstrates the psychological reality of story structures.

Finally, Cirilo and Foss (1980) showed that, in an SPR experiment, subjects spent more time reading a sentence when it was high in the structure of one story than when it was low in the structure of a different story. They explained this result by assuming that subjects could use the (partially computed) hierarchical structure to decide which sentences were important, and therefore required more attention.

A more general hierarchical model

Stories, and in particular the restricted set of folk tales that fall within the domain of story grammars, comprise only a small subset of texts. Kintsch and van Dijk (1978; van Dijk and Kintsch, 1983) put forward a more general theory of hierarchical structure in text representations, which can, in principle, be applied to any kind of text. Kintsch and van Dijk, like story grammarians, assume that a set of propositions can be extracted from a text, and that those propositions capture (part of) its content. This idea is taken from Kintsch's earlier work (e.g. 1974), though Kintsch never formulated an algorithm for extracting sets of propositions from texts. An adequate theory of text understanding that incorporated Kintsch's proposal would have to provide such an algorithm.

Kintsch and van Dijk's explanation of better memory for high-level propositions is different from that of story grammarians. On their theory it is not the position of these propositions in the hierarchical representation that makes them easier to remember. Kintsch and van Dijk propose that information from different propositions is integrated in a short-term memory buffer with limited capacity. Integration occurs in cycles, and a proposition is retained in the buffer only if it is predicted to be useful for further integration. The longer a proposition remains in the buffer, the better it is remembered. In the original model, integration depended only on *argument overlap* between the propositions, but van Dijk and Kintsch (1983) now recognize that other factors may be important.

Kintsch and van Dijk's account of integration disguises the fact that the notion of argument overlap is a problematic one for them. They face the following dilemma. On the one hand it could be that the arguments in propositions are referentially tagged (that is they have arbitrary labels that distinguish different things of the same kind), in which case a separate account is needed of how the tagging takes place – an account of how two expressions in a text are determined to be coreferential or non-coreferential. If arguments are referentially tagged it is difficult to see why propositions need to be integrated in a short-term memory buffer. On the other hand, if the arguments are not referentially tagged, then the mere repetition of an argument does not guarantee identity of reference, and the integration process cannot work properly. Consider the sentence:

A fat man drank a beer and then another fat man drank a beer.

The propositional content of the first clause in this sentence (ignoring tense) is, on Kintsch's theory:

(DRINK MAN BEER) & (FAT MAN)

The second clause has the same content. The word *another* indicates that the two fat men are different. The two clauses should be represented as:

(DRINK MAN23 BEER) & (FAT MAN23)
(DRINK MAN57 BEER) & (FAT MAN57)

However, in order to ensure that the two men have different referential tags (and there are problems about the beer, too) the question of which noun phrases are coreferential and which are not must be resolved. As Kintsch does not specify the details of the process that extracts propositions, he is at liberty to claim that *it* will solve this problem, but not that *he* has.

Problems with hierarchical models

Despite their apparent success in explaining empirical findings, story grammars face a number of conceptual difficulties. The first arises from the fact that the units of story structure are propositions. The proposition corresponds to the word or morpheme in the analysis of sentences, but propositions and words differ in one crucial respect. The lexical category of a word is stored in the mental lexicon, so there is no problem in deciding under which nodes (e.g. N, V, DET) a lexical item can be inserted into a phrase marker. The set of propositions, unlike the set of words, is indefinitely large. There can be no list of propositions and their categories, corresponding to the lexicon, and no story grammarian has described how the category of a proposition should be computed. A story grammar tree can be forced on to a story by assuming that the propositions of the story are members of the required categories but, if story grammars are to have explanatory power, there must be independent evidence about the categories to which propositions belong.

A second problem is that, unlike syntacticians, story grammarians have given little consideration to mathematical arguments for and against particular kinds of grammar – finite-state, phrase-structure or transformational. Most story grammars are phrase-structure grammars, though Mandler and Johnson (1977) introduced both deletion and reordering transformations. Deletion transformations account for missing items in stories. For example, a character's goal may not be explicitly stated. Mandler and Johnson proposed that deleted constituents should be inferable, a condition that corresponds loosely to Chomsky's (1964) stipulation that a constituent can be deleted only if it is identical to one elsewhere in the sentence. An alternative treatment of such constituents would be to allow them to be optional in the phrase-structure rules, though this analysis might cause problems for semantic interpretation. Reordering transformations relate, for example, normal and 'flashback' versions of the same story. However, the rejection of transformations from sentence grammars, discussed in chapter 2, raises the question of whether relations between stories should be treated structurally. Mathematical arguments are crucial for justifying the framework within which grammars should be constructed at a particular level of linguistic analysis, whether it be the sentence or the story, and unless story grammarians can provide arguments similar to those of syntacticians, the use of a particular type of grammar to analyse stories remains unjustified.

Third, unlike sentence grammars, which ideally generate all and only the grammatical sentences of a language, story grammars are intended to analyse only a small subset of stories. However, unless the set of such stories can be described independently, there is a danger of circularity – the grammar is intended to analyse just those stories that fit its rules.

An alternative explanation of the 'story grammar' findings

If story grammars are rejected, how can the findings that they purport to explain be accounted for? The principal theme of these findings is that some parts of a text are more important than others, and are therefore attended to more closely, remembered better and included in summaries. Story grammarians explain these facts by proposing that important information occurs higher in story grammar parse trees than unimportant information.

It is possible to reject story grammars, but still maintain that the facts in a text are hierarchically related to one another – the hierarchy may not be specific to stories. For example, the structure that story grammarians discern in simple folk tales is primarily that of the main character's goals and subgoals. Such hierarchies explain how people behave both in and out of stories. Since information about goal structures is not specific to stories, it need not be duplicated in a knowledge structure that is (i.e. a story grammar). Rather, knowledge of goal structures is one more aspect of knowledge about the world that is required for language understanding (cf. Black and Bower, 1980).

More generally, there are a number of ways in which the facts in a text can be related to one another. The more important kinds of relation, none of which is specific to text, are: temporal, spatial, logical, causal, intentional and moral (Miller and Johnson-Laird, 1976). Some of these relations have hierarchical structure, but others do not. No adequate account of how and when these relations are computed is yet available, either in psychology or in AI, though their computation is an important aspect of text comprehension, as the 'story grammar' results show. Furthermore, Garnham, Oakhill and Johnson-Laird (1982) could not account for all of the difficulty produced by jumbling up the sentences in a story in terms of referential continuity. The reason is that a jumbled story presents a bizarre sequence of events that cannot be understood easily in terms of how things usually happen. Such a story is *implausible*, and people find it difficult to remember things that do not fit their expectations.

A theory of story understanding based on story grammars assumes that there is something special about the way stories are understood. There is no evidence that this is so. All of the experimental results can be explained in terms of knowledge about the world. In the case of the findings about folk tales, all that is necessary, in most cases, is to recast an explanation that appeals to the level of a proposition in a story grammar tree with one in terms of level in a hierarchy of goals. In jumbled stories, including those in which referential continuity is restored, there is no readily comprehensible goal structure. To understand other kinds of text different kinds of knowledge are required, but little, if any of that knowledge is specific to stories.

These conclusions mesh well with the theory of mental models. Since a model is similar to the part of the world that it represents, the same kinds of inference that make sense of events in the world can be used to elaborate representations of texts describing those events. For example, the proper understanding of a story may require the identification of the characters' wants and goals from their actions. Similarly, wants and goals may have to be inferred from the actions that a person is seen to perform, if those actions are to be correctly understood. Therefore, although goal structures can be indefinitely complex, and knowledge about them must be stored as a set of rules, or grammar (cf. Bruce and Newman, 1978), these rules should not be thought of as a *story* grammar.

Pragmatic and rhetorical significance

The processes described so far determine the content of a discourse, in the sense of the situation that it is about. However, there is more to understanding a discourse than discovering this situation. It is also necessary to determine what points a speaker or writer is trying to make. Furthermore, readers and listeners have their own reasons for studying texts, and these reasons affect the way they process them.

The effects that a writer or speaker intends to produce can be divided into those that depend on general conventions about the use of language and those that do not – what Austin (1962) called illocutionary and perlocutionary effects, respectively. The *illocutionary force* of an utterance is part of its pragmatic meaning, and determines whether it is to be understood as, say, a description, a question, a command or a promise. The intentional production of certain *perlocutionary effects*, such as persuading someone of the truth of a statement, was traditionally taught as *rhetoric*.

In psycholinguistics a broader view can be taken of the *rhetorical significance* of a text for a particular reader or listener on a particular occasion. For example, one person might search a book for a specific fact, whereas another might study the whole text in detail as part of a university course. Both the structure of the text and the strategy of the reader determine how easily the required information can be extracted.

The study of pragmatic meaning is comparatively recent in both AI and psychology. The network-based understanding systems of the early 1970s largely ignored this aspect of meaning. They operated in two modes – one in which they learned facts, and another in which they answered questions. Cohen, Allen and Perrault (1982) argue that a realistic language understanding system should not be restricted to answering questions, but should be able to engage in dialogues. They demonstrate, by analysing interactions between people and both real and simulated programs, that participants in dialogues implicitly assume that the person (or machine) with which they are interacting can compute their wants and goals on the slenderest of evidence, and use these wants and goals to determine the illocutionary force of the numerous indirect speech acts that occur in dialogues. The work of Cohen *et al.* shows that constructing a theory of how people compute pragmatic meaning is difficult, perhaps more difficult than theorizing about semantic interpretation. Such a theory might expect to borrow ideas from linguistics. However, the most influential pragmatic theory in that discipline, that of Grice (see chapter 5), is not explicit enough to provide the basis for a performance theory, although parts of it have been formalized, for example by Gazdar (1979). At present, psycholinguists look to AI rather than linguistics for ideas on the pragmatic interpretation of utterances.

Procedural semantics is particularly suited to providing an account of pragmatic meaning. First, it can describe how word meanings – themselves represented as procedures – combine to form sentence meanings, since a procedure in a high-level programming language can perform all the combinatorial operations of model-theoretic semantics. Second, since sentence meanings are also procedures or *programs*, they can just as well be commands or questions as descriptions. The parallel between utterances and programs was originally drawn by Davies and Isard (1972), who also compared understanding with compiling a program, and responding with running it.

Experiments on pragmatic interpretation

A number of psycholinguistic experiments have investigated memory for the pragmatic content of utterances, principally their illocutionary force. Schweller, Brewer and Dahl (1976) showed that, in a cued recall task, people recalled an explicit speech act, such as:

The housewife spoke to the manager about the increased meat prices.

When they had been presented with a implicit one:

The housewife complained to the manager about the increased meat prices.

Furthermore, they falsely recognized a sentence describing an expected perlocutionary effect of an utterance, for example:

The English Professor bored his students with a dull story about Jane Austen.

when they had been presented only with the speech act:

The English Professor told his students a dull story about Jane Austen.

The most extensively studied question about pragmatic interpretation in psycholinguistics is whether indirect speech acts (see chapter 5) are understood as though they were idioms, or whether their literal meanings are first computed, and then rejected as impossible or implausible in the context. Clark and Lucy (1975) first provided evidence that the literal meaning of indirect requests is computed, by showing that requests conveyed by sentences with implicitly negative words, such as *unless* (e.g. *I'll be very sad unless you open the door*), take longer to understand than matched requests without them (e.g. *I'll be very happy if you open the door*).

More recently Clark (1979; Clark and Schunk, 1980) has pointed out that the *politeness* of indirect requests depends on their literal meaning and, has argued that because people are sensitive to this aspect of requests – polite requests receive polite replies – literal meaning must be computed. The importance of the politeness of requests is further emphasized by Kemper and Thissen's (1981) finding that the wording of (unexpectedly) polite requests by high-status speakers and of (unexpectedly) impolite requests by low status speakers is well remembered. However, not all evidence favours the view that the literal meaning of indirect speech acts is computed (Gibbs, 1979, 1983), and Clark concedes (e.g. Clark and Schunk, 1980) that many indirect speech acts may be understood as idioms. An obvious example is the greeting *how do you do?*

Experiments on rhetorical significance

Kemper and Thissen's finding illustrates the further point that when some aspect of the wording of an utterance violates expectations, and hence, according to Gricean principles, should convey information, it is well remembered. This idea was also supported in a series of experiments by Bates and Kintsch and their colleagues. Kintsch and Bates (1977) showed that, five days after a lecture, students could remember the exact wording of asides and jokes, though they had forgotten how the academic content of the lecture had been phrased. This distinction between jokes and academic content is not surprising since the wording of a joke is more likely to be important in making a point. Keenan, MacWhinney and Mayhew (1977) performed a similar experiment, but included a control to ensure that the jokes and asides were not simply more memorable sentences. They confirmed that it was not the wording itself that made the sentences easy to remember but the fact that it was important to the point being made.

Bates, Masling and Kintsch (1978) and Bates, Kintsch, Fletcher and Giuliani (1980) investigated memory for explicit and anaphoric reference in 'natural' conversations – mainly from television soap operas. Again they found good retention of surface form, particularly for explicit forms of reference. They hypothesized that explicit forms of reference are *marked*, and anaphoric forms unmarked. Marked forms are more likely to carry pragmatically important information, and are therefore better remembered.

As well as the phrasing of a text affecting the way it is processed, the reader's or listener's goals are also important. Pichert and Anderson (1977; Anderson and Pichert, 1978) asked two sets of subjects to read a passage about a house from different perspectives – that of a potential home-buyer and that of a burglar. Potential home buyers tended to remember details about the fabric of the house, whereas burglars remembered valuable items that were portable. However, Anderson and Pichert (1978) showed that a shift in perspective *after the first recall* could trigger memory of details that had previously not been produced. This result suggests that the findings must be explained at least partly in terms of retrieval of information from memory, and not encoding.

Summary

The comprehension of discourse and text is the goal of the language understanding system. The meaning of a discourse depends on the meaning of the sentences in it, though the distinction between sentence meaning and text meaning is not always a useful one in psycholinguistics – even a single sentence in use is a mini-discourse.

Compositional aspects of sentence meaning have been described both in linguistics and in AI. The first semantic theory in generative grammar was that of Katz and Fodor, which produced sentence meanings by amalgamating word meanings in a manner determined by the syntactic structure of the sentence. Recently a more rigorous theory with the same underlying principle – model-theoretic semantics – has become popular in linguistics. It could be incorporated into a psychological theory of how word meanings contribute to a specification of the kind of situation that a sentence describes.

Katz and Fodor's theory provided the context in which psycholinguistic interest switched from syntax to semantics. It was shown that people cannot remember the syntactic structure of sentences, when they can still remember their meaning. However, Katz and Fodor's theory did not lead directly to any psycholinguistic experiments, and AI formalisms, particularly semantic networks and the related propositional representations had more influence in psychology. Semantic networks inspired experiments that showed that all the information about an individual is stored around a single memory node, regardless of how that individual was described on a particular occasion. More generally, people remember what the world would be like if what they heard or read was true. Representations of the content of sentences contain items corresponding not to linguistic elements, but to things in the world – people, things, actions and events – and relations between them.

Semantic network theory failed to provide an account of how information in a text is converted into a model-like representation in memory. The theory of mental models, together with an account of the semantic processing of anaphoric expressions, fills this gap, and goes some way to explaining how information from different parts of a text is integrated. Sometimes knowledge about the world is also necessary to effect this integration, and when it is, it is used on-line.

World knowledge can also be used to make merely elaborative inferences. For example, implicit case fillers may be made explicit, or general terms instantiated. Despite indirect evidence to the contrary, it now appears that elaborative inferences are not made as a text is read, but only when they are required, for example, to answer questions.

Long-term memory must be highly structured if it is to be useful in text comprehension. There have been a number of suggestions, particularly in AI, as to what kinds of structures it contains, but none of these proposals has been strongly supported. Neither has the question of how information is accessed from memory during text comprehension been resolved.

Lack of a particular item of knowledge may make a text difficult to understand, for example, because a crucial bridging inference cannot be made. However, ignorance of the overall context in which a text should be interpreted – that is ignorance of what knowledge is needed to understand it – has much more drastic effects.

The theory of mental models answers a number of questions about the way the local structure of texts is computed. Texts also have a more global structure, and one suggestion is that this structure should be analysed using story grammars that are similar to sentence grammars. A more plausible alternative is that structure in stories derives primarily from structure in the situations that they describe. Many kinds of knowledge may be used to link together facts in a story. Some of them, for example knowledge about goals and subgoals, impose a hierarchical structure on to the story, others do not. Texts are easy to understand in so far as they conform to knowledge of how things usually happen in the world.

To understand a discourse or text it is necessary to grasp its point as well as the situation that it is about. The pragmatic meaning of an utterance depends on knowledge about communicative acts and the participants in them. It is often expressed indirectly. The rhetorical intentions of producers of discourse also affects its interpretation, as do the goals of readers and listeners.

8

The structure of the
language processor

In the preceding chapters the major component processes of language understanding have been described. These processes can be divided into three groups: word-level processes, syntactic processes, and what Forster (1979) has called message-level processes – that is to say, those processes that compute the various aspects of the meaning of a discourse or text. The first set of processes determines, on the basis of perceptual and contextual inputs, what words have been presented to the understanding system; the second set computes the structural relations between the words; the last set uses these structural relations, together with context, to ascertain the import or *significance* (Johnson-Laird, 1977b) of what has been said. These three sets of processes can be ordered with respect to one another in the following sense. All the words in a sentence could, in principle, be recognized before any syntactic structure has been assigned, but a complete syntactic analysis cannot be generated before any words have been recognized. Similarly, parsing could precede the interpretation of a sentence or text, but interpretation cannot proceed in the absence of any syntactic information. However, these logical considerations place only weak constraints on how the three sets of processes work together. Once the lower-level processes have produced partial analyses, those at a higher level can begin their computations, and their outputs *may* be fed back to lower levels.

Psycholinguists have asked two main questions about how the three processors operate. First, at what point in a sentence do the syntactic and message-level processors begin their computations? Although there is strong introspective evidence that words are recognized almost as soon as they are read, this evidence does not show when a more detailed understanding is achieved. Further analysis could be delayed, for example, until a sentence or clause boundary is reached. Second, do the lower-level subprocessors act independently of the higher-level ones, or can information flow back through system? Two subsidiary questions are: if information is passed back, what information and when?

When is syntactic and semantic analysis performed?

Early psycholinguistic research assumed that the clause was the basic unit in comprehension. This assumption is consistent with the grammatical theory of *Aspects* (Chomsky, 1965), in which each deep structure clause is a complete 'sentence' with explicit subject and objects, and describes a single action, event, state or process. Furthermore, the Derivational Theory of Complexity (see chapter 4) claimed that underlying clauses are recovered from the surface form of a sentence by reversing transformations. Since transformations relate complete phrase markers to one another, the Derivational Theory suggests that much syntactic and semantic processing must be delayed to a point at which a complete phrase marker is available – that is a clause boundary. A number of experimental findings supported this hypothesis. First, as described in chapter 3, MacKay (1966) showed that the presence of an ambiguous word in a sentence fragment caused a delay in starting a completion of that sentence. Bever, Garrett and Hurtig's (1973) follow-up to this experiment showed that the effect was restricted to cases in which the completion began in the same clause as the ambiguous word. This pattern of results was taken to indicate that ambiguities are resolved at the end of the clause in which they occur, and that if there is insufficient information to resolve the ambiguity, an arbitrary decision is made. Resolution of an ambiguity generally requires message-level processing.

A second experiment that supported the clausal processing hypothesis was carried out by Caplan (1972). In his experiment subjects listened to sentences such as:

Make your calls after six, because night rates are lower.
Whenever one telephones at night, rates are lower.

They then had to decide whether a word had occurred in the sentence. For the above sentences, the word was *night*. This word is exactly the same distance from the end of each sentence – the final four words of the two sentences were made acoustically identical by tape splicing. However, in the first sentence *night* is in the final clause, and in the second it is in the penultimate clause. Caplan found that the time to respond 'yes' was shorter when the word was in the final clause. He took this result to show that the surface representation of this clause is held in a more readily accessible form than that of preceding clauses, because that clause has not been completely analysed.

Finally Jarvella (see 1979 for a summary), in a series of experiments, provided direct evidence that people have better verbatim memory for the clause that they are currently processing than for previous clauses.

This evidence for the special status of the current clause in memory has sometimes been taken to support a strong version of the claim that syntactic and semantic processing are performed at clause boundaries. On this version of the hypothesis *only* the surface form of the current clause is encoded before the clause boundary, and all higher-level processing occurs at this point. It is difficult to find a clear statement of that hypothesis in the psycholinguistic literature, though it is often attributed to Fodor, Bever and Garrett (1974). The experiments described above provide only weak support for the hypothesis. They show only that the current clause is represented differently in immediate memory from information further back in the passage. They do not rule out the possibility that some syntactic and message-level analysis has been performed on the current clause. However, the strong version of the hypothesis does generate testable predictions – predictions that are known to be incorrect.

Many people would claim that introspective evidence refutes the idea that syntactic and semantic processing are delayed to clause boundaries. In neither reading nor listening does it seem that understanding comes only at the end of clauses. Furthermore, the existence of single-clause garden path sentences suggests that it does not. If no analysis were performed until the end of the sentence, the garden path could not be recognized before that point. In practice it usually is. However, introspection is an unreliable source of information about language processing and, as noted above, the feeling of comprehension in the middle of a clause may simply come from the recognition of familiar words.

Marslen-Wilson (1973, 1975, 1976) demonstrated experimentally that syntactic and semantic analyses have been computed before clause boundaries. He used the shadowing technique in which subjects listen to a passage over headphones, and have to repeat back the words as soon as possible after they hear them. Marslen-Wilson deliberately corrupted some of the words in his passages. For example, he changed *company* to *compsiny*. These corruptions were restored to their correct form, even by the closest shadowers, who lagged only 250 milliseconds, or about one syllable, behind what they were listening to. However, such restorations depended on the corruption occurring in a syntactically and semantically appropriate context. Marslen-Wilson argued that the restorations were guided by syntactic and semantic analyses, and that these analyses must have been computed within the clause. He further argued that his results supported an interactive model of the language processor (see below), but these two arguments are independent of one another. His experiments refute the hypothesis that syntactic and semantic processing is delayed to clause boundaries. Partial analyses are developed word by word as clauses are processed.

How is the language understanding system organized?

If syntactic and semantic analysis occurred only at the end of clauses, then word recognition would, of necessity, be largely unaffected by the operations of the parser and the message-level processor, though syntactic processing might be influenced by the computation of meaning. However, since both parsing and interpretation take place almost immediately, either might affect lexical access. It is, of course, an empirical question whether the processors do influence each other's operations – a question that is usually couched in the following way: do the components of the language understanding system operate serially and independently (Forster, 1979) or do they interact with one another (Marslen-Wilson, 1975; Marslen-Wilson and Welsh, 1978; Marslen-Wilson and Tyler, 1980)? A model in which the processors act serially and independently is called an *autonomy model*, since the operation of lower-level processors is not governed by what happens at higher levels in the system. Although autonomous and interactive models of the language processor are conceptually distinct, Norris (1982) argues that it is more difficult to distinguish between them empirically than has usually been assumed.

Norris points out that discussions of the structure of the language processor have been marred by a lack of clarity about some crucial concepts. One obvious requirement is a precise statement of what is meant by serial, independent operation of subprocessors. Serial operation does not mean that, for example, in analysing a sentence *all* word-level processing takes place before all syntactic processing. While the current word is being identified, the previous words may be undergoing syntactic analysis. The subprocessors operate serially if there is a strict order in which they receive information about a given part of the input. Information flows through the system in one direction only (see Figure 8.1). The word-level processor receives the input first and passes its analysis on to the syntactic processor. The syntactic processor is not able to send information back to the word-level processor,

Figure 8.1 Serial model of the language processor

and so lexical access cannot be affected by the syntactic (or semantic) analysis of the rest of the sentence. It may appear that this definition of serial operation makes any serial model incompatible with some of the findings discussed in chapter 3. That chapter described a number of effects of context on the identification of words, and these effects suggest that semantic analysis influences word recognition. However, as will be explained below, serial models *can* explain effects of context on the identification of words.

In addition to a clear specification of what it means to say that processors are autonomous, a precise definition of interaction is also required. An *interactive* model of the language understanding system is one in which information can be exchanged between two of the processors during the performance of a task (Norris, 1982). In an interactive model there may therefore be some parallel processing. For example, the word-level processor could pass its output to both the syntactic and message-level processors directly if these two interact. However, because of the logical dependence between the subprocessors, strictly parallel models, in which either two or all three processors analyse the same input simultaneously and independently, are not possible.

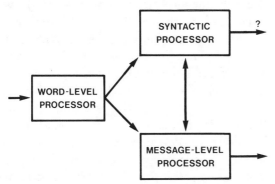

Figure 8.2 An interactive model of the language processor

Figure 8.2 shows one example of an interactive model. In this model, word-level processing is autonomous, but parsing may be influenced by the interpretation of the message. The query by the output of the parser indicates that a phrase marker may or may not be one of the outputs. The essential output is the interpretation of the sentence or text. In other interactive models, information can be exchanged between the word-level processor and the syntactic and message-level processors.

Many different interactive models of the language understanding system can be constructed. Not only is there a choice of which processors can exchange information, but also there is a choice of what information can pass from one processor to another. Crain and Steedman (1985) distinguish between weak and strong forms of interaction, using the parser and the message-level processor as an example. In the case of weak interaction, the message-level processor is able to signal to the parser only that a certain parse should be discontinued because it does not have a sensible interpretation. In a more powerful interactive model, the message processor can *direct* the parser to attempt one analysis rather than another. Marslen-Wilson (see the account of Tyler and Marslen-Wilson's, 1977, experiment below) implies that this second, strong, form of interaction characterizes the human language processor. A final parameter of interactive models is the set of conditions under which the processors exchange information.

It follows from the above discussion that simply to say that the language understanding system is interactive is not to propose a model of that system. If testable predictions are to be made, a particular interactive model must be developed in which the parameters mentioned above take specific values.

There are many interactive models of the language processor. Are there also many autonomy models? It has sometimes been assumed, at least implicitly, that there is only one such model – one in which the word-level processor identifies each word and then passes it to the parser, and in which the parser then analyses each clause before passing a single phrase marker to the message-level processor. However, there *are* parameters on which serial models can vary. One of these is the number of outputs that a processor can pass to the next one at any one time. Another is how often it produces these outputs. It is widely accepted that the parser may produce several analyses in parallel. This possibility was discussed in chapter 4. Furthermore, since message-level analyses are developed word by word, and natural languages have many local syntactic ambiguities, it is probable that the parser, even if it is autonomous, often passes several possible syntactic analyses on to the message-level processor. If multiple outputs are allowed in interactive models, they must also be permitted in serial models. In an autonomous system the message-level processor attempts to decide between alternative parses on the basis of message-level information. If it fails, it must wait for further output from the parser to resolve the ambiguity.

It has less frequently been recognized that, during the analysis of one word, the word-level processor might repeatedly pass sets of candidates for the identity of that word to the syntactic processor, which could then attempt to produce parses incorporating each possibility. Those word candidates that could not be fitted into a phrase marker would be rejected on syntactic grounds, without any violation of the assumption of autonomy (see Norris, 1982).

A serial model that produces multiple outputs behaves differently from one that is restricted to a single output for each input of the appropriate type (a word for the word-level processor, and a clause for the parser) from each of its subprocessors. Data that refute one serial model may therefore be compatible with another. A number of Marslen-Wilson's arguments against serial models rely on the implicit assumption that the word-level processor produces just one output for each word that it analyses (see Norris, 1982). Norris has shown that Marslen-Wilson's findings can be accounted for by a serial model with frequent multiple outputs from the word recognition system.

One further potential source of confusion must be mentioned, before empirical work on the structure of the language processor is discussed. An interaction between subprocessors in the language understanding system is *not* the same as a statistical interaction between, say, syntactic and semantic factors in an experiment. Both serial and interactive models may predict statistical interactions.

Experimental studies of the structure of the language understanding system

Almost all empirical work on the structure of the language processor has addressed only the question of whether there is interaction between the processors. No specific interactive model has been formulated and tested, though Marslen-Wilson, the chief proponent of the interactive view, believes that information can be exchanged between any pair of processors.

> information at each level can constrain and guide simultaneous processing at other levels. (1975, 227)

However, Marslen-Wilson does not specify in detail what information can pass between the processors or when it can do so. Forster (1979) gives the most detailed presentation of a serial model. At the centre of his model is the series of processors illustrated in Figure 8.1. However, the model has two additional components. First, each processor is in two-way contact with the mental lexicon. Second, each processor passes its output to a General Problem Solver (GPS) that is responsible for making decisions and generating responses (see Figure 8.3). The processors themselves do not produce responses – such as 'yes' or 'no' in a lexical decision experiment – they only analyse their inputs. The GPS is in two-way contact with general conceptual knowledge.

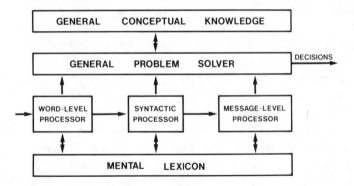

Figure 8.3 Forster's model of the language processor
(*Source* Forster, 1979)

Forster claims that the autonomy hypothesis has one major advantage over the interactive view. It rules out more possibilities, and is therefore more easily testable. He argues that the autonomy hypothesis should, therefore, be adopted until there is adequate evidence that it is incorrect. However, it will emerge from the discussion below that Forster's claim is true only of the simplest autonomy model, and not of his own.

Is word-level processing autonomous?

This section considers the question of whether syntactic or message-level analysis can affect lexical *access*. An example of a syntactic effect on word recognition would be if nouns were easier to identify in contexts such as *the little black....* in which they are syntactically highly probable. Chapter 3 described some effects of semantic context in experiments that investigated lexical access. The most robust of these effects is that an associative context speeds lexical decision. *Butter* is recognized more quickly after *bread* than in a neutral or inappropriate context. Is this evidence for a message-level effect on lexical access? Forster claims not. He explains associative priming by postulating a semantic network of connections between related words *in the lexicon*. In his model the word-level processor is in two-way contact with the lexicon. Therefore associative priming does not violate the principle of autonomy.

It is more difficult to account for the effects of *sentential* context on word recognition without claiming that the message-level processor influences lexical access. In sentences such as:

On the train the man read his *paper.*

in which there are no strong associations between the individual words in the context-providing sentence fragment, and the word to be identified (*paper*), a network of connections in the lexicon cannot account for the speeding of word recognition. Such effects have been found in a number of experiments, and Forster has tried to reconcile them with the autonomy view. The experiments will be described first, and then Forster's account of the results will be presented.

Schuberth and Eimas (1977) and Fischler and Bloom (1979) report experiments in which appropriate sentential context speeded lexical decisions. For example, subjects responded more quickly to *shoes*, following:

She cleaned the dirt from her

than following the 'neutral' context:

xxx xxxxxxx xxx xxxx xxxx xxx

Stanovich and West (1979) obtained similar results in a pronunciation experiment.

Further evidence that sentential context affects lexical access comes from a phoneme-monitoring experiment by Morton and Long (1976). Although Foss and Gernsbacher (1983) argue that the materials used in this experiment were not ideal, it will be discussed in detail for two reasons. First, it illustrates the kind of detailed argument that is necessary in discussions of the structure of the language processor. Second, Mehler (in preparation) has shown that when more appropriate materials are used, the results are the same.

Morton and Long chose pairs of words beginning with the same phoneme, one word that was highly probably in a given sentential context, and another that was possible but not very likely, for example:

He sat reading the book (probable)/bill (unlikely) until it
was time to go home for his tea.

The result of the experiment was that /b/ in *book* was detected faster than /b/ in *bill*. How is this result to be explained?

The answer to this question is not obvious, for the following reason. The target phoneme is at the beginning of the word whose recognition should be speeded by context. It might, therefore, be possible to respond to that phoneme before the word has been identified, in which case phoneme-monitoring time could not decide whether context had speeded lexical access. However, Cutler and Norris (1979) and Foss and Blank (1980) argue that there are two ways of responding in the phoneme-monitoring task. A response can be derived from a phonemic analysis of the word containing the target phoneme. This is the case in which the word need not have been accessed from the lexicon before the response is made. Alternatively, a response can be based on the phonological representation of the word containing the phoneme, after that word has been accessed. It might be thought that the first way of responding would always be quicker, particularly if the recognition of a spoken word depends on the recognition of its constituent phonemes. However, although it has often been implicitly assumed, for example in the research of the early 1970s on 'units of perception' in reading (e.g. Savin and Bever, 1970), that responses based on a low-level analysis can be made more quickly than those based on a high-level analysis, this plausible assumption may be incorrect, for reasons discussed by Foss and Swinney (1973).

Foss and Swinney make the following observation. Although the language understanding system must be able to analyse phonemes, it is not designed to produce awareness of phonemes, or to make responses based on the presence of particular phonemes. Recognizing individual words, though not the principal concern of the language understanding system, is a more natural task for it. It follows that, even if phonemes are analysed before words, a response based on the phonemic level of analysis might be slower than a response generated from the output of the word-level processor, because it is hard to make decisions about phonemes. The fact that Morton and Long obtained a reduction in phoneme-monitoring even when the target phoneme was in the contextually primed word suggests that many responses in phoneme-monitoring experiments *are* derived from phonological representations of words. If subjects were able to respond by considering only the phonemic analysis, then there would have been no effects of word-level variables such as contextual probability. Furthermore, even if phoneme-monitoring responses are based on the lexical level of analysis, Morton and Long would have obtained no effect, unless sentential context speeded word recognition. Their results, therefore, support the claim that it does.

Foss and Gernsbacher's criticism of Morton and Long's experiment arose from their demonstration (1983, Experiment 4) that phoneme-monitoring time is positively correlated with the duration of the vowel following the target phoneme. Foss and Gernsbacher (1983, Experiment 5) used the words from Morton and Long's experiment that contained the target phonemes, and showed that, even out of context, the highly probable words produced shorter phoneme-monitoring times – they had shorter vowels. In Mehler's experiment, which produced the same results as Morton and Long's, vowel duration was controlled.

There is therefore a body of evidence to suggest that sentential context speeds lexical access. Its effect cannot be explained in terms of connections between words in the lexicon, because sentential context does not always depend on word associations. Furthermore, Foss (1982) has demonstrated that sentential context effects, even when they do depend partly on associated words, behave differently from ordinary associative effects – they last much longer. In an auditorily presented list of words, such as:

> Group the examined the entire gills the and fins the of fish caught in the river Nile.

there was no evidence that the association between *gills* and *fins* and *fish* speeded lexical access of *fish*. Phoneme monitoring time for the /k/ in *caught* was the same as when *gills* and *fins* were replaced with much weaker associates of *fish*, *spots* and *stripes*. However, in a sentence made up of the same words, and with the same spacing between the related words:

> The entire group examined the gills and fins of the fish caught in the river Nile.

there was a reduction in phoneme-monitoring time on the /k/ in *caught* when the high associates were present compared to the condition with the low associates. The implication of this finding is that, in a sentential context, *fish* is identified more quickly when the preceding words are related to it, freeing more capacity for a rapid response to the /k/ in the next word. (Note that, in this experiment, phoneme-monitoring is quicker on the word *after* the one whose identification has been speeded by context, so the explanation given for Morton and Long's results does not apply.) Foss hypothesizes that the effects of sentential context should be explained by invoking the notion of a mental model. However, he has a more linguistic notion of mental models than Johnson-Laird and Garnham (1980), since he allows such representations to share lexical concepts with sentences. Foss is therefore able to assume that the representation of items in a mental model allows their names to remain available for priming. Similar effects cannot occur with lists of words.

It therefore appears that the most natural explanation of the effects of sentential context on word recognition is that the message-level processor interacts with the word-level processor. Indeed, in the logogen model (see chapter 3) the effect of sentential context is explained by assuming that the cognitive system, after computing a representation of context, can prime logogens before the next word is presented. However, there is no *exchange* of information between the logogen system (the word-level processor in that model) and the cognitive system (the message-level processor) during the identification of an individual word, so only a limited form of interaction between the two systems takes place. However, even this form of interaction is forbidden in a pure autonomy model. Is there any way that such a model can account for the effects of sentential context?

Forster claims that there is. The explanation of the results of Morton and Long's experiment assumes that decisions based on word-level analysis become available before those based on phonemes, even though phonemes are analysed before words. Similarly, decisions at the message level may become available before those at the word level, since the understanding system is primarily intended to decode messages rather than to recognize individual words. Forster is therefore, able to provide an explanation of effects of sentential context on lexical decisions (e.g. in the experiments of Schuberth and Eimas, 1977, and Fischler and Bloom, 1979, mentioned above), though his explanation does not apply directly to the phoneme-monitoring or word-naming results. His explanation is as follows. When the word *shoes* is presented in context it is identified by an autonomous word recognition system. This processor passes its output to both the syntactic processor and the GPS. The GPS finds it comparatively difficult to produce a 'yes' response based on the output from the word-level processor. It is not designed to make such decisions. While the GPS is computing its lexical decision from the output of the word recognition system, *shoes* is incorporated into the representations constructed by the higher-level processors. Since *shoes* is the last word in the sentence, and it fits the expectations of these processors, they assimilate it rapidly. The message-level processor constructs a coherent interpretation for the sentence, and passes this interpretation on to the GPS. Since the message makes sense, the GPS rapidly deduces that a word was presented, otherwise no comprehensible message would have resulted. Because the GPS is designed to analyse messages, it handles message-level information with great speed, and is sometimes able to produce a 'yes' answer for the lexical decision before the output from the word recognition system has determined a response. Thus lexical *decision* time has been reduced, even though lexical *access* time has remained constant. There has been no interaction between the processors, and the principle of autonomy has been maintained.

The lesson to be learned from this discussion is that recent versions of the autonomy model, particularly those in which the autonomous processors pass their outputs to a powerful problem solving system, are harder to refute than the original version. The introduction of the GPS into an autonomy model of the language processor tends to rob that model of the feature that originally made it attractive, namely its testability. Similarly, multiple-output autonomy models are harder to refute that those that produce only single outputs. None of the evidence presented in this chapter or in chapter 3 is incompatible with a modified version of the autonomy thesis, so it cannot be concluded that word recognition is influenced by the syntactic or message-level processor.

Is syntactic processing autonomous?

This section addresses a question that both psycholinguists and AI researchers have investigated: is the human sentence parsing mechanism autonomous, or is syntactic analysis aided, or even guided, by interpretation at the message level?

In chapter 2 Chomsky's principle of the autonomy of syntax from semantics was mentioned. This principle must be clearly distinguished from the claim that syntactic *processing* is independent of semantic, or message-level, processing. Chomsky's formal autonomy principle is a stipulation about the way in which the fundamental concepts in syntactic theory, such as noun phrase, phrase-structure rule, and transformation, should be defined. It states that their definitions should not contain any semantic terms. Thus Chomsky's view is different from, for example, writers of school textbooks on grammar, in which syntactic classes are defined by what their members *refer* to. An example of such a definition is that the verb is the part of speech that names actions, events, states and processes. For Chomsky a term such as *verb* is defined implicitly by its role in syntactic theory, and not by reference to anything outside of syntax.

By contrast, autonomy of syntactic processing means that the parser does not exchange information with the message-level processor in the course of analysing a sentence, but simply passes its analyses to the message-level processor. It is possible to take different views on the questions of formal autonomy and processing autonomy. It can even be argued that the positions that combine opposite views on the two issues are more plausible that those that do not. If syntactic categories are semantically defined, then semantic interpretation itself should be straightforward, and is unlikely to be of any help to the parser. However, if syntax is formally autonomous, then it may permit structures that are uninterpretable. In such cases the semantic processor could signal to the parser that the analysis should be discontinued.

Artificial Intelligence Discussions of autonomy in AI have frequently been marred by confusions between formal and processing autonomy. However, some projects have genuinely addressed questions about interaction between processes. For example, in Winograd's (1972) SHRDLU, semantic analysis and knowledge of the world affect the choices that the parser makes between alternative syntactic structures. Consider the command:

Put the block in the box on the table.

This command is ambiguous – the block could be in the box to start with or it might have to be placed in the box. If SHRDLU knows that there is no block in a box, then it can use its knowledge of the world to reject one potential analysis of *the block in the box* (on the assumption that the command is a sensible one) and discontinue parses of the sentence based on that analysis. However, the psychological relevance of this aspect of SHRDLU is unclear. Winograd claims that the interactive nature of his language processor is essential to its efficient functioning.

> The key to the function of language as a means of communication is in the way that these areas [knowledge base, semantics, grammar] interact. (1973, 180)

However, he provides no evidence in support of this claim, and a non-interactive version of SHRDLU could be written, in which the message processor decided between all possible parses at the end of each clause. Furthermore, the factors that determine what is efficient for a computer may have only tangential relevance to how the human language understanding system has developed. Only in extreme cases might the unworkability of a method of computation in a computer simulation suggest its implausibility as a model of human performance.

Unlike Winograd's writings, many other discussions in AI that purport to be about interaction between syntactic and semantic processing are largely about formal autonomy. For example, in the language understanding programs written by Schank and his colleagues (see Schank, 1975) the definitions of structural categories make use of semantic concepts, and therefore violate Chomsky's principle of formal autonomy. Schank refers to this aspect of his programs by saying that comprehension is 'semantics-driven'. This description suggests that semantic analysis guides parsing. Indeed, Schank claims that syntactic analysis is not always necessary.

> The rules of French grammar are not crucial in understanding French. (1975, 12)

On these points he is the victim of the same confusion between syntax and semantics as the Generative Semanticists (see chapter 2). A structural (that is syntactic) analysis of a sentence is easily confused with a semantic one if the grammar violates the formal autonomy principle. A 'semantic' grammar may have syntactic categories such as AGENT and LOCATION, with the result that the *syntactic* structure of a sentence displays its meaning transparently and can be mistaken for a semantic representation. It then appears that the sentence has been interpreted without recourse to syntactic analysis. However, the interpretation is performed by the person looking at what is a structural (*syntactic*) analysis of the sentence. The occurrence of a symbol such as AGENT (rather than, say, NP) in a phrase marker does not determine what that symbol *means*. Another reason why analysis by a semantic grammar seems to bypass syntax is that a semantic grammar for analysing discourse about a specific domain of knowledge is comparatively simple (see for example, Bruce, 1982, who presents a grammar for analysing questions about business trips), and 'semantic' phrase markers have little structure. The major problem with simple semantic grammars is that they do not generalize to other knowledge domains.

From Schank's descriptions of his programs it is impossible to tell whether syntactic and semantic processors interact. The reason is that Schank does assume the structural descriptions constructed by his program to be semantically transparent, and no proper *semantic* interpreter is provided. However, he certainly claims that higher-order message-level processes, such as the use of scripts to interpret and expand the information in a sequence of sentences, influence analysis at the sentence level (e.g. Schank and Abelson, 1977). To use Schank's favourite example, once the topic of a passage has been identified as a visit to a restaurant, the restaurant script, which contains information about typical sequences of events in restaurants, becomes active, and can be used to predict what people and events will be mentioned in subsequent sentences, and what roles they will play. Since role names (e.g. AGENT, INSTRUMENT) are structural categories in Schank's representational system, message-level processing guides parsing. Therefore, even if there is no syntactic-semantic interaction in Schank's programs, there is certainly an interaction between his 'semantic' sentence parsers and the message-level processor.

Psycholinguistics In the psycholinguistic literature there are a number of experiments that purport to demonstrate syntactic–semantic interaction in human sentence comprehension. One set of these experiments compared reversible and non-reversible passives. Non-reversible passives, such as:

The cake was eaten by the florist.

are easier to understand than reversible passives, such as:

The chemist was praised by the doctor.

In fact, non-reversible passives are no more difficult to understand than their corresponding actives (Slobin, 1966). The ease with which non-reversible passives are understood could be explained by assuming that people use case-frame analysis, as described in chapter 4. A verb such as *eat* requires an animate subject. A florist is animate, but a cake is not therefore of the two NPs in the non-reversible passive sentence, only one, *the florist*, can refer to the logical (or underlying) subject of the verb *eat*, i.e. the thing that does the eating. The main relation expressed by the sentence must therefore be (EAT FLORIST CAKE) rather than (EAT CAKE FLORIST). Thus semantic cues in non-reversible passives reduce the amount of syntactic processing that must be done. For the reversible passives a full parse is needed to produce the correct interpretation, but for the non-reversible passives all that is required is the identification of the verb and the NPs.

However, there is reason to doubt whether Slobin's results reflect processing that happens as sentences are read. First, Gough (1966) produced the same pattern of results as Slobin using the same task – the sentence-picture verification task – even when he presented the picture 3 seconds after the sentence. This finding suggests that the difference between reversible and non-reversible passives should be explained in terms of processes that compare the sentence and the picture, rather than those that analyse the sentence itself. Second, Forster and Olbrei (1973) argued that non-reversible passives are typically more plausible than reversible ones, and are likely to be understood more quickly for that reason. When they controlled for plausibility, Forster and Olbrei found no difference in comprehensibility between reversible and non-reversible passives either in sentence classification, in which subjects have to decide whether strings of words are sentences, or in RSVP. Both tasks come closer to measuring on-line processing than does sentence-picture verification. However, it should be pointed out that message-level processing is not strictly necessary either to perform sentence classification or to recall sentences after RSVP.

Somewhat more convincing evidence for interaction between the parser and the message-level processor comes from an experiment by Quinn (reported by Steedman and Johnson-Laird, 1978). Quinn presented subjects with sentences such as:

The man took the boy to the girl.
The man took the girl the boy.
The man took the coat to the girl.
The man took the girl the coat.

The first and third of these sentences have an explicit cue to their syntactic structure. The word *to* indicates that the final NP is the indirect object of *took*, and that the preceding NP must therefore be its direct object. In the second and fourth sentences the final four words are potentially ambiguous. The two NPs could be the indirect and direct objects, respectively, of *took*, but they could also be the beginning of a conjoined direct object. For example, the second sentence could continue:

The man took the girl the boy and the puppy to the zoo.

In the third and fourth sentences there is a message-level cue to the role of the people or things denoted by the two NPs. It is much more likely that a coat would be taken to a girl than that a girl would be taken to a coat. Furthermore, the final four words of the fourth sentence, *the girl the coat*, are less likely to be the beginning of a conjoined direct object than are the words *the boy the girl*. The result of the experiment was that the dative-shifted sentences (the second and fourth) were more difficult to unders-tand than those with the explicit syntactic cue – the subjects' task was to press a button when they had understood the sentence, and then to answer a question. However, the effect was considerably reduced when there was a cue at the message level to the roles of the objects mentioned after the verb. The difficulty of parsing the V NP NP construction was reduced by plausibility, a non-syntactic cue. The simplest explanation of this result, and the one implicit in Steedman and Johnson-Laird's brief discussion, is that plausibility has its effect by sending information back to the parser telling it to discontinue one of its analyses (in this case the one in which *the girl the coat* is the beginning of a list of conjoined NPs). If the parser has fewer analyses to pursue it can proceed more quickly with the ones that remain under consideration, and the message-level processor, too, will have its subsequent work reduced. However, there are explanations of Quinn's result that are consistent with the autonomy hypothesis. One such explana-tion is that the parser computes in their entirety all possible analyses and passes those analyses to the message-level processor, where the ambiguity is resolved. Semantic cues help the message processor with this resolution, and hence reduce the difference in processing difficulty between a sentence with a local ambiguity (for example, *the man took the girl the coat*) and a matched sentence without that ambiguity (for example, *the man took the coat to the girl*). Quinn's experiment does not therefore decide conclusively against autonomy.

The experiments described so far have attempted to demonstrate an interac-tion between syntactic and message-level processors by taking measures for the processing of complete sentences. However, if Marslen-Wilson is correct in claiming that interactive processing occurs all the time, then it should be possible to find evidence for interaction within a sentence. Tyler and Marslen-Wilson (1977) devised a technique that was intended to identify such interaction. They presented the beginning of a sentence over headphones, for example:

> If you walk too near the runway, landing planes...
> If you've been trained as a pilot, landing planes...

A word, either *is* or *are*, was then presented visually and subjects had to say it as quickly as possible. The phrase *landing planes* is ambiguous between a 'planes that are landing' and an 'activity of landing planes' reading. These two readings are appropriate in the first and second sentence fragments, respectively. The natural continuation of the first is therefore *are* and that of the second *is*. The results of the experiment were that the appropriate continuation word was pronounced more quickly than the inappropriate one. Tyler and Marslen-Wilson took this result to be evidence for a message-level influence on parsing. However, it must be pointed out that this interpretation commits them to the rather implausible claim that the meaning of the first clause in the first fragment produces a *general* bias towards analysing the first two words of any following clause as ADJ N rather than V-ing N, whereas the first clause of the second fragment produces the opposite bias. However, these biases could lead to mistakes or difficulties in understanding such sentence fragments as:

> If you've been trained as a pilot, approaching storms. ...

An alternative, non-interactive explanation of Tyler and Marslen-Wilson's results has been suggested by Forster (1979). He claims that both of the syntactic analyses of *flying planes* are generated, whatever the preceding context, and that the ambiguity is resolved at the message level. There is no further recourse to syntactic information, and no interaction. Forster assumes that the resolution of the ambiguity occurs in the short time between the end of the auditorily presented sentence fragment, and the visual presentation of the continuation word. He is therefore committed to the view that the shorter this time can be made the smaller the difference in pronunciation latencies for *is* and *are* should be. However, it is difficult to turn this commitment into a clear prediction, since Forster could claim that the processing is very rapid, and that no experimental technique could detect it.

One final set of findings that suggest an interaction between the parser and the message-level processor come from experiments on the comprehension of garden path sentences (Crain and Steedman, 1985; Milne, 1982). Crain and Steedman argue that if parsing is independent of higher-level processing, then a syntactic structure that produces a garden path in one instance should always produce one. They attempt to demonstrate that this prediction of the autonomy theory is false. Consider the sentence:

The teachers taught by the Berlitz method passed the test.

It does produce a garden path, since *taught* is plausible as a main verb following the subject NP *the teachers*, whereas, in the correct analysis of the sentence *taught by the Berlitz method* is a reduced object-relative clause, and *passed* is the main verb. However, in the structurally identical sentence:

The children taught by the Berlitz method passed the test.

it is less plausible that the children did the teaching, and more plausible that *the children* should be the head noun phrase of an object-relative, and hence the direct object of *taught*. Crain and Steedman found that, in a sentence classification task, the first of these sentences was much more frequently classified as ungrammatical than the second. They also found grammaticality judgements were affected by biasing contexts that occurred before potential garden path sentences. Similarly Milne (1982) showed that of the following potential garden path sentences:

The granite rocks during the earthquake.
The granite rocks were by the seashore.
The table rocks during the earthquake.

only the first was difficult to understand. This result suggests that the analysis of the first three words in the sentence is determined by plausibility, and that the last part of the sentence is difficult to parse if it does not fit with the chosen interpretation.

Can the results of Crain and Steedman and of Milne be explained by a non-interactive theory? The standard ploy would be to argue that even in garden path sentences all parses are passed to the message-level processor, and it is there that factors such as plausibility have their effect. However, this argument is a little less plausible than in the explanation of Quinn's results, since if all parses are computed, it is difficult to see why some garden paths are so hard to recover from, given that they describe quite likely situations.

An impasse?

With a little ingenuity it has proved possible to explain away all the empirical evidence that apparently favours an interactive view of the structure of the language processor. This fact raises two questions. First, why have experimental tests failed to resolve the autonomy vs interaction issue? Second, is there any empirical evidence that *is* relevant to its resolution?

The answer to the first question is that interactionists have greatly underestimated the power of serial models, partly because of the way that such models have usually been presented. Multiple-output serial models are much less restricted in their capabilities than those that produce only single outputs, but they are not so easily falsified. Because the power of serial models has not been recognized, the experiments that purported to distinguish between interactive and autonomy theories did not do so.

There are two answers to the second question. The first is that, because there are many different autonomous and interactive models it is difficult to design a single experiment to resolve the general question of whether the language processor is interactive. The second is that certain kinds of very powerful interactive models are incompatible with established findings. First, models in which syntactic and semantic context *guide* lexical access cannot explain the results of some of the experiments on lexical ambiguity (e.g. Swinney, 1979) described in chapter 3. These experiments show that, even in strongly biasing contexts, all the meanings of an ambiguous word are accessed initially. Second, the claim that message-level processing guides parsing is hard to reconcile with the findings of Rayner, Carlson and Frazier (1983), who studied the eye movements of subjects reading structurally ambiguous sentences. They found that both the pattern of fixations and that of regressive eye movements were always the same for a given syntactic structure, regardless of whether the interpretation was plausible. For example, when reading a garden path sentence such as:

The florist sent the flowers was very pleased.

subjects made regressive eye movements from *was pleased* to *florist sent*, which were interpreted by Rayner *et al.* as an attempt to recover from a garden path. A similar pattern of regressive eye movements occurred in the reading of

The performer sent the flowers was very pleased.

in which the less common syntactic structure (reduced relative clause) has a highly plausible interpretation. No such regressions were made when reading a control sentence with the more common syntactic structure (main clause).

The performer sent the flowers and was very pleased with herself.

These results suggest that, on initial reading, a single syntactic analysis is computed on the basis of *syntactic* frequency, or, at least, alternative analyses are very quickly discontinued. If this interpretation is correct, then the parser is not influenced by message-level processing, and results such as those of Crain and Steedman must either arise at the message level, or reflect the influence of plausibility on syntactic reanalysis.

It is therefore possible to obtain indirect evidence *against* certain forms of interaction. Information that could be used by an interactive processor does not, in fact, have its predicted effects on lexical access or syntactic analysis. However, as Norris (in press) argues, a case for a limited form of weak interaction can be made, at least to explain recovery from garden paths. The most difficult garden path sentences for an autonomy model to cope with are those such as Frazier and Fodor's (1978):

Tom said that Bill will take the cleaning out yesterday.

In this sentence the meaning of the correct parse is plausible. Message-level information cannot be used to reject that analysis. Conversely the (garden path) parse that underlies the reading initially obtained is syntactically well-formed. There is no syntactic information to show that its interpretation is nonsensical. Although it would be possible to explain recovery from this garden path at the message level – all parses are passed to the message processor and interpreted one at a time in order of syntactic frequency – Norris argues that this account is both unparsimonious and inconsistent with what is known about limitations on short-term memory in language processing. In particular, memory for syntactic structure is rapidly lost (see chapter 7), so it is unlikely that all parses are retained while the message processor tries to interpret the sentence. Norris proposes instead that when there is no message-level information to decide between two possible parses, the less frequent is terminated. This account implies that the message-level processor will sometimes have to send information back to the parser to tell it to continue with an infrequent analysis, or to restart it, if the more frequent structure was a garden path.

Summary

There are three main groups of subprocessors in the language understanding system – lexical, syntactic and message level. All three kinds of processing are initiated soon after linguistic information is input. Suggestions that syntactic and semantic processing is delayed to major clause boundaries can be rejected, though the current clause does have special status in immediate memory – its surface form is more readily available than that of previous clauses. One plausible hypothesis is that information – including some information about surface form – is transferred into a more permanent memory store at clause boundaries, and the detailed representation of surface form is erased from immediate memory.

The question of how the processors work together is a more difficult one to resolve. The hypothesis that they operate serially and independently is, in its simplest form, easier to test than the hypothesis that they interact, but it has been modified by Forster and by Norris so that it too is difficult to refute.

There are many alternative models of the structure of the language processor. They vary on such parameters as the number of outputs produced at one time by each processor, the processors that are in direct communication with one another, and the information that can be communicated between them. In testing these models a number of sources of confusion must be avoided. In particular, processing interaction should be distinguished from statistical interaction, and formal autonomy from autonomy of processing.

Although many experiments have suggested that interaction between processors occurs in comprehension, and particularly that the message-level processor affects word recognition and parsing, none of the evidence is conclusive. However, not only is there indirect evidence against the more powerful kinds of strong interactive model, but there are also plausible arguments to suggest that a limited amount of weak interaction occurs in the language processor.

9

Language production and its relation to comprehension

Although this book is about psycholinguistics – the study of the mechanisms that govern language use – it has focused on understanding rather than production. The reason for this emphasis was explained in chapter 1. It is easier to study language understanding than language production, and comprehension has therefore been more widely investigated. However, a number of methods for the study of speaking and writing have been developed, and it is sometimes argued (e.g. Butterworth, 1980a) that the operation of the language processor can be examined more directly in production than in comprehension. Butterworth supports this claim by noting that the *output* of the production system – speech or writing – is more tangible than that of the comprehension system – mental representations. The properties of such representations can be determined only by indirect methods, but speech and writing are more easily analysed. Nevertheless, the tighter experimental control that can be exercised in studies of comprehension continues to guarantee their favour among psycholinguists.

Most studies of language production have investigated spoken rather than written language. This preference arises partly because theories of production make predictions about its temporal characteristics. In the case of speech these characteristics can be measured from tape recordings, whereas more complex recording techniques (e.g. for forearm muscle activity) are required in investigations of handwriting (see for example, Wing, 1978; Viviani and Terzuolo, 1983). Furthermore, since speaking is a more natural activity than writing, the temporal pattern of speech reflects more closely the linguistically important processes of language production than does the temporal pattern of writing.

Psycholinguistic questions about language production

The questions that psycholinguists ask about language production parallel those about language understanding, though they do not necessarily receive parallel answers. There are, therefore, two main sets of questions about production. The first concerns the subprocessors of the production system, and how each performs its task (cf. chapters 3, 4, 6, 7). The second is directed to the overall structure of the system (cf. chapter 8). In the study of production, unlike comprehension, the second set of questions has received more attention than the first.

There are two principal questions about structure, which correspond to those in chapter 8. One is: how do the subprocessors work together – is the correct model of the production system serial or interactive? The other is analogous to the question about the locus of syntactic and semantic processing in comprehension. The related problem in production is how far *in advance* the syntactic and semantic properties of a sentence have been decided. Is the form of a clause finalized before it is spoken, or can some computations be delayed until after it has been started?

More general questions about planning in language production can also be asked. Planning takes place at many levels, from determining the overall purpose of a conversation or text to deciding on the particular words to convey the message and how they are to be articulated. Chapter 7 described how knowledge of plans and goals is used in the *interpretation* of stories. However, speakers and writers not only need to know about plans in order to describe actions in a comprehensible way, but also have to plan their own productions.

Methods of Studying Production

Language production has been studied in three main ways. The oldest and most popular method is to investigate cases in which it goes wrong, and to infer what happens in normal production. This approach parallels the study of visual perception via visual deficits and optical illusions. The second method is to carry out experiments with normal subjects, and the third is to write computer programs.

Failures of the production system

The production system can fail in several ways, some more drastic than others. Almost all speech contains some disfluencies. Their incidence varies from speaker to speaker, and from context to context but, except in extreme cases, they do not cause comprehension problems. The most common types of disfluency are hesitations, pauses, ums and ahs, corrections, false starts, repetitions, interjections, stuttering and slips of the tongue.

Aphasia   In the mid-nineteenth century Broca and Wernicke established that injuries to certain areas of the brain cause gross speech deficits, called aphasias. In Broca's aphasia, damage to part of the left frontal lobe leads to very hesitant and broken, though largely comprehensible, speech. In Wernicke's aphasia, damage further back in the left hemisphere results in fluent, but meaningless speech. On the basis of these findings some sketchy ideas about how parts of the brain contribute to language production were formulated. This tradition is continued in the work of Geschwind (1972), who provides a useful overview of the approach. This work will not be discussed in detail, as its implications for psycholinguistic theories of language production are far from obvious.

More recently, data from brain-damaged patients have been used to test psycholinguistic theories derived from studies of normal language use. However, attention has focused primarily on the dyslexias – disorders of reading – and hence on language perception rather than production (see e.g. Coltheart, Patterson and Marshall, 1980; Marshall, Coltheart and Patterson, in press)

Speech errors   The speech of aphasics is so different from that of normals, either in content or form, or both, that it is difficult to draw conclusions about ordinary language production from it. An alternative approach is to investigate production errors in normal speakers and writers. In recent years the most important evidence about language production has come from speech errors (for example, Fromkin, 1973, 1980; Cutler, 1982). The speech errors that psycholinguists study are the slips of the tongue discussed by Freud (1901/1960), whose interests were rather different from those of modern psycholinguists. More importantly, speech errors were first studied from a psycholinguistic point of view by Meringer and Mayer (1895/1978).

Each author classifies speech errors in a slightly different way. Garnham, Shillcock, Brown, Mill and Cutler (1981) suggest a seven-way classification: anticipations, perseverations, omissions, additions, exchanges, substitutions and blends. A second dimension on which speech errors can be classified is the kind of linguistic unit that is, for example, added or substituted. Garnham *et al.* distinguish between errors at four levels: segments (distinctive features or phonemes), syllables or morphemes, words and larger units. Some examples of speech errors, taken from Garnham *et al.* (1981), are shown in Table 9.1. Garnham *et al.*'s data allow a conservative estimate of the frequency of speech errors – about one error for every 1800 words.

A number of generalizations about speech errors have been formulated. Three of them are particularly important, though, as Cutler (1981) points

Table 9.1 Examples of speech errors

Type	Target utterance	Error
anticipation	the new Mel Brooks film	the new Bel
perseveration	practical classes	practical kr
omission	British	Britsch
omission (haplology)	never lets	nets
addition	better off than	better off-wise than
exchange	on a table round you	round a table on you
substitution	engineering job	engineering degree
substitution ('malapropism')	she'd burnt a couple... burst a couple	burst
substitution (derivation error)	these are oral contraceptives	these are oral contraception
blend	hilarity OR hysterics	hilarics

out, care must be taken in evaluating them. Some speech errors are easier to detect than others, so errors that violate the laws may be difficult to hear rather than uncommon. Wells (1951) formulated the First Law of Slips of the Tongue – each speech error results in a sequence of sounds that is permitted in the language being spoken. Thus a speech error in English should never result in a sound such as /btir/, since English words cannot begin with /b/ followed by /t/. The second law is that, for segmental errors, the beginning of a syllable can exchange only with the beginning of another syllable, and similarly for middles and ends of syllables. The final generalization is that segmental errors tend to occur within major syntactic constituents, and word errors across syntactic boundaries. A consequence of this third law is that sounds often shift between lexical categories, for example from a noun to a verb, since a constituent typically contains only one item from a category. When words exchange, however, they usually exchange with other items from the same class.

Hesitations and pauses   A third case in which the language production system *may* not be working optimally is when speech contains hesitations or pauses. Although such disfluencies are not, strictly speaking, errors, they do indicate points at which processing load may be high. By determining when the production system becomes overloaded, the kinds of processing it performs can be inferred. However, care is needed in interpreting the occurrence of pauses, in particular. Goldman-Eisler (1968) stressed the connection between pauses and planning. However, speakers need not pause every time they plan. Some spontaneous speech is fluent, even though it is not planned in advance. Furthermore, some pauses are primarily for breathing, and others are stylistic – they make the point of the utterance clearer. Such pauses do not reflect difficulties in production. (See Dechert and Raupach, 1980, for a review of recent work on the temporal characteristics of speech.)

Controlled production experiments

The second method of studying production is in controlled experiments. In these experiments subjects are given a stimulus – perhaps a word or pair of words to include in a sentence, or a picture to describe – and they have to generate a word, a sentence or a longer stretch of speech. The rationale for this procedure is as follows. In language production a message is converted into words. Normally the message is selected by the speaker or writer. In controlled production experiments part of the message is provided. These studies therefore address the question of how difficult it is to put certain ideas into words. The most common measure in such experiments is the time taken to begin speaking. This time reflects the difficulty of formulating a response. When longer stretches of discourse are generated, temporal patterns in the speech can be analysed.

Computer programming

The major use of computer programming in the study of language production has been to model high-level planning. Syntactic processing (Kempen and Hoenkamp, in press) and the structure of the production system (Dell and Reich, 1980) have also been studied.

An outline of language production

The account of comprehension in the previous chapters explains how linguistically conveyed information is converted into an internal representation, or mental model, of a situation in the real or an imaginary world. The mind contains many such representations, derived from both language and perception. A theory of language production must describe how such representations are converted into speech or writing.

In the study of comprehension, some processes, for example the extraction of visual features from printed words, are too peripheral to be studied by *cognitive* psychologists. It is assumed that their outputs can be described, and that those outputs form the inputs to the language understanding system.

Similarly, in production there are peripheral processes, such as the control of articulatory movements, that psycholinguists do not investigate, though other psychologists study them with profit.

Only a brief sketch of a theory of language production can be given and the discussion will again focus on speaking rather than writing. Such a theory has components that correspond to those of a theory of comprehension. At the highest level, production is guided by the speaker's overall goals and plans, which are reflected in the points that he or she wishes to make. As was mentioned in chapter 7, making a point successfully is a skill that may have to be taught. One aspect of this skill is taking account of context – making sure that what one says is pragmatically appropriate. The simplest way to account for pragmatic influences on production – and they are ubiquitous (see Gazdar, 1980) – is to assume that speakers have a representation of the context in which their utterances are produced, and writers one of the context in which their texts will be interpreted. Both speakers and writers must also follow general pragmatic principles such as the Co-operative Principle and those governing speech acts. A representation of context indicates what information is available to the hearer, and can therefore be presupposed. It determines what import, or illocutionary force, the utterance has, and how its actual meaning differs from its literal meaning.

Given a representation of context, and a message to convey, speakers use semantic knowledge to construct a literal meaning that can be used to express the intended meaning. Psycholinguists usually assume that there is a mental language in which such meanings can be expressed. Fodor (1976; Fodor, Fodor and Garrett, 1975) has proposed that the *language of thought*, or *mentalese*, is very close to natural language and hence differs from person to person. The more common view (for example, Schank, 1972) is that it is the same, or at least that it shares many properties, for speakers of different languages.

The final task of the cognitive part of the production system is to convert the chosen literal meaning into a sentence fragment, complete sentence or set of sentences. To accomplish this task it uses the syntactic and phonological rules of the language, and the lexicon. The fact that words must be chosen to express specific semantic contents implies that there is a third way of accessing the mental lexicon in addition to the phonological and orthographic routes discussed in chapter 3 – one using syntactic and semantic features (cf. Forster, 1976).

One misunderstanding must be avoided in thinking about theories of language production. Such theories are not intended to predict what a person will say when, but only to explain how utterances are produced when the decision to speak has been made. A parallel limitation in the natural sciences is that a theory of gravitation does not predict when a stone will fall, only how it falls if it does.

Empirical investigations of planning

High-level planning

Many AI projects, including a number that were primarily addressed to the problems of language understanding (for example, Winograd's, 1972, SHRDLU, and Schank's, 1975, MARGIE), have attempted to produce programs with realistic output. Such programs need not construct sentences in the same way that people do, but they must construct similar sentences in similar contexts. This work and other AI research on language production from the same period was therefore addressed to the question of how the appropriate response is chosen on the basis of previous context, knowledge about the other speaker, and knowledge about the world. Although these programs offer some insights into human language production, there are two issues about which they have little to say. First, the programs make no attempt to model the temporal structure of planning. They construct sentences and then type them out. Second, because they respond only to specific requests and commands, the programs engage in comparatively little high-level planning. They do not, for example, select topics for conversation.

SHRDLU is able to make some use of discourse context and world knowledge in selecting its responses, though the syntactic complexity of its output is restricted. A more sophisticated program that extended Winograd's work was written by Davey (see Davey and Longuet-Higgins, 1978). This program produces descriptions of games of noughts and crosses (tic-tac-toe). Its output not only specifies the moves in a game, but also indicates tactical relations between them by its use of conjunctions such as *but*, *because* and *although*. The program demonstrates how knowledge of what is being described affects the structure of discourse. However, although Davey's program produces coherent, well-planned descriptions, it does not take part in conversations.

A program that is able to converse – with another copy of itself – was written by Power (1979). The two copies of Power's program can be thought of as robots that inhabit a very simple world. These robots have goals, such as getting in and out of a door that can be opened from only one side, which they must co-operate to achieve. They are therefore led to converse. The importance of Power's program is that it shows how high-level plans influence what is said. Its main failing as a model of language production is that it cannot generate ordinary conversational English from its plans. The part of the program that understands what is said is responsible for its most obvious deficiency – its long-winded preamble to every interchange. This part of the program cannot deduce the force of an utterance from its form and its context – in particular, it cannot interpret an utterance as a question unless it has been prefaced with *May I ask you something?* A program like Power's could produce more natural discourse if it had knowledge of the conditions under which different speech acts were appropriate. Cohen and Perrault (1979) describe a program that has this knowledge. Although its outputs are in a LISP-like notation rather than English, it does not have to signal every speech act overtly. The quality of its output is further improved by the fact that the program knows, or can find out, the wants and beliefs of the person it is addressing.

A further aspect of language production that depends on the wants and beliefs of the addressee is the giving of helpful answers to questions that have incorrect presuppositions. Steedman (see Steedman and Johnson-Laird, 1978) has begun to tackle this problem in a program that answers questions about particles moving in a one dimensional world. If it is asked:

Did particle X hit particle Y at time 2?

and X never hit Y, it can respond:

X did not hit Y. X hit Z.

rather than simply saying 'no'. This program illustrates one of the crucial skills required in conversation, the ability to work out the 'best' answer when there is no strictly correct one.

AI research has pinpointed many of the important questions about high-level (pragmatic) influences on planning. However, there have been few psycholinguistic studies of planning at this level. One study that bears on this issue was carried out by Osgood (1971). He asked subjects to describe a series of events, one at a time, and then analysed the sentences that were produced. He was interested in, when, for example, definite descriptions were used in preference to indefinite ones (*the ball* vs *a ball*), and when qualifying adjectives were included (*the white ball* vs *the ball*). He found that indefinite articles were usually used only when an object was first introduced, and that adjectives were included when they were necessary to distinguish between two objects of the same kind. Osgood argued from these results that speakers are sensitive to the information their audience needs, and that they tailor what they say accordingly.

Planning sentences and clauses

Most psychological work on planning has addressed two questions: what aspects of a message make planning difficult, and when does planning takes place?

In an attempt to answer the first question, subjects have been asked to construct sentences containing words or pairs of words, and a variety of word-level variables has been shown to influence performance on this task. Taylor (1969) demonstrated that subjects started speaking sooner when the words were concrete rather than abstract, and sooner when they were common rather than rare. Rosenberg (1977) showed that it is easier to produce sentences containing related words than unrelated words, and Jarvella (reported in 1977) found that, when subjects had to make up a sentence containing two finite verbs they preferred to place the main clause before the subordinate clause regardless of which verb they chose as the main verb. Jarvella originally attempted to argue from this result to a transformational theory of production, though his arguments were criticized by Fodor, Bever and Garrett (1974, 414–18).

In a more complex experiment Tannenbaum and Williams (1968) asked subjects to describe pictures using either active or passive sentences. Before they saw each picture the subjects read a paragraph in which either the subject or the object of the sentence that they were intended to produce was the topic. When the surface subject of the active form was the topic, the active sentence was produced more quickly than the passive, but there was no difference when focus was on the surface subject of the passive. This result is similar to those from comprehension experiments designed to test the Derivational Theory of Complexity (see chapter 4). It shows that the ease of producing a sentence cannot be predicted from its syntactic form alone, but that semantic and pragmatic factors also exert an influence. Unfortunately Tannenbaum and Williams did not follow the usual practice and report the time to begin speaking. They reported one measure that included both this latency and the time to say the sentence. This measure is therefore contaminated by differences in the lengths of the sentences that were produced.

The most intensively studied question in the planning of speech is when it occurs. In sentence comprehension Fodor, Bever and Garrett's (1974) hypothesis that major syntactic and semantic processing is delayed to clause boundaries proved to be incorrect – parsing and interpretation begin almost immediately. The corresponding hypothesis in sentence production is that major syntactic and semantic decisions are taken before a clause is begun. This conjecture is plausible, since there is often introspective evidence that a sentence has been planned before it is said.

Fodor *et al.* suggested that the fundamental unit of planning is the *surface structure* clause, and Boomer (1965) proposed the *phonemic* clause, which corresponds closely to the surface structure clause. These ideas are supported by the fact that hesitations tend to occur towards the beginning of such clauses (Boomer, 1965; Hawkins, 1971) where short-term memory load is high – most of the clause is occupying that store, and that pauses often occur before them (Goldman-Eisler, 1972), presumably for planning.

Another piece of evidence that syntactic units play a role in language production comes from a study by Maclay and Osgood (1959). They examined repetitions in speech recorded from lectures at a psycholinguistic conference, and noted that speakers almost always went back to a major constituent boundary, regardless of where they stopped. To take an artificial example, a speaker who intends to say *pass me that mat*, but says *pass me this. . .*, usually continues *pass me this. . . that mat*. However, a speaker who says *pass me that new. . .*would also return to the beginning of the noun phrase *pass me that new. . . that old mat*, even though the word *that* is repeated. However, the relevance of these findings to a model of language production is not clear. Speakers may go back to constituent boundaries not because of any property of the production system, but in order to make what they say comprehensible.

Ford and Holmes (1978) point out that these early studies failed to consider the role of *deep structure* – as opposed to surface structure – clauses in planning. Every surface clause boundary corresponds to a deep clause boundary, but the reverse is not true. For example, the sentence:

I began working a lot harder.

contains two deep structure clauses, but only one finite verb, *began*. There is a deep but not a surface clause boundary between *began* and *working*. Ford and Holmes asked subjects to speak spontaneously on preselected topics, and at the same time to listen for tones and press a button whenever they heard one. The time to respond to a tone was taken as an indication of processing load at the time when it occurred. The results were that tone-monitoring time increased towards the end of deep structure clauses, regardless of whether they corresponded to surface structure clauses. Ford (1982) showed that pauses in spontaneous speech also provide evidence for the importance of deep clauses in planning.

It should not be concluded that these results support a transformational model of production. Deep clauses correspond to semantic units. Indeed, Ford and Holmes (1978) favoured a semantic account of their findings, and Ford (1982) argues that her data are incompatible with a transformational model. They indicate clause by clause planning, which is inconsistent with the idea that underlying phrase markers are planned as single units, and clauses then moved away from their underlying positions by transformations.

In a recent experiment Holmes (1984) asked subjects to continue stories portraying stereotypical sequences of events. In these circumstances more than one sentence was planned at a time, and the number of surface clauses – rather than the number of deep clauses – determined the time taken to plan a sentence. When people do not have to think so much about what they are going to say, their productions have different characteristics from when they are extemporizing.

Further evidence that the unit of planning can be larger than a single clause comes from Garrett's (1975) study of speech errors. Garrett found that many word exchanges occur across *clause* boundaries, suggesting that at some stage two clauses are being planned together.

The structure of the language production system

As with comprehension, some workers have suggested that in language production the subprocessors work serially and independently (e.g. Garrett, 1975, 1980; Shattuck-Hufnagel, 1979), while others have claimed that production is an interactive process (e.g. Butterworth, 1980b; Dell and Reich, 1980; Stemberger, 1985). In the best-worked-out serial model – Garrett's – there are a comparatively large number of subprocessors, and in particular there are two responsible for syntax. Interactive models centre around the familiar lexical, syntactic and message-level processors.

An interactive model of production is one in which the selection of particular words may affect the choice of syntax, and both may influence the message. This latter influence may at first seem counterintuitive, but it could reflect the common impression of not knowing exactly what one is going to say before putting it into words. As with comprehension, interactive models of production are, as a class, very powerful, in the sense that they can accommodate a wide range of data. Hence it is difficult to refute the claim that the production system is interactive. However, particular interactive models do make specific predictions. Simple serial models are less powerful, but they can be upgraded by allowing multiple outputs from the subprocessors. As in comprehension the effect is that later processors get a chance to choose between these outputs at their own level of analysis.

Garrett's serial model of production

The most important aspect of Garrett's model is the inclusion of two syntactic subprocessors, which Garrett calls functional and positional. At the earlier functional level the syntactic and semantic properties of the main lexical items are chosen, and the syntactic relations between them (their functions) are determined. At the positional level the syntactic structure of the sentence is chosen together with its intonational contour and inflectional morphemes (e.g. plural markers for nouns and verbs, past tense endings for verbs, function words). Garrett calls this representation, before the phonetic forms of the content words have been inserted, the *planning frame*. He uses speech error data of three kinds to argue for the independence of the two levels.

First, as noted above, content words tend to exchange across constituent boundaries, whereas sounds exchange within constituents. Furthermore, content words usually exchange with other words of the same syntactic category, whereas sounds exchange between categories. Garrett argues that these data are best explained by assuming that word exchanges arise at the functional level – words maintain their function, but are inserted into a representation of the wrong phrase or clause. Sound exchanges, by contrast, occur later in the production process. Garrett proposes that when phrases have been assembled for output they are held in a short-term store where segments may be altered or transposed. The limited size of this store explains why segmental errors occur only within phrases.

Second, when words exchange, they *strand* their inflectional endings and sentential stress, and *accommodate* to their new environment. For example:

It makes the AIR warmer to breathe

becomes:

It makes the WARM breather to air

(Garrett, 1980). Inflectional endings also accommodate. For example, if *eating marathon* becomes *meating arathon* a preceding indefinite article is changed from *an* to *a* (Fromkin, 1971). Garrett argues that inflections assume their phonetic shape late in production, after the phonological representations of the content words have been inserted into the planning frame, and that they take a form appropriate to what actually appears in the planning frame.

Third, Garrett assumes that items in the planning frame are always in the correct order. He therefore argues that exchanges between inflectional morphemes should never occur, though such morphemes may shift on to an adjacent word, if a lexical item is inserted in the wrong place in the planning frame. His corpus of errors supports these predictions.

Problems for Garrett's model

Some speech error data are incompatible with Garrett's theory in its original form. Dell and Reich (1981) show that Garrett's model makes predictions about the *relative frequencies* of certain types of error. Their data show three patterns that are incompatible with these predictions. First, sound exchanges produce words rather than non-words more often than would be expected, if such exchanges are not influenced by whether the outcome is a word. In Garrett's model they should not be, since they happen in an output buffer that has no access to lexical information. Second, words that blend tend to be phonologically related, though according to Garrett blends occur before phonological look up. Third, phonological and semantic influences on word substitution are not independent. On Garrett's account they should be, since semantic errors arise at the functional stage, and phonological errors are produced when words are inserted into the planning frame.

Dell and Reich propose a relatively minor modification to Garrett's model to account for these data. In their model it is not possible, as Garrett assumes, to access functional and phonological information about a word separately. Each subprocessor of the production system communicates with the mental lexicon, and when a word is accessed all the information about it becomes active. To a lesser degree, related words are also activated. If noise in the system or some outside influence causes the wrong word to have the highest activation level, then it will be wrongly selected. Similarly, choice of the sounds that make up a word may be influenced by the phonological representations of words related to it.

Dell and Reich's first observation – that speech errors commonly produce words rather than non-words – is similar to one made by Baars, Motley and MacKay (1975), who invented a technique for eliciting spoonerisms. Subjects were asked to pronounce pairs of words such as *barn door*. If this pair had been preceded by three pairs in which the first word began with /d/ and the second with /b/, then a high proportion of subjects produced the spoonerism *darn bore*. However, spoonerisms were less frequent if the exchange of the initial sounds did not produce words. For example, fewer subjects swapped the /d/ and /b/ in *dart board* since neither *bart* nor *doard* is a(n American) word. Baars *et al.*'s explanation of the fact that speech errors tend to produce words is different from Dell and Reich's. They propose that the *output* of the production system is *monitored*, and that non-words are often detected and corrected. More recently, Baars and Motley and their colleagues (see Baars, 1980, for a summary) have found evidence that other laboratory-induced slips of the tongue tend to produce sense rather than nonsense, and have argued that speech is monitored at many levels. Dell and Reich (1981) explain the same phenomena without positing an explicit monitor. In their model sense tends to be produced because of spreading activation and the exchange of information between processors. For example, words are favoured over non-words, because non-words do not have lexical entries that can be activated.

Stemberger (1985) reports data that are more difficult for Garrett's model to explain, such as exchanges between inflectional morphemes. Stemberger favours an interactive model of production based on McClelland and Rumelhart's (1981; Rumelhart and McClelland, 1982) interactive activation model of word recognition. However, it would be possible to account for his data in a serial model with different levels, or levels with different properties, from those of Garrett's. Even more than in comprehension, insufficient attention has been paid to the general properties of serial and interactive models.

The relation between production and comprehension

There are two main psycholinguistic questions about the relation between production and comprehension. First, which aspects of utterances reflect constraints on the production system and which are produced largely or solely for the benefit of listeners? Second, to what extent do production and comprehension share mechanisms and processes? Part of the answer to the first question is, of course, that speakers and writers should always try to speak and write comprehensibly. However, the directive to be comprehensible is a vague one, whose consequences are difficult to determine. A more specific question, to which some attention has been given, is: to what extent are pauses indicative of constraints on production, and to what extent do they simply aid comprehension?

The role of pausing

A disfluency gives little indication of the processes that gave rise to it. A pause, for example, may be made simply to breathe, or it may indicate planning of the next part of the utterance. Henderson, Goldman-Eisler and Skarbek (1965) noted that actors and orators tend to breathe at major constituent boundaries so as to facilitate understanding. In an experimental study, they found that the placement of breathing pauses was better in reading aloud than in spontaneous speech, indicating that, when the planning load is reduced, more attention can be directed to aiding comprehension.

Do comprehension and production share rule systems?

The most parsimonious theory about the relation between comprehension and production, which should be adopted until there is evidence against it, is one in which the two make use of the same knowledge base. For example, from a psycholinguistic point of view, grammatical rules are neutral between the generation and analysis of sentences. The same rules can be used both to assign syntactic structure in production, and to compute it in comprehension. Nevertheless, it has been argued that there are different lexicons for comprehension and production, and that there are different syntactic rules.

These arguments are most plausible in the case of child language. For example, the forms of a word that a child recognizes and produces are so different that some writers (e.g. Menn, 1983) consider that the postulation of two lexicons is justified. Similarly, adults' reading vocabularies are different from – usually much larger than – their speaking vocabularies. A simple explanation of this fact would be that adults have two mental lexicons. However, there are other explanations that do not require this unnecessary duplication of information. The most straightforward depends on the fact that a person can recognize many words and understand them in context, but cannot define or pronounce them. These words have entries in the mental lexicon, but their entries do not contain, or point to, a full specification of sound or meaning. Furthermore, these entries may be marked as incomplete – people often know that they are unsure about a word. In production, entries with incomplete meanings will not usually be accessed, and if they are, it will be impossible to decide whether they are suitable for conveying the message. If a word with an unknown sound is accessed by a speaker, it will pose a pronunciation problem, and may well be rejected.

Similarly, it is not necessary to postulate two lexicons or two sets of syntactic rules for speaking and writing. Although spoken and written language differ considerably, the discrepancies can be readily explained. For example, there are different memory constraints on speaking and writing and different social conventions governing what is suitable in each medium. Even in the case of child language the argument for two different lexicons is not compelling. The same phonological representation could be used by different sets of rules – those for perception and those for production – to produce different results, particularly given that the young child speaks with an imperfectly developed articulatory system.

As with words, people can understand syntactic constructions that they never use. However, this observation does not force the conclusion that grammars for perception and comprehension differ. Fay (1980) put forward a different argument in favour of this idea. He accepts that the Derivational Theory of Complexity is incorrect (see chapter 4) and that transformations are not used in comprehension. However, he argues that some speech errors suggest the use of transformations in production. For example, a speaker who intended to say:

I know where a top for it is.

actually said:

I know where is a top for it.

Fay explains this error as a misapplication of the transformation of subject–auxiliary inversion, proposed to explain the formation of questions. For example, the subject *a top for it*, and the auxiliary verb, *is*, in the affirmative sentence *a top for it is on the table* change places in questions such as *where is a top for it*? However, as Ford (1982) observes, any linguistic theory that gives a satisfactory account of subject–auxiliary inversion can offer an explanation of such speech errors. They are produced when an attempt is made to apply two syntactic rules at the same time – one for forming affirmative sentences and one for forming questions.

One lexicon for comprehension and production   Generally speaking the sub-processors of the language production system have not been studied in detail. The exception is the lexicon – a number of observations have been made about its organization and these bear on the relation between comprehension and production. Brown and McNeill (1966) experimentally induced the tip of the tongue state by reading definitions of rare words, such as *nepotism*, *cloaca* and *ambergris*. When in that state subjects were able to provide a surprising amount of information about the target word in an indirect way. For example, their incorrect guesses, which they usually knew to be incorrect, often had the same initial phoneme, same number of syllables and the same stress pattern as the target – typical responses to the definition of *sampan* were *Siam* and *Cheyenne*. These observations suggest that the production lexicon is organized according to the phonological properties of words.

Fay and Cutler (1977) drew the same conclusion from their study of speech errors in which a similar sounding word substitutes for the one intended, for example *burnt* for *burst* or *magician* for *musician*. They called such errors *malapropisms*, though they are not the errors of ignorance perpetrated by Sheridan's Mrs Malaprop. The substituted words resembled the intended words in the same way that Brown and McNeill's erroneous responses resembled the defined words. Fay and Cutler argue that malapropisms result from errors in retrieving words from the lexicon, which must therefore be arranged so that words of similar length, sound and stress pattern are close to each other. They point out that speech *production* does not demand such an organization of the lexicon, though word recognition does. They therefore argue that there is one lexicon for perception and production.

Finally, although language comprehension and language production probably use the same linguistic knowledge, it is unlikely that they share procedures for using that knowledge. The two systems use linguistic rules for different purposes, and hence require different kinds of processing.

Summary

Language production is harder to study systematically than comprehension because it is more difficult to control in the laboratory. However, an advantage of studying the production system is that its output is more tangible than that of the comprehension system.

Psycholinguists ask questions about the structure of the production system, about the operation of its subprocessors and about the relation between comprehension and production. The three main ways of studying production are by examining disfluencies, by carrying out controlled production experiments and by writing computer programs. Disfluencies include hesitations and pauses, speech errors and the major disruption of speech in aphasia. Speech errors have been most intensively studied, and by examining the kinds of error that occur, it is possible to draw conclusions about the structure of the language production system.

A theory of language production must explain how different kinds of knowledge – knowledge of the world, and rhetorical, pragmatic, semantic, syntactic, phonological and lexical knowledge of the language – work together to convert a mental representation of a situation in the world into a discourse that makes a point. Although models of production are not expected to predict what a particular person will say when, they must explain how utterances that are appropriate to the context can be chosen. A model of production must therefore include knowledge of conversational structure and goals.

The modelling of high-level skills required for language production has been carried out mainly in AI. In psycholinguistics, attention has focused on local planning of sentences and clauses, and on a particular serial model of language production – that of Garrett.

Experiments in which subjects produce single sentences to include given words have examined the question of what makes an idea difficult to express. Studies in which longer stretches of speech have been produced have shown that the 'deep structure clause', or the corresponding semantic unit, is the unit of planning in spontaneous speech on an unexpected topic. However, when less thought is required, people can plan further ahead and in larger units – surface clauses rather than underlying clauses.

Garrett argues for two separate syntactic stages in production – the functional and the positional – and uses speech error data to support his claim. However, some patterns of speech errors are incompatible with his model and it cannot be maintained in its original form. Nevertheless, the case for an interactive model is not well established. Even more than in comprehension, the properties of serial and interactive models have not been investigated in detail.

There are a number of plausible arguments to suggest that people have separate lexicons and separate sets of syntactic rules for comprehension and production. However, none of these arguments withstands close scrutiny. In the case of word-level processing there is strong evidence from the tip of the tongue phenomenon and from speech errors that there is a single lexicon for production and comprehension.

10

Overview and future directions

This book has presented the central topics of psycholinguistics from the perspectives of cognitive psychology and, more especially, the new discipline of cognitive science. It has discussed the basic mechanisms and processes that mediate language use in normal adults, and has emphasized that an account of them should be both *well specified* and *principled*. General principles that are vaguely stated are of little scientific value, but neither are specific ideas that have no general import. In particular, a computer program that simulates language use is not a psycholinguistic theory, though it may embody one. If the program is to run, every stage of its operation must be specified. But the fact that a program produces realistic output does not necessarily mean that it is based on important cognitive principles. However, programming does have a place in psycholinguistic research – two major advantages accrue from turning ideas into programs. First, a program can be used to investigate the role of a general principle in an overall model of language use. Second, the writing of a program may itself suggest new theoretical ideas – a point that is often not appreciated by non-programmers.

AI formalisms are useful in the development of well specified theories, but psycholinguists should be wary of adopting all aspects of the AI approach to language understanding. In particular, many practitioners of AI (e.g. Feigenbaum, 1977), though not all (see for example, Marr, 1982), draw a parallel between their discipline and engineering, and view AI as an applied science, which has the goal of producing complete working systems. By contrast, psycholinguists are primarily concerned with discovering principles that provide an understanding of how people use language – principles that can be applied in the same way as those of any other scientific theory.

As well as using the formalisms of AI, psycholinguists have borrowed ideas from linguists and logicians, who study language itself without reference to processing mechanisms. There has been much controversy about the relation between linguistics and psycholinguistics. However, as is often the case in such debates, the arguments have had little influence on the work of either linguists or psychologists, except that Chomsky's claims about the psychological reality of transformational grammar were part of the reason for importing it into psycholinguistic theory. Chomsky's contention that linguistic rules are in the mind is, in any case, difficult to interpret. People may assign the same syntactic structures to sentences and texts as a grammar does, even if the language processor does not directly incorporate that grammar. What is true, however, is that in so far as linguistic theory is correct, grammars specify the functions (in the mathematical sense) that *should* be computed in the understanding of sentences and text. Psycholinguistic theory must therefore describe the procedures that are used to compute those functions in comprehension and production and, in conjunction with theories of other cognitive processes, it should also explain why people make mistakes – why they misunderstand or say the wrong thing.

The importance of linguistic theory in psychological accounts of language understanding is not universally accepted. A number of AI language understanding programs (e.g. those of Schank and his colleagues), and some psychological theories of text comprehension (e.g. those of Kintsch and his colleagues) ignore standard linguistic treatments of either syntax or semantics or both. Their proponents claim, either implicitly or explicitly, that linguistic grammars are irrelevant to the way people understand language. Such programs and theories appear to offer simpler accounts of language processing than those that produce linguistically motivated analyses, but they do so by restricting themselves to a limited set of sentence types, with no indication of how they can be generalized to the cases that complicate syntax and semantics. However, psycholinguistic theory must explain how people understand a wide range of constructions. Although 'tricks' may be used to analyse simple sentences, the claim that linguistic work on syntax and semantics is irrelevant to psychology is, to say the least, premature.

In attempting to understand a complex system, such as the language processor, it is customary to divide the overall problem into subproblems. In the case of the language processor a number of subprocessors have been identified – the word recognition system, the parser, and the processors that compute various aspects of the meaning of text – and have been studied separately. There are some general constraints on the sequence of operation of these processors. For example, in comprehension the *lowest-level* processor, the word recognizer, must begin its work before the higher-level ones have anything to analyse, whereas in production an outline of the message to be conveyed must be decided, before suitable syntax and vocabulary can be chosen. However, it is not necessary to assume that the processors work in strict serial order, nor that the output from an early process is independent of what happens later. As chapter 8 discussed, the question of whether such interaction occurs is still an open one.

Since the focus of this book has been comprehension rather than production, this overview will describe the subprocessors of the language understanding system in the order in which they receive information in comprehension. The first major task of the understanding system is to recognize the words presented to it. Once a word has been identified, information about it can be retrieved from the mental lexicon – the mental equivalent of a dictionary – and made available to the higher-level processors. There are two main proposals about the way the lexicon is accessed. One is that perceptual and contextual information is passed directly to a set of word detectors (logogens). The other is that the information is used in an ordered search through the lexicon, or some part of it. Recent models of word recognition combine the two proposals. For example, in Becker's verification model a list of candidate words is generated by direct access, and then searched for an exact match to the input. In such models the processes of lexical access and word recognition are separate. Candidate lists are generated from the lexicon, implying that at least some information has been accessed from it before the word has been uniquely identified.

There has been rapid progress in the study of word recognition in the last twenty years, and a number of recalcitrant phenomena are now succumbing to theoretical analysis. Context effects, especially inhibitory effects of inappropriate context, have proved particularly difficulty to explain. The most popular approach is to propose an additional attentional mechanism to account for them. Apart from the effects of context, and of frequency and stimulus quality, models of word recognition must also be able to describe how the correct meaning of an ambiguous word is selected, and to explain why the sound of a word may influence recognition of its written form. A step towards a more unified theory of word recognition is Norris's checking model, in which the mechanism that resolves ambiguities also explains the effects of context, both facilitatory and inhibitory, without appeal to attentional factors.

Word recognition is followed by syntactic analysis – the grouping of words into structural units. The apparent success of AI programs that do not use a full set of syntactic rules suggests that people, too, may *sometimes* be able to interpret text without completing a parse. For example, they may be able to use case frames and selectional restrictions in the way described in chapter 4. However, sentences with no such constraints on their interpretation are not usually misunderstood. In these instances structural information must be used, though not necessarily to generate complete phrase markers. It may be required only locally in the course of constructing a semantic representation or a mental model. Nevertheless, in the absence of semantic cues, all of the syntactic relations between words and phrases in a sentence have to be computed, if it is to be correctly understood.

Interest in parsing has only recently revived in psycholinguistics. A number of models of the human sentence parsing mechanism have been proposed, and subjected to empirical test. The proposals have all emphasized the computation of syntactic surface structure. This emphasis is appropriate, since an increasing number of linguists believe that surface structure is the only level of syntactic representation. There is every indication that parsing will become a more popular research topic in psycholinguistics over the next few years, as methods of deciding among the competing theories are developed, and some of the current issues of debate are resolved.

The computation of syntactic relations is not the normal *goal* of language understanding. Rather, this computation is a step towards semantic interpretation, since the meaning of a sentence depends both on the meanings of the words in it, and on the way in which those words are grouped together. Information about word meanings is stored in semantic memory, and becomes available when words are accessed from the lexicon. Since the mid-1970s there has been little psycholinguistic research on the question of how word meanings are mentally represented. At that time the importance of the distinction between typical and atypical exemplars of a concept had been accepted, and both feature and network models had been modified to take account of it. It had also become apparent that the debate between proponents of feature models and network models could not be resolved without making unmotivated assumptions about the processes that operate on word meanings. At present the only approach to word meaning that is active is procedural semantics. Its most important claim is that the components of a word's meaning need not correspond to other words, but may be procedures that manipulate mental models.

A major obstacle to the production of an adequate theory of semantic memory is the still underestimated diversity of the kinds of meaning that words can have (Wittgenstein, 1953; Armstrong, Gleitman and Gleitman, 1983). Although semantic networks and procedural semantics are equivalent to Universal Turing Machines and therefore in principle capable of expressing any computable function, and hence any plausible candidate for a word's meaning, they have not been used in a sufficiently flexible manner. Before further progress is made in the psycholinguistic study of word meanings, some new ideas are needed about the forms that they can take.

Psycholinguists have tended to ignore the purely semantic aspects of sentence meaning – those that determine what situations a sentence could be used to describe. However, a promising development is the recognition of the relevance to theories of sentence comprehension of formal semantics, which provides a detailed account of how the meanings of complex expressions are built up from those of their parts. Formal semantics could provide the basis of a psycholinguistic theory of how semantic representations are computed. Another welcome development is the application of formal semantics, by linguists and formal logicians, to units larger than single sentences. Sentences are not understood in isolation, and psycholinguists must be sensitive to the way that the structure of a text contributes to its meaning, if they are to explain how people understand and produce texts.

The initial impact of formal semantic theories is likely to be on computer modelling. They will suggest general algorithms that compute the meanings of sentences – algorithms that need not ignore large classes of sentences. As psycholinguistics become more familiar with formal semantics, they should produce ideas about how people construct semantic representations of discourse, which can be tested experimentally.

Semantic interpretation, in the restricted sense of that term, does not result in a full understanding of a conversation or text. What Johnson-Laird (1977b) calls its *significance* depends on pragmatic factors, and on knowledge about the world. Given the literal meaning of a discourse or text – its truth conditions if it is a description – pragmatic theory specifies what additional information it is intended to convey (its implicatures), what it takes for granted (its presuppositions) and whether it is intended as, say, a description, a set of instructions or a series of questions (its illocutionary force). Knowledge about the world is used chiefly to provide connections that are not explicit in the text between the events that it describes, and hence to allow the construction of a coherent model of the situation that it is *most probably* about. World knowledge can also be used to elaborate the information in a text in other ways, but such elaboration is usually only carried out for a specific purpose, for example, to answer a question.

Recent work in AI has shown how difficult it is, in general, to determine the intended meaning of an utterance from its literal meaning. Large amounts of knowledge about the world, and in particular about people's goals, wants and beliefs, must often be mobilized for this task. Psychological research on pragmatic interpretation has been restricted to investigating how the literal meaning of indirect requests affects the way they are understood. The refinement of programs that understand pragmatic meaning, and a more thorough acquaintance with recent attempts to formalize Grice's ideas, should suggest a wider range of hypotheses for experimental test.

In both AI and psychology there have been intensive investigations of the use of knowledge about the world in comprehension. In psychology it has been shown that inferences needed to produce a coherent interpretation of a text are made as the text is read, and a way of reconciling the conflicting findings on when elaborative inferences are drawn has recently been suggested (Garnham, 1982). From AI have come many accounts of how knowledge is stored in long-term memory and accessed for text comprehension. Some general principles that unify these ideas are urgently required.

The interpretation of a discourse or text is achieved by co-operation between the subprocessors of the language understanding system. As has been stressed, they may not operate in a strictly serial order – the question of how they are organized is an empirical one. It is possible to write computer programs that work either serially or interactively, and it has been claimed (for example, by Winograd, 1973) that interactive (or *heterarchical*) models are more efficient. Two points should be borne in mind when assessing this claim. First, what is efficient for the subset of a language that a particular program understands may not be efficient for the language as a whole. Second, the human language processor is subject to different constraints from an AI program. What is efficient for a program may not be efficient for a person, though some general lessons about which algorithms can feasibly be used to compute a function may be learned from both programming itself, and from the theory of computation. In the next few years it is unlikely that computer modelling will lead to advances in our understanding of how the subprocessors of the human language understanding system interact with one another. Progress will depend on careful consideration of relevant experimental evidence. However, one important lesson must be drawn from recent experience of addressing this problem. A prerequisite for any advance is a clear account of what is meant by interaction, or the lack of it, between processors.

In the past there has been less work on language production than on comprehension. At present there is a growing interest in production. In particular, the study of speech errors and other disfluencies has led to the formulation of detailed models of production. This work is likely to continue over the next few years, and to result in clarification of the processes of language production and their relation to comprehension.

Although this book has focused on the central processes of language understanding in normal adults, there are many other aspects of language use that have in the past been studied under the heading of 'psycholinguistics', and that will continue to receive attention. However, such topics as language development, speech perception, language pathology and the relation between language and thought are likely, in the future, to be studied by specialists with different interests from those who pursue the topics covered in this book. Word recognition, parsing and the computation of meaning will be the central interests of research on natural language processing in cognitive psychology, and more especially in the emerging discipline of cognitive science. Psychologists, AI workers, linguists and logicians studying language have more interests in common than do psychologists from different branches of the discipline. Future research on these topics will therefore tend to be pursued under the heading of cognitive science, and the cross-fertilization that has already taken place between its subdisciplines suggests that the coming decade will be a time of great progress in our understanding of language understanding.

References

Anderson, A., Garrod, S.C. and Sanford, A.J. (1983) The accessibility of pronominal antecedents as a function of episode shifts in narrative text. *Quarterly Journal of Experimental Psychology 35A*, 427–40.

Anderson, J.R. (1976) *Language, Memory, and Thought*. Hillsdale, NJ: Lawrence Erlbaum.

Anderson, J.R. and Bower, G.H. (1973) *Human Associative Memory*. Washington, DC: Winston.

Anderson, J.R. and Hastie, R. (1974) Individuation and reference in memory: Proper names and definite descriptions. *Cognitive Psychology 6*, 495–514.

Anderson, R.C. and Ortony, A. (1975) On putting apples into bottles: A problem of polysemy. *Cognitive Psychology 7*, 167–80.

Anderson, R.C. and Pichert, J.W. (1978) Recall of previously unrecallable information following a shift in perspective. *Journal of Verbal Learning and Verbal Behavior 17*, 1–12.

Anderson, R.C., Pichert, J.W., Goetz, E.T, Schallert, D.L., Stevens, K.V. and Trollip, S.R. (1976) Instantiation of general terms. *Journal of Verbal Learning and Verbal Behavior 15*, 667–79.

Antos, S.J. (1979) Processing facilitation in a lexical decision task. *Journal of Experimental Psychology: Human Perception and Performance 5*, 527–45.

Armstrong, S., Gleitman, L. and Gleitman, H. (1983) What some concepts might not be. *Cognition 13*, 263–308.

Austin, J.L. (1962) *How to Do Things with Words*. Oxford: Oxford University Press. (Edited by J.O. Urmson.)

Baars, B.J. (1980) On eliciting predictable speech errors in the laboratory. In V.A. Fromkin (ed.) *Errors in Linguistic Performance: Slips of the Tongue, Ear, Pen and Hand*. New York: Academic Press.

Baars, B.J., Motley, M.T. and MacKay, D.G. (1975) Output editing for lexical status in artificially elicited slips of the tongue. *Journal of Verbal Learning and Verbal Behavior 14*, 382–91.

Bahrick, H.P. (1970) Two-phase model for prompted recall. *Psychological Review* 77, 215 – 22.

Barclay, J.R. (1973) The role of comprehension in remembering sentences. *Cognitive Psychology* 5, 229 – 54.

Barclay, J.R., Bransford, J.D., Franks, J.J., McCarrell, N.C. and Nitsch, K. (1974) Comprehension and semantic flexibility. *Journal of Verbal Learning and Verbal Behavior 13*, 471 – 81.

Bar-Hillel, Y. (1967) Dictionaries and meaning rules. *Foundations of Language 3*, 409 – 14.

Baron, J. (1973) Phonemic stage not necessary for reading. *Quarterly Journal of Experimental Psychology 25*, 241 – 6.

Bartlett, F.C. (1932) *Remembering: A Study in Experimental and Social Psychology.* Cambridge: Cambridge University Press.

Barwise, J. and Perry, J. (1984) *Situations and Attitudes.* Cambridge, MA: MIT Press.

Bates, E, Kintsch, W., Fletcher, C. and Giuliani, V. (1980) On the role of pronominalization and ellipsis in texts: Some memory experiments. *Journal of Experimental Psychology: Human Learning and Memory 6*, 676 – 91.

Bates, E., Masling, M. and Kintsch, W. (1978) Recognition memory for aspects of dialogue. *Journal of Experimental Psychology: Human Learning and Memory 4*, 187 – 97.

Becker, C.A. (1976) Allocation of attention during visual word recognition. *Journal of Experimental Psychology: Human Perception and Performance 2*, 556 – 66.

Becker, C.A. and Killion, T.H. (1977) Interaction of visual and cognitive effects in word recognition. *Journal of Experimental Psychology: Human Perception and Performance 3*, 389 – 407.

Bever, T.G. (1970) The cognitive basis for linguistic structures. In J.R. Hayes (ed.) *Cognition and the Development of Language.* New York: Wiley.

Bever, T.G., Garrett, M.F. and Hurtig, R. (1973) The interaction of perceptual processes and ambiguous sentences. *Memory and Cognition 1*, 277 – 86.

Bever, T.G., Lackner, J.R. and Kirk, R. (1969) The underlying structures of sentences are the primary units of immediate speech processing. *Perception and Psychophysics 5*, 225 – 31.

Black, J.B. and Bower, G.H. (1980) Story understanding as problem solving. *Poetics 9*, 223 – 50.

Black, J.B. and Wilensky, R. (1979) An evaluation of story grammars. *Cognitive Science 3*, 213 – 30.

Bloomfield, L. (1933) *Language.* New York: Holt, Rinehart, & Winston.

Boomer, D.S. (1965) Hesitation and grammatical encoding. *Language and Speech 8*, 148–58.

Brachman, R.J. (1979) On the epistemological status of semantic nets. In N.V. Findler (ed.) *Associative Networks: Representation and Use of Knowledge by Computers*. New York: Academic Press.

Brame, M.K. (1978) *Base-Generated Syntax*. Seattle, WA: Noit Amrofer.

Bransford, J.D., Barclay, J.R. and Franks, J.J. (1972) Sentence memory: A constructive versus interpretive approach. *Cognitive Psychology 3*, 193–209.

Bransford, J.D. and Franks. J.J. (1971) The abstraction of linguistic ideas. *Cognitive Psychology 3*, 331–50.

Bransford, J.D. and Johnson, M.K. (1972) Contextual prerequisites for understanding: Some investigations of comprehension and recall. *Journal of Verbal Learning and Verbal Behavior 11*, 717–26.

Bransford, J.D. and McCarrell, N.C. (1975) A sketch of a cognitive approach to comprehension. In W.B. Weimar and D.S. Palermo (eds) *Cognition and the Symbolic Processes*. Hillsdale, NJ: Lawrence Erlbaum.

Bresnan, J.W. (1978) A realistic transformational grammar. In M. Halle, J.W. Bresnan and G.A. Miller (eds) *Linguistic Theory and Psychological Reality*. Cambridge, MA: MIT Press.

Brown, R. and McNeill, D. (1966) The 'tip of the tongue' phenomenon. *Journal of Verbal Learning and Verbal Behavior 5*, 325–37.

Bruce, B.C. (1982) Natural communication between a person and a computer. In W.G. Lehnert and M.H. Ringle (eds) *Strategies for Natural Language Processing*. Hillsdale, NJ: Lawrence Erlbaum.

Bruce, B.C. and Newman, D. (1978) Interacting plans. *Cognitive Science 2*, 195–233.

Butterworth, B.L. (1980a) Introduction: A brief review of methods of studying language production. In B.L. Butterworth (ed.) *Language Production, vol. 1: Speech and Talk*. London: Academic Press.

Butterworth, B.L. (1980b) Some constraints on models of language production. In B.L. Butterworth (ed.) *Language Production, vol. 1: Speech and Talk*. London: Academic Press.

Cairns, H.S. and Kamerman, J. (1975) Lexical information processing during sentence comprehension. *Journal of Verbal Learning and Verbal Behavior 14*, 170–9.

Caplan, D. (1972) Clause boundaries and recognition latencies for words in sentences. *Perception and Psychophysics 12*, 73–6.

Caramazza, A., Grober, E.H., Garvey, C. and Yates, J. (1977) Comprehension of anaphoric pronouns. *Journal of Verbal Learning and Verbal Behavior 16*, 601–9.

Carnap, R. (1952) Meaning postulates. *Philosophical Studies 3*, 65–73.

Charniak, E. (1977) A framed PAINTING: The representation of a common sense knowledge fragment. *Cognitive Science 1*, 355–94.

Chomsky, N. (1956) Three models for the description of language. *IRE Transactions on Information Theory IT-2*, 113–24. Reprinted in R.D. Luce, R.R. Bush and E. Galanter (1965, eds) *Readings in Mathematical Psychology, vol. II*. New York: Wiley.

Chomsky, N. (1957) *Syntactic Structures*. The Hague: Mouton.

Chomsky, N. (1959) A review of B.F. Skinner's 'Verbal Behavior'. *Language 35*, 26–58.

Chomsky, N. (1964) *Current Issues in Linguistic Theory*. The Hague: Mouton.

Chomsky, N. (1965) *Aspects of the Theory of Syntax*. Cambridge, MA: MIT Press.

Chomsky, N. (1972) *Language and Mind* (enlarged edn). New York: Harcourt Brace Jovanovich.

Chomsky, N. (1981) *Lectures on Government and Binding*. Dordrecht: Foris.

Cirilo, R.K. and Foss, D.J. (1980) Text structure and reading time for sentences. *Journal of Verbal Learning and Verbal Behavior 19*, 96–109.

Clark, H.H. (1973) The language-as-fixed-effect fallacy: A critique of language statistics in psychological research. *Journal of Verbal Learning and Verbal Behavior 12*, 335–59.

Clark, H.H. (1974) Semantics and comprehension. In T.A. Sebeok (ed.) *Current Trends in Linguistics, vol. 12: Linguistics and Adjacent Arts and Sciences*. Mouton: The Hague.

Clark, H.H. (1977) Bridging. In P.N. Johnson-Laird and P.C. Wason (eds) *Thinking: Readings in Cognitive Science*. Cambridge: Cambridge University Press.

Clark, H.H. (1979) Responding to indirect speech acts. *Cognitive Psychology 11*, 430–77.

Clark, H.H. and Clark, E.V. (1977) *Psychology and Language: An Introduction to Psycholinguistics*. New York: Harcourt Brace Jovanovich.

Clark, H.H. and Haviland, S.E. (1974) Psychological processes as linguistic explanation. In D. Cohen (ed.) *Explaining Linguistic Phenomena*. Washington, DC: Hemisphere Publishing.

Clark, H.H. and Lucy, P. (1975) Understanding what is meant from what is said: A study in conversationally conveyed requests. *Journal of Verbal Learning and Verbal Behavior 14*, 56–72.

Clark, H.H. and Schunk, D.H. (1980) Polite responses to polite requests. *Cognition 8*, 111–43.

Clark, H.H. and Sengul, C.J. (1979) In search of referents for noun phrases and pronouns. *Memory and Cognition* 7, 35 – 41.

Clifton, C., Kurtz, I. and Jenkins, J.J. (1965) Grammatical relations as determinants of sentence similarity. *Journal of Verbal Learning and Verbal Behavior 4*, 112 – 7.

Cohen, P.R., Allen, J.F. and Perrault, C.R. (1982) Beyond question answering. In W.G. Lehnert and M.H. Ringle (eds) *Strategies for Natural Language Processing.* Hillsdale, NJ: Lawrence Erlbaum.

Cohen, P.R. and Perrault, C.R. (1979) Elements of a plan-based theory of speech acts. *Cognitive Science 3*, 177 – 212.

Collins, A.M. and Loftus, E.F. (1975) A spreading-activation theory of semantic processing. *Psychological Review 82*, 407 – 28.

Collins, A.M. and Quillian, M.R. (1969) Retrieval time from semantic memory. *Journal of Verbal Learning and Verbal Behavior 8*, 240 – 7.

Collins, A.M. and Quillian, M.R. (1972) Experiments on semantic memory and language comprehension. In L.W. Gregg (ed.) *Cognition in Learning and Memory.* New York: Wiley.

Coltheart, M. (1978) Lexical access in simple reading tasks. In G. Underwood (ed.) *Strategies of Information Processing.* London: Academic Press.

Coltheart, M., Davelaar, C., Jonasson, J.T. and Besner, D. (1977) Access to the internal lexicon. In S. Dornic (ed.) *Attention and Performance VI.* New York: Academic Press.

Coltheart, M., Patterson, K. and Marshall, J.C. (1980, eds) *Deep Dyslexia.* London: Routledge & Kegan Paul.

Conrad, C. (1972) Cognitive economy in semantic memory. *Journal of Experimental Psychology 92*, 149 – 54.

Corbett, A.T. and Dosher, B.A. (1978) Instrument inferences in sentence encoding. *Journal of Verbal Learning and Verbal Behavior 17*, 479 – 91.

Crain, S. and Steedman, M.J. (1985) On not being led up the garden path: The use of context by the psychological parser. In D. Dowty, L. Karttunen and A. Zwicky (eds) *Natural Language Parsing.* Cambridge: Cambridge University Press.

Crowder, R.G. (1982) *The Psychology of Reading.* New York: Oxford University Press.

Cutler, A. (1981) The reliability of speech error data. *Linguistics 19*, 561 – 82.

Cutler, A. (1982, ed.) *Slips of the Tongue and Language Production.* Amsterdam: Mouton.

Cutler, A. and Norris, D.G. (1979) Monitoring sentence comprehension. In W.E. Cooper and E.C.T. Walker (eds) *Sentence Processing: Psycholinguistic Studies Presented to Merrill Garrett.* Hillsdale, NJ: Lawrence Erlbaum.

Davey, A.C. and Longuet-Higgins, H.C. (1978) A computational model of discourse production. In R.N. Campbell and P.T. Smith (eds) *Advances in the Psychology of Language: Formal and Experimental Approaches.* New York: Plenum.

Davies, D.J.M. and Isard, S.D. (1972) Utterances as programs. In D. Michie (ed.) *Machine Intelligence 7.* Edinburgh: Edinburgh University Press.

Dechert, H.W. and Raupach, M. (1980, eds) *Temporal Variables in Speech.* The Hague: Mouton.

Dell, G.S. and Reich, P.A. (1980) Toward a unified model of slips of the tongue. In V.A. Fromkin (ed.) *Errors in Linguistic Performance: Slips of the Tongue, Ear, Pen and Hand.* New York: Academic Press.

Dell, G.S. and Reich, P.A. (1981) Stages in sentence production: An analysis of speech error data. *Journal of Verbal Learning and Verbal Behavior 20*, 611 – 29.

van Dijk, T.A. and Kintsch, W. (1983) *Strategies of Discourse Comprehension.* New York: Academic Press.

Dooling, D.J. and Christiaansen, R.E. (1977) Levels of encoding and retention of prose. In G.H. Bower (ed.) *The Psychology of Learning and Motivation 11.* New York: Academic Press.

Dooling, D.J. and Lachman, R. (1972) Effects of comprehension on retention of prose. *Journal of Experimental Psychology 88*, 216 – 22.

Dooling, D.J. and Mullet, R.L. (1973) Locus of thematic effects in retention of prose. *Journal of Experimental Psychology 97*, 404 – 6.

Dowty, D.R., Peters, P.S. and Wall, R. (1981) *An Introduction To Montague Semantics.* Dordrecht: Reidel.

Dreyfus, H.L. (1979) *What Computers Can't Do: The Limits of Artificial Intelligence* (revised edn). New York: Harper & Row.

Dyer, M.G. (1983) *In-Depth Understanding: A Computer Model of Integrated Processing for Narrative Comprehension.* Cambridge, MA: MIT Press.

Ehrlich, K. and Johnson-Laird, P.N. (1982) Spatial descriptions and referential continuity. *Journal of Verbal Learning and Verbal Behavior 21*, 296 – 306.

Epstein, W. (1961) The influence of syntactical structure on learning. *American Journal of Psychology 74*, 80 – 5.

Fahlman, S.E. (1979) *NETL: A System for Representing and Using Real-World Knowledge.* Cambridge, MA: MIT Press.

Fay, D. (1980) Performing transformations. In R. Cole (ed.) *Perception and Production of Fluent Speech.* Hillsdale, NJ: Lawrence Erlbaum.

Fay, D. and Cutler, A. (1977) Malapropisms and the structure of the mental lexicon. *Linguistic Inquiry 8*, 505 – 20.

Feigenbaum, E.A. (1977) The art of artificial intelligence, I: Theories and case studies of knowledge engineering. *Proceedings of the 5th International Joint Conference on Artificial Intelligence.* Cambridge, MA, August 1977.

Fillmore, C.J. (1968) The case for case. In E. Bach and R.T. Harms (eds) *Universals in Linguistic Theory.* New York: Holt, Rinehart & Winston.

Fillmore, C.J. (1971) Types of lexical information. In D.D. Steinberg and L.A. Jakobovits (eds) *Semantics: An Interdisciplinary Reader in Philosophy, Linguistics and Psychology.* Cambridge: Cambridge University Press.

Fillmore, C.J. (1975) An alternative to checklist theories of meaning. *Proceedings of the Berkeley Linguistics Society 1,* 123 – 31.

Fischler, I. and Bloom, P.A. (1979) Automatic and attentional processes in the effects of sentence contexts on word recognition. *Journal of Verbal Learning and Verbal Behavior 18,* 1 – 20.

Flagg, P.W. and Reynolds, A.G. (1977) Modality of presentation and blocking in sentence recognition memory. *Memory and Cognition 5,* 111 – 15.

Fodor, J.A. (1976) *The Language of Thought.* Hassocks, Sussex: Harvester.

Fodor, J.A. and Bever, T.G. (1965) The psychological reality of linguistic segments. *Journal of Verbal Learning and Verbal Behavior 4,* 414 – 20.

Fodor, J.A, Bever, T.G. and Garrett, M.F. (1974) *The Psychology of Language: An Introduction to Psycholinguistics and Generative Grammar.* New York: McGraw-Hill.

Fodor, J.A. and Garrett, M.F. (1966) Some reflections on competence and performance. In J. Lyons and R.J. Wales (eds) *Psycholinguistic Papers.* Edinburgh: Edinburgh University Press.

Fodor, J.A. and Garrett, M.F. (1967) Some syntactic determinants of sentential complexity. *Perception and Psychophysics 2,* 289 – 96.

Fodor, J.A., Garrett, M.F. and Bever, T.G. (1968) Some syntactic determinants of sentential complexity, II: Verb structure. *Perception and Psychophysics 3,* 453 – 61.

Fodor, J.D., Fodor, J.A. and Garrett, M.F. (1975) The psychological unreality of semantic representations. *Linguistic Inquiry 6,* 515 – 31.

Fodor, J.D. and Frazier, L. (1980) Is the human sentence parsing mechanism an ATN. *Cognition 8,* 417 – 59.

Ford, M. (1982) Sentence planning units: Implications for the speaker's representation of meaningful relations underlying sentences. In J.W. Bresnan (ed.) *The Mental Representation of Grammatical Relations.* Cambridge, MA: MIT Press.

Ford, M. and Holmes, V.M. (1978) Planning units and syntax in sentence production. *Cognition 6,* 35 – 53.

Forster, K.I. (1976) Accessing the mental lexicon. In R.J. Wales and E.C.T. Walker (eds) *New Approaches to Language Mechanisms.* Amsterdam: North Holland.

Forster, K.I. (1979) Levels of processing and the structure of the language processor. In W.E. Cooper and E.C.T. Walker (eds) *Sentence Processing: Psycholinguistic Studies Presented to Merrill Garrett*. Hillsdale, NJ: Lawrence Erlbaum.

Forster, K.I. and Chambers, S.M. (1973) Lexical access and naming time. *Journal of Verbal Learning and Verbal Behavior 12*, 627–35.

Forster, K.I. and Olbrei, I. (1973) Semantic heuristics and syntactic analysis. *Cognition 2*, 319–47.

Foss, D.J. (1970) Some effects of ambiguity upon sentence comprehension. *Journal of Verbal Learning and Verbal Behavior 9*, 699–706.

Foss, D.J. (1982) A discourse on semantic priming. *Cognitive Psychology 14*, 590–607.

Foss, D.J. and Blank, M.A. (1980) Identifying the speech code. *Cognitive Psychology 12*, 1–31.

Foss, D.J. and Gernsbacher, M.A. (1983) Cracking the dual code: Toward a unitary model of phoneme identification. *Journal of Verbal Learning and Verbal Behavior 22*, 609–32.

Foss, D.J. and Hakes, D.T. (1978) *Psycholinguistics: An Introduction to the Psychology of Language*. Englewood Cliffs, NJ: Prentice-Hall.

Foss, D.J. and Jenkins, C.J. (1973) Some effects of context on the comprehension of ambiguous sentences. *Journal of Verbal Learning and Verbal Behavior 12*, 577–89.

Foss, D.J. and Swinney, D.A. (1973) On the psychological reality of the phoneme: Perception, identification and consciousness. *Journal of Verbal Learning and Verbal Behavior 12*, 246–57.

Frazier, L. and Fodor, J.D. (1978) The sausage machine: A new two-stage parsing model. *Cognition 6*, 291–325.

Frege, G. (1879/1972) Conceptual notation: A formula language of pure thought modelled upon the formula language of arithmetic. In T.W. Bynum (ed. and trans.) *Conceptual Language and Related Articles*. Oxford: Oxford University Press. (First published in German in 1879, Halle: L. Nerbert.)

Freud, S. (1901/1960) *The Psychopathology of Everyday Life* (A. Tyson, trans.) In *The Standard Edition of the Complete Psychological Works of Sigmund Freud, vol. VI*. London: Hogarth.

Fromkin, V.A. (1971) The non-anomalous nature of anomalous utterances. *Language 47*, 27–52.

Fromkin, V.A. (1973) *Speech Errors as Linguistic Evidence*. The Hague: Mouton.

Fromkin, V.A. (1980) *Errors in Linguistic Performance: Slips of the Tongue, Ear, Pen and Hand*. New York: Academic Press.

Garnham, A. (1979) Instantiation of verbs. *Quarterly Journal of Experimental*

Psychology 31, 207–14.

Garnham, A. (1981a) Mental models as representations of discourse and text. Unpublished D. Phil. thesis, University of Sussex.

Garnham, A. (1981b) Anaphoric reference to instances, instantiated and non-instantiated categories: A reading-time study. *British Journal of Psychology* 72, 377–84.

Garnham, A. (1982) Testing psychological theories about inference making. *Memory and Cognition 10*, 341–9.

Garnham, A. (1983a) Why psycholinguists don't care about DTC: A reply to Berwick and Weinberg. *Cognition 15*, 263–9.

Garnham, A. (1983b) What's wrong with story grammars. *Cognition 15*, 145–54.

Garnham, A. (1984) Effects of specificity on the interpretation of anaphoric noun phrases. *Quarterly Journal of Experimental Psychology 36A*, 1–12.

Garnham, A., Oakhill, J.V. and Johnson-Laird, P.N. (1982) Referential continuity and the coherence of discourse. *Cognition 11*, 29–46.

Garnham, A., Shillcock, R.C., Brown, G.D.A., Mill, A. and Cutler, A. (1981) Slips of the tongue in the London-Lund corpus of spontaneous conversation. *Linguistics 19*, 805–17.

Garrett, M.F. (1970) Does ambiguity complicate the perception of sentences? In G.B. Flores d'Arcais and W.J.M. Levelt (eds) *Advances in Psycholinguistics*. Amsterdam: North-Holland.

Garrett, M.F. (1975) The analysis of sentence production. In G.H. Bower (ed.) *The Psychology of Learning and Motivation 9*. New York: Academic Press.

Garrett, M.F. (1980) Levels of processing in sentence production. In B.L. Butterworth (ed.) *Language Production, vol. 1:Speech and Talk*. London: Academic Press.

Garrett, M.F., Bever, T.G. and Fodor, J.A. (1966) The active use of grammar in sentence perception. *Perception and Psychophysics 1*, 30–2.

Garrod, S.C. and Sanford, A.J. (1977) Interpreting anaphoric relations: The integration of semantic information while reading. *Journal of Verbal Learning and Verbal Behavior 16*, 77–90.

Garrod, S.C. and Sanford, A.J. (1981) Bridging inferences and the extended domain of reference. In J. Long and A. Baddeley (eds) *Attention and Performance IX*. Hillsdale, NJ: Lawrence Erlbaum.

Gazdar, G.J.M. (1979) *Pragmatics: Implicature, Presupposition, and Logical Form*. New York: Academic Press.

Gazdar, G.J.M. (1980) Pragmatic constraints on linguistic production. In B.L. Butterworth (ed.) *Language Production, vol. 1:Speech and Talk*. London: Academic Press.

Gazdar, G.J.M. (1981) Unbounded dependencies and coordinate structure. *Linguistic Inquiry 12*, 155 – 84.

Gazdar, G.J.M. (1982) Phrase structure grammar. In G.K. Pullum and P. Jacobson (eds) *The Nature of Syntactic Representation.* Dordrecht: Reidel.

Geschwind, N. (1972) Language and the brain. *Scientific American 226(4)*, 76 – 83.

Gibbs, R.W. (1979) Contextual effects in understanding indirect requests. *Discourse Processes 2*, 1 – 10.

Gibbs, R.W. (1983) Do people always process the literal meaning of indirect requests? *Journal of Experimental Psychology: Learning, Memory, and Cognition 9*, 524 – 33.

Glass, A.L. and Holyoak, K.J. (1975) Alternative conceptions of semantic memory. *Cognition 3*, 313 – 39.

Glushko, R. (1979) The organization and activation of orthographic knowledge in reading aloud. *Journal of Experimental Psychology: Human Perception and Performance 5*, 674 – 91.

Goetz, E.T., Anderson, R.C. and Schallert, D.L. (1981) The representation of sentences in memory. *Journal of Verbal Learning and Verbal Behavior 20*, 369 – 81.

Goldiamond, I. and Hawkins, W.F. (1958) Vexierversuch: The logical relationship between word-frequency and recognition obtained in the absence of stimulus words. *Journal of Experimental Psychology 56*, 457 – 63.

Goldman-Eisler, F. (1968) *Psycholinguistics: Experiments in Spontaneous Speech.* London: Academic Press.

Goldman-Eisler, F. (1972) Pauses, clauses, sentences. *Language and Speech 15*, 103 – 13.

Gough, P.B. (1966) The verification of sentences: The effects of delay of evidence and sentence length. *Journal of Verbal Learning and Verbal Behavior 5*, 492 – 6.

Gough, P.B. and Cosky, M.J. (1977) One second of reading again. In N.J. Pistellan, D.B. Pisoni and G.R. Potts (eds) *Cognitive Theory, vol. 2.* Hillsdale, NJ: Lawrence Erlbaum.

Greene, J. (1972) *Psycholinguistics: Chomsky and Psychology.* Harmondsworth: Penguin.

Grice, H.P. (1975) Logic and conversation. In P. Cole and J.L. Morgan (eds) *Syntax and Semantics 3: Speech Acts.* New York: Seminar Press.

Grober, E.H., Beardsley, W. and Caramazza, A. (1978) Parallel function in pronoun assignment. *Cognition 6*, 117 – 33.

Grosz, B. (1981) Focusing and description in natural language dialogues. In A.K. Joshi, B.L. Webber and I.A. Sag (eds) *Elements of Discourse*

Understanding. Cambridge: Cambridge University Press.

Gumenik, W.E. (1979) The advantage of specific terms over general terms as cues for sentence recall: Instantiation or retrieval? *Memory and Cognition* 7, 240 – 4.

Hakes, D.T. (1971) Does verb structure affect sentence comprehension? *Perception and Psychophysics 10*, 229 – 32.

Hakes, D.T. (1972) Effects of reducing complement constructions on sentence comprehension. *Journal of Verbal Learning and Verbal Behavior 11*, 278 – 86.

Hakes, D.T. and Foss, D.J. (1970) Decision processes during sentence comprehension: Effects of surface structure reconsidered. *Perception and Psychophysics 8*, 413 – 16.

Halliday, M.A.K. (1970) Language structure and language function. In J. Lyons (ed.) *New Horizons in Linguistics.* Harmondsworth: Penguin.

Halliday, M.A.K. and Hasan, R. (1976) *Cohesion in English.* London: Longman.

Haviland, S.E. and Clark, H.H. (1974) What's new? Acquiring new information as a process in comprehension. *Journal of Verbal Learning and Verbal Behavior 13*, 512 – 21.

Hawkins, P.R. (1971) The syntactic location of hesitation pauses. *Language and Speech 14*, 277 – 88.

Heider, E.R. (1972) Universals in color naming and memory. *Journal of Experimental Psychology 93*, 10 – 20.

Henderson, A., Goldman-Eisler, F. and Skarbek, A. (1965) Temporal patterns of cognitive activity and breath control in speech. *Language and Speech 9*, 207 – 16.

Henderson, L. (1982) *Orthography and Word Recognition in Reading.* London: Academic Press.

Hendrix, G.G. (1979) Encoding knowledge in partitioned networks. In N.V. Findler (ed.) *Associative Networks: Representation and Use of Knowledge by Computers.* New York: Academic Press.

Hogaboam, T.W. and Perfetti, C.A. (1975) Lexical ambiguity and sentence comprehension: The common sense effect. *Journal of Verbal Learning and Verbal Behavior 14*, 265 – 75.

Hollan, J.D. (1975) Features and semantic memory: Set-theoretic or network model? *Psychological Review 82*, 154 – 5.

Holmes, V.M. (1979) Accessing ambiguous words during sentence comprehension. *Quarterly Journal of Experimental Psychology 31*, 569 – 89.

Holmes, V.M. (1984) Sentence planning in a story continuation task. *Language and Speech 27*, 115 – 34.

Holmes, V.M. and Forster, K.I. (1972) Perceptual complexity and understanding sentence structure. *Journal of Verbal Learning and Verbal Behavior 11*, 148 – 56.

Holyoak, K.J. and Glass, A.L. (1975) The role of contradictions and counterexamples in the recognition of false sentences. *Journal of Verbal Learning and Verbal Behavior 14*, 215 – 39.

Isard, S.D. (1974a) What would you have done if. . .? *Theoretical Linguistics 1*, 233 – 55.

Isard, S.D. (1974b) Changing the context. In E.L. Keenan (ed.) *Formal Semantics of Natural Language*. Cambridge: Cambridge University Press.

Jackendoff, R.S. (1972) *Semantic Interpretation in Generative Grammar*. Cambridge, MA: MIT Press.

Jarvella, R.J. (1977) From verbs to sentences: Some experimental studies of predication. In S. Rosenberg (ed.) *Sentence Production: Developments in Research and Theory*. Hillsdale, NJ: Lawrence Erlbaum.

Jarvella, R.J. (1979) Immediate memory and discourse processing. In G.H. Bower (ed.) *The Psychology of Learning and Motivation 13*. New York: Academic Press.

Johnson, M.K., Bransford, J.D. and Solomon, S. (1973) Memory for tacit implications of sentence. *Journal of Experimental Psychology 98*, 203 – 5.

Johnson-Laird, P.N. (1970) The interpretation of quantified sentences. In G.B. Flores d'Arcais and W.J.M. Levelt (eds) *Advances in Psycholinguistics*. Amsterdam: North-Holland.

Johnson-Laird, P.N. (1974) Experimental psycholinguistics. *Annual Review of Psychology 25*, 135 – 60.

Johnson-Laird, P.N. (1977a) Procedural semantics. *Cognition 5*, 189 – 214.

Johnson-Laird, P.N. (1977b) Psycholinguistics without linguistics. In N.S. Sutherland (ed.) *Tutorial Essays in Psychology vol. 1*. Hillsdale, NJ: Lawrence Erlbaum.

Johnson-Laird, P.N. (1980) Mental models in cognitive science. *Cognitive Science 4*, 71 – 115.

Johnson-Laird, P.N. (1981) Mental models of meaning. In A.K. Joshi, B.L. Webber and I.A. Sag (eds) *Elements of Discourse Understanding*. Cambridge: Cambridge University Press.

Johnson-Laird, P.N. (1982a) Formal semantics and the psychology of meaning. In S. Peters and E. Saarinen (eds) *Processes, Beliefs, and Questions*. Dordrecht: Reidel.

Johnson-Laird, P.N. (1982b) Propositional representations, procedural semantics, and mental models. In J. Mehler, E.C.T. Walker and M.F. Garrett (eds) *Perspectives on Mental Representation: Experimental and Theoretical Studies of Cognitive Processes and Capacities*. Hillsdale, NJ: Lawrence Erlbaum.

Johnson-Laird, P.N. (1983) *Mental Models: Towards a Cognitive Science of Language, Inference, and Consciousness.* Cambridge: Cambridge University Press.

Johnson-Laird, P.N. and Garnham, A. (1980) Descriptions and discourse models. *Linguistics and Philosophy 3*, 371–93.

Johnson-Laird, P.N., Gibbs, G. and de Mowbray, J. (1978) Meaning, amount of processing, and memory for words. *Memory and Cognition 6*, 372–5.

Johnson-Laird, P.N., Herrmann, D.J. and Chaffin, R. (1984) Only connections: A critique of semantic networks. *Psychological Bulletin 96*, 292–315.

Johnson-Laird, P.N., Robins, C. and Velicogna, L. (1974) Memory for words. *Nature 251*, 704–5.

Johnson-Laird, P.N. and Stevenson, R. (1970) Memory for syntax. *Nature 227*, 412.

Johnson-Laird, P.N. and Wason, P.C. (1977) Introduction to inference and comprehension. In P.N. Johnson-Laird and P.C. Wason (eds) *Thinking: Readings in Cognitive Science.* Cambridge: Cambridge University Press.

Jones, G.V. (1982) Stacks not fuzzy sets: An ordinal basis for prototype theory of concepts. *Cognition 12*, 281–90.

de Jong, G. (1982) An overview of the FRUMP system. In W.G. Lehnert and M.H. Ringle (eds) *Strategies for Natural Language Processing.* Hillsdale, NJ: Lawrence Erlbaum.

Kamp, J.A.W. (1979) Events, instants and temporal reference. In R. Bauerle, U. Egli and A. von Stechow (eds) *Semantics from Different Points of View.* Berlin: Springer.

Kamp, J.A.W. (1981) A theory of truth and semantic representation. In J. Groenendijk, T. Janssen and M. Stokhof (eds) *Formal Methods in the Study of Language.* Amsterdam: Mathematical Centre Tracts.

Kant, I. (1787/1929) *Critique of Pure Reason.* N. Kemp-Smith (trans.). London: Macmillan.

Kaplan, R.M. (1972) Augmented transition networks as psychological models of sentence comprehension. *Artificial Intelligence 3*, 77–100.

Kaplan, R.M. and Bresnan, J.W. (1982) Lexical-functional grammar: A formal system for grammatical representation. In J.W. Bresnan (ed.) *The Mental Representation of Grammatical Relations.* Cambridge, MA: MIT Press.

Karttunen, L. (1976) Discourse referents. In J.D. McCawley (ed.) *Syntax and Semantics 6: Notes from the Linguistic Underground.* New York: Academic Press.

Karttunen, L. and Peters, P.S. (1979) Conventional implicature. In C-Y. Oh and D.A. Dineen (eds) *Syntax and Semantics 11: Presupposition.* New York: Academic Press.

Katz, J.J. (1981) *Language and Other Abstract Objects.* Oxford: Blackwell.

Katz, J.J. and Fodor, J.A. (1963) The structure of a semantic theory. *Language* *39*, 170 – 210.

Katz, J.J. and Postal, P.M. (1964) *An Integrated Theory of Linguistic Descriptions.* Cambridge, MA: MIT Press.

Kay, J. and Marcel, A. (1981) One process, not two, in reading aloud: Lexical analogies do the work of non-lexical rules. *Quarterly Journal of Experimental Psychology 33A*, 397 – 413.

Keenan, J.N., MacWhinney, B. and Mayhew, D. (1977) Pragmatics in memory: A study of natural conversation. *Journal of Verbal Learning and Verbal Behavior 16*, 549 – 60.

Kempen, G. and Hoenkamp, E. (in press) Incremental procedural grammar for sentence production. *Cognitive Science.*

Kemper, S. and Thissen, D. (1981) Memory for the dimensions of requests. *Journal of Verbal Learning and Verbal Behavior 20*, 552 – 63.

Kempson, R.M. (1975) *Presuppostion and the Delimitation of Semantics.* Cambridge: Cambridge University Press.

Kimball, J. (1973) Seven principles of surface structure parsing in natural language. *Cognition 2*, 15 – 47.

Kintsch, W. (1970) Models for free recall and recognition. In D.A. Norman (ed.) *Models of Human Memory.* New York: Academic Press.

Kintsch, W. (1974) *The Representation of Meaning in Memory.* Hillsdale, NJ: Lawrence Erlbaum.

Kintsch, W. and Bates, E. (1977) Recognition memory for statements from a classroom lecture. *Journal of Experimental Psychology: Human Learning and Memory 3*, 150 – 9.

Kintsch, W. and van Dijk, T.A. (1978) Towards a model of text comprehension and reproduction. *Psychological Review 85*, 363 – 94.

Kleiman, G.M. (1975) Speech recoding in reading. *Journal of Verbal Learning and Verbal Behavior 14*, 323 – 39.

Kripke, S.A. (1963) Semantical considerations on modal logic. *Acta Philosophica Fennica 16*, 83 – 94.

Kuhn, T.S. (1962) *The Structure of Scientific Revolutions.* Chicago, IL: Chicago University Press.

Lackner, J.R. and Garrett, M.F. (1972) Resolving ambiguity: Effects of biasing context in the unattended ear. *Cognition 1*, 359 – 72.

Lakoff, G.P. (1972) Structural complexity in fairy tales. *The Study of Man 1*, 128 – 90.

Landauer, T.K. and Freedman, J.L. (1968) Information retrieval from long-term memory: Category size and recognition time. *Journal of Verbal*

Learning and Verbal Behavior 7, 291–5.

Lehnert, W. (1982) Plot units: A narrative summarization structure. In W.G. Lehnert and M.H. Ringle (eds) *Strategies for Natural Language Processing.* Hillsdale, NJ: Lawrence Erlbaum.

Levelt, W.J.M. (1974) *Formal Grammars in Linguistics and Psycholinguistics III: Psycholinguistic Applications.* The Hague: Mouton.

Levy, B.A. (1978) Speech analysis during sentence processing: Reading vs. Listening. *Visible Language 12*, 81–101.

Liberman, A.M. (1970) The grammars of speech and language. *Cognitive Psychology 1*, 301–23.

Lyons, J. (1977) *Semantics* (2 vols). Cambridge: Cambridge University Press.

McClelland, J.L. (1979) On the time relation of mental processes: An examination of systems of processes in cascade. *Psychological Review 86*, 287–330.

McClelland, J.L. and Rumelhart, D.E. (1981) An interactive model of context effects in letter perception. Part 1: An account of basic findings. *Psychological Review 88*, 375–407.

MacKay, D.G. (1966) To end ambiguous sentences. *Perception and Psychophysics 1*, 426–36.

MacKay, D.G. (1972) Input testing in the detection of misspellings. *American Journal of Psychology 85*, 121–7.

MacKay, D.G. (1973) Aspects of the theory of comprehension, memory and attention. *Quarterly Journal of Experimental Psychology 25*, 22–40.

Maclay, H. and Osgood, C.E. (1959) Hesitation phenomena in spontaneous English speech. *Word 15*, 19–44.

Mandler, J.M. (1984) *Stories, Scripts, and Scenes: Aspects of Schema Theory.* Hillsdale, NJ: Lawrence Erlbaum.

Mandler, J.M. and Johnson, N.S. (1977) Remembrance of things parsed: Story structure and recall. *Cognitive Psychology 9*, 111–51.

Mani, K. and Johnson-Laird, P.N. (1982) The mental representation of spatial descriptions. *Memory and Cognition 10*, 181–7.

Marcus, M.P. (1980) *A Theory of Syntactic Recognition for Natural Language.* Cambridge, MA: MIT Press.

Marks, L.E. and Miller, G.A. (1964) The role of semantic and syntactic constraints in the memorization of English sentences. *Journal of Verbal Learning and Verbal Behavior 3*, 1–5.

Marr, D. (1982) *Vision.* San Francisco, CA: Freeman.

Marshall, J.C., Coltheart, M. and Patterson, K. (in press, eds) *Surface Dyslexia and Surface Dysgraphia.* London: Lawrence Erlbaum.

Marslen-Wilson, W.D. (1973) Linguistic structure and speech shadowing at very short latencies. *Nature 244*, 522–3.

Marslen-Wilson, W.D. (1975) Sentence perception as an interactive parallel process. *Science 189*, 226–8.

Marslen-Wilson, W.D. (1976) Linguistic descriptions and psychological assumptions in the study of sentence perception. In R.J. Wales and E.C.T. Walker (eds) *New Approaches to Language Mechanisms.* Amsterdam: North-Holland.

Marslen-Wilson, W.D. and Tyler, L.K. (1980) The temporal structure of spoken language understanding. *Cognition 8*, 1–71.

Marslen-Wilson, W.D. and Welsh, A. (1978) Processing interactions and lexical access during word recognition in continuous speech. *Cognitive Psychology 10*, 29–63.

Martin, R.C. (1982) The pseudohomophone effect: The role of visual similarity in non-word decisions. *Quarterly Journal of Experimental Psychology 34A*, 395–409.

Mehler, J. (in preparation) Word transition probability and phoneme identification.

Mehler, J. and Carey, P.W. (1967) Role of surface and base structure in the perception of sentences. *Journal of Verbal Learning and Verbal Behavior 6*, 335–8.

Mehler, J., Segui, J. and Carey, P.W. (1978) Tails of words: Monitoring ambiguity. *Journal of Verbal Learning and Verbal Behavior 17*, 29–35.

Menn, L. (1983) Development of articulatory, phonetic and phonological capabilities. In B.L. Butterworth (ed.) *Language Production vol. 2: Development, Writing and Other Language Processes.* London: Academic Press.

Meringer, R. and Mayer, K. (1895/1978) *Versprechen und Verlesen: Eine Psychologisch-Linguistische Studie.* Stuttgart: Goschen. (Reissued in 1978. Amsterdam: John Benjamins.)

Meyer, D.E. and Schvaneveldt, R.W. (1971) Facilitation in recognizing pairs of words: Evidence of a dependence between retrieval operations. *Journal of Experimental Psychology 90*, 227–35.

Meyer, D.E., Schvaneveldt, R.W., and Ruddy, M.G. (1974) Functions of graphemic and phonemic codes in visual word recognition. *Memory and Cognition 2*, 309–21.

Miller, G.A. (1951) *Language and Communication.* New York: McGraw-Hill.

Miller, G.A. and Isard, S.D. (1963) Some perceptual consequences of linguistic rules. *Journal of Verbal Learning and Verbal Behavior 2*, 217–28.

Miller, G.A. and Johnson-Laird, P.N. (1976) *Language and Perception.* Cambridge: Cambridge University Press.

Milne, R.W. (1982) Predicting garden path sentences. *Cognitive Science 6*,

349 – 73.

Milsark, G. (1983) On length and structure in sentence parsing. *Cognition 13*, 129 – 34.

Minsky, M. (1975) A framework for representing knowledge. In P.H. Winston (ed.) *The Psychology of Computer Vision.* New York: McGraw-Hill.

Mitchell, D.C. (1982) *The Process of Reading: A Cognitive Analysis of Fluent Reading and Learning to Read.* Chichester: Wiley.

Montague, R. (1968) Pragmatics. In R. Klibansky (ed.) *Contemporary Philosophy: A Survey.* Florence: La Nuova Italia Editrice. (Chapter 3 of Thomason, 1974.)

Montague, R. (1970) Pragmatics and intensional logic. *Synthese 22*, 68 – 94. (Chapter 4 of Thomason, 1974.)

Montague, R. (1973) The proper treatment of quantification in ordinary English. In H.J.J. Hintikka, J. Moravcsik and P. Suppes (eds) *Approaches to Natural Language: Proceedings of the 1970 Stanford Workshop on Grammar and Semantics.* Dordrecht: Reidel. (Chapter 8 of Thomason, 1974.)

Morris, C. (1938) *Foundations of the Theory of Signs.* Chicago, IL: Chicago University Press.

Morton, J. (1969) Interaction of information in word recognition. *Psychological Review 76*, 165 – 78.

Morton, J. (1970) A functional model for memory. In D.A. Norman (ed.) *Models of Human Memory.* New York: Academic Press.

Morton, J. (1979) Word recognition. In J. Morton and J.C. Marshall (eds) *Psycholinguistics Series 2: Structures and Processes.* London: Elek.

Morton, J. (1982) Disintegrating the lexicon: An information processing approach. In J. Mehler, E.C.T. Walker and M.F. Garrett (eds) *Perspectives on Mental Representation: Experimental and Theoretical Studies of Cognitive Processes and Capacities.* Hillsdale, NJ: Lawrence Erlbaum.

Morton, J. and Long, J. (1976) Effect of word transition probability on phoneme identification. *Journal of Verbal Learning and Verbal Behavior 15*, 43 – 51.

Moyer, R.S. and Bayer, R.H. (1976) Mental comparison and the symbolic distance effect. *Cognitive Psychology 8*, 228 – 46.

Neely, J.H. (1977) Semantic priming and retrieval from lexical memory: Roles of inhibitionless spreading activation and limited capacity attention. *Journal of Experimental Psychology: General 106*, 226 – 54.

Norris, D.G. (1982) Autonomous processes in comprehension: A reply to Marslen-Wilson and Tyler. *Cognition 11*, 97 – 101.

Norris, D.G. (1984) The effects of frequency, repetition and stimulus quality in visual word recognition. *Quarterly Journal of Experimental Psychology*

36A, 507–18.

Norris, D.G. (in press) Syntactic and semantic aspects of comprehension. In Th. Balmer (ed.) *Cognitive Dynamics vol. 1.*

Ogden, C.K. and Richards, I.A. (1923) *The Meaning of Meaning.* London: Routledge & Kegan Paul.

Ortony, A. and Anderson, R.C. (1977) Definite descriptions and semantic memory. *Cognitive Science 1*, 74–83.

Osgood, C.E. (1971) Where do sentences come from? In D.D. Steinberg and L.A. Jakobovits (eds) *Semantics: An Interdisciplinary Reader in Philosophy Linguistics and Psychology.* Cambridge: Cambridge University Press.

Paris, S.G. and Lindauer, B.K. (1976) The role of inference in children's comprehension and memory for sentences. *Cognitive Psychology 8*, 217–27.

Parkin, A.J. (1984) Redefining the regularity effect. *Memory and Cognition 12*, 287–92.

Peters, P.S. and Ritchie, R.W. (1973) On the generative power of transformational grammars. *Information Sciences 6*, 49–83.

Pichert, J.W. and Anderson, R.C. (1977) Taking different perspectives on a story. *Journal of Educational Psychology 69*, 309–15.

Popper, K.R. (1959) *The Logic of Scientific Discovery.* London: Hutchinson.

Posner, M.I. and Snyder, C.R.R. (1975) Facilitation and inhibition in the processing of signals. In P.M.A. Rabbitt and S. Dornic (eds) *Attention and Performance V.* New York: Academic Press.

Postman, L. and Keppel, G. (1970, eds) *Norms of Word Association.* New York: Academic Press.

Potts, G.R. (1972) Information processing strategies used in the encoding of linear orderings. *Journal of Verbal Learning and Verbal Behavior 11*, 727–40.

Potts, G.R. (1973) Memory for redundant information. *Memory and Cognition 1*, 467–70.

Potts, G.R. (1974) Storing and retrieving information about ordered relationships. *Journal of Experimental Psychology 103*, 431–9.

Power, R.J. (1979) The organization of purposeful dialogues. *Linguistics 17*, 107–52.

Propp, V. (1928/1968) *Morphology of the Folktale.* Austin, TX: University of Texas Press.

Putnam, H. (1970) Is semantics possible? In H. Kiefer and M. Munitz (eds) *Languages, Belief and Metaphysics (Contemporary Philosophic Thought: The International Philosophy Year Conferences at Brockport, vol. 1).* New York: State University of New York Press.

Putnam, H. (1975) The meaning of 'meaning'. In K. Gunderson (ed.)

Language, Mind and Knowledge: Minnesota Studies in the Philosophy of Science VII. Minneapolis, MN: Minnesota University Press.

Quillian, M.R. (1968) Semantic memory. In M. Minsky (ed.), *Semantic Information Processing.* Cambridge, MA: MIT Press.

Ratcliff, R. and McKoon, G. (1978) Priming in item recognition: Evidence for the propositional structure of sentences. *Journal of Verbal Learning and Verbal Behavior 17*, 403–17.

Rayner, K., Carlson, M. and Frazier, L. (1983) The interaction of syntax and semantics during sentence processing: Eye movements in the analysis of semantically biased sentences. *Journal of Verbal Learning and Verbal Behavior 22*, 358–74.

Reicher, G.M. (1969) Perceptual recognition as a function of the meaningfulness of the stimulus material. *Journal of Experimental Psychology, 81*, 275–80.

Reinhart, T. (1983) *Anaphora and Semantic Interpretation.* London: Croom Helm.

Reitman, J.S. and Bower, G.H. (1973) Storage and later recognition of exemplars of concepts. *Cognitive Psychology 4*, 194–206.

Rieger, C. (1979) Five aspects of a full-scale story comprehension model. In N.V. Findler (ed.) *Associative Networks: Representation and Use of Knowledge by Computers.* New York: Academic Press.

Riesbeck, C.K. (1982) Realistic language comprehension. In W.G. Lehnert and M.H. Ringle (eds) *Strategies for Natural Language Processing.* Hillsdale, NJ: Lawrence Erlbaum.

Ringle, M.H. and Bruce, B.C. (1982) Conversation failure. In W.G. Lehnert and M.H. Ringle (eds) *Strategies for Natural Language Processing.* Hillsdale, NJ: Lawrence Erlbaum.

Rips, L.J., Shoben, E.J. and Smith, E.E. (1973) Semantic distance and the verification of semantic relations. *Journal of Verbal Learning and Verbal Behavior 12*, 1–20.

Rips, L.J., Smith, E.E., and Shoben, E.J. (1975) Set-theoretic and network models reconsidered: A comment on Hollan's 'Features and semantic memory'. *Psychological Review 82*, 156–7.

Rosch, E. (1973) Natural categories. *Cognitive Psychology 4*, 328–50.

Rosch, E. (1978) Principles of categorization. In E. Rosch and B. Lloyd (eds) *Categorization and Cognition.* Hillsdale, NJ: Lawrence Erlbaum.

Rosch, E. and Mervis, C.B. (1975) Family resemblances: Studies in the internal structure of categories. *Cognitive Psychology, 7*, 573–605.

Rosch, E., Mervis, C.B., Gray, W., Johnson, D. and Boyes-Braem, P. (1976) Basic objects in natural categories. *Cognitive Psychology 8*, 382–439.

Rosenberg, S. (1977) Semantic constraints on sentence production: An experimental approach. In S. Rosenberg (ed.) *Sentence Production: Developments in Research and Theory.* Hillsdale, NJ: Lawrence Erlbaum.

Rubenstein, H., Garfield, L. and Millikan, J.A. (1970) Homographic entries in the internal lexicon. *Journal of Verbal Learning and Verbal Behavior 9,* 487 – 92.

Rubenstein, H., Lewis, S.S. and Rubenstein, M.A. (1971) Evidence for phonemic recoding in visual word recognition. *Journal of Verbal Learning and Verbal Behavior 10,* 645 – 57.

Rumelhart, D.E. (1975) Notes on a schema for stories. In D.G. Bobrow and A.M. Collins (eds) *Representation and Understanding: Studies in Cognitive Science.* New York: Academic Press.

Rumelhart, D.E., Lindsay, P.H. and Norman, D.A. (1972) A process model for long-term memory. In E. Tulving and W. Donaldson (eds) *Organization of Memory.* New York: Academic Press.

Rumelhart, D.E. and McClelland, J.L. (1982) An interactive model of context effects in letter perception. Part 2: The perceptual enhancement effect and some tests and extensions of the model. *Psychological Review 89,* 60 – 94.

Rumelhart, D.E. and Ortony, A. (1977) The representation of knowledge in memory. In R.C. Anderson, R.J. Spiro and W.E. Montague (eds) *Schooling and the Acquisition of Knowledge.* Hillsdale, NJ: Lawrence Erlbaum.

Sachs, J.S. (1967) Recognition memory for syntactic and semantic aspects of connected discourse. *Perception and Psychophysics 2,* 437 – 42.

Sag. I.A. and Hankamer, J. (1984) Toward a theory of anaphoric processing. *Linguistics and Philosophy 7,* 325 – 45.

Sanford, A.J. and Garrod, S.C. (1980) Memory and attention in text comprehension: The problem of reference. In R.S. Nickerson (ed.) *Attention and Performance VIII,* Hillsdale, N.J.: Lawrence Erlbaum.

Sanford, A.J. and Garrod, S.C. (1981) *Understanding Written Language: Explorations in Comprehension Beyond the Sentence.* Chichester: Wiley.

Sanford, A.J., Garrod, S.C. and Bell, E, (1979) Aspects of memory dynamics in text comprehension. In M.M. Gruneberg, P.E. Morris and R.N. Sykes (eds), *Practical Aspects of Memory: Proceedings of the International Conference.* London: Academic Press.

Savin, H.B. and Bever, T.G. (1970) The nonperceptual reality of the phoneme. *Journal of Verbal Learning and Verbal Behavior 9,* 295 – 302.

Schaeffer, B. and Wallace, R. (1969) Semantic similarity and the comprehension of word meanings. *Journal of Experimental Psychology 82,* 343 – 6.

Schaeffer, B. and Wallace, R. (1970) The comparison of word meanings. *Journal of Experimental Psychology 86*, 144 – 52.

Schank, R.C. (1972) Conceptual dependency: A theory of natural language understanding. *Cognitive Psychology 3*, 552 – 631.

Schank, R.C (1973) Identification of conceptualizations underlying natural language. In R.C. Schank and K.M. Colby (eds) *Computer Models of Thought and Language.* San Francisco, CA: Freeman.

Schank, R.C. (1975) *Conceptual Information Processing.* Amsterdam: North-Holland.

Schank, R.C. (1982) Reminding and memory organization: An introduction to MOPs. In W.G. Lehnert and M.H. Ringle (eds) *Strategies for Natural Language Processing.* Hillsdale, NJ: Lawrence Erlbaum.

Schank, R.C. and Abelson, R.P. (1977) *Scripts, Goals, Plans and Understanding.* Hillsdale, NJ: Lawrence Erlbaum.

Scholtz, K. and Potts, G.R. (1974) Cognitive processing of linear orderings. *Journal of Experimental Psychology 102*, 323 – 6.

Schuberth, R.E. and Eimas, P.D. (1977) Effects of context on the classification of words and non-words. *Journal of Experimental Psychology: Human Perception and Performance 3*, 27 – 36.

Schvaneveldt, R.W., Meyer, D.E. and Becker, C.A. (1976) Lexical ambiguity, semantic context, and visual word recognition. *Journal of Experimental Psychology: Human Perception and Performance 2*, 243 – 56.

Schweller, K.G., Brewer, W.F. and Dahl, D.A. (1976) Memory for illocutionary forces and perlocutionary effects of utterances. *Journal of Verbal Learning and Verbal Behavior 15*, 325 – 37.

Searle, J.R. (1969) *Speech Acts: An Essay in the Philosophy of Language.* Cambridge: Cambridge University Press.

Seidenberg, M.S., Waters, G.S., Barnes, M.A. and Tanenhaus, M.K. (1984) When does irregular spelling or pronunciation influence word recognition? *Journal of Verbal Learning and Verbal Behavior 23*, 383 – 404.

Seidenberg, M.S., Waters, G.S., Sanders, M. and Langer, P. (1984) Pre- and postlexical loci of contextual effects on word recognition. *Memory and Cognition 12*, 315 – 28.

Shannon, C.E. and Weaver, W. (1949) *The Mathematical Theory of Communication.* Urbana, IL: University of Illinois Press.

Shattuck-Hufnagel, S. (1979) Speech errors as evidence for a serial ordering mechanism in sentence production. In W.E. Cooper and E.C.T. Walker (eds) *Sentence Processing: Psycholinguistic Studies Presented to Merrill Garrett.* Hillsdale, NJ: Lawrence Erlbaum.

Sheldon, A. (1974) The role of parallel function in the acquisition of relative clauses in English. *Journal of Verbal Learning and Verbal Behavior 13*, 272–81.

Simmons, R.F. (1973) Semantic networks: Their computation and use for understanding English sentences. In R.C. Schank and K.M. Colby (eds) *Computer Models of Thought and Language*. San Francisco, CA: Freeman.

Singer, M. (1979) The temporal locus of inference in the comprehension of brief passages: Recognizing and verifying implications about instruments. *Perceptual and Motor Skills 49*, 539–50.

Singer, M. (1980) The role of case-filling inferences in the comprehension of brief passages. *Discourse Processes 3*, 185–201.

Singer, M. (1981) Verifying the assertions and implications of language. *Journal of Verbal Learning and Verbal Behavior 20*, 46–60.

Skinner, B.F. (1957) *Verbal Behavior*. New York: Appleton-Century-Crofts.

Slobin, D.I. (1966) Grammatical transformations and sentence comprehension in childhood and adulthood. *Journal of Verbal Learning and Verbal Behavior 5*, 219–27.

Slobin, D.I. (1971) *Psycholinguistics*. Glenview, IL: Scott Foresman.

Sloman, A. (1978) *The Computer Revolution in Philosophy: Philosophy, Science, and Models of Mind*. Hassocks, Sussex: Harvester.

Slowiaczek, M.L. and Clifton, C. (1980) Subvocalization and reading for meaning. *Journal of Verbal Learning and Verbal Behavior 19*, 573–82.

Small, S. and Rieger, C. (1982) Parsing and comprehending with word experts (a theory and its realization). In W.G. Lehnert and M.H. Ringle (eds) *Strategies for Natural Language Processing*. Hillsdale, NJ: Lawrence Erlbaum.

Smith, E.E., Shoben, E.J. and Rips, L.J. (1974) Structure and process in semantic memory: A featural model for semantic decisions. *Psychological Review 81*, 214–41.

Stanners, R.F. and Forbach, G.B. (1973) Analysis of letter strings in word recognition. *Journal of Experimental Psychology 98*, 31–5.

Stanovich, K.E. and Bauer, D. (1978) Experiments on the spelling-to-sound regularity effect in word recognition. *Memory and Cognition 6*, 115–23.

Stanovich, K.E. and West, R.F. (1979) Mechanisms of sentence context effects in reading: Automatic activation and conscious attention. *Memory and Cognition 7*, 77–85.

Steedman, M.J. and Johnson-Laird, P.N. (1978) A programmatic theory of linguistic performance. In R.N. Campbell and P.T. Smith (eds) *Advances in the Psychology of Language: Formal and Experimental Approaches*. New York: Plenum.

Stemberger, J. (1985) An interactive activation model of language production. In A.W. Ellis (ed.) *Progress in the Psychology of Language I*.

London: Lawrence Erlbaum.

Stenning, K. (1977) Articles, quantifiers and their encoding in textual comprehension. In R.O. Freedle (ed.) *Discourse Production and Comprehension* (Discourse Processes: Advances in Research and Theory, vol. 1). Norwood, NJ: Ablex.

Stenning, K. (1978) Anaphora as an approach to pragmatics. In M. Halle, J.W. Bresnan and G.A. Miller (eds) *Linguistic Theory and Psychological Reality.* Cambridge, MA: MIT Press.

Strawson, P.F. (1950) On referring. *Mind 59*, 320 – 44.

Sutherland, N.S. (1966) Discussion of 'Some reflections on competence and performance' by J.A. Fodor and M.F. Garrett. In J. Lyons and R.J. Wales (eds) *Psycholinguisitic Papers.* Edinburgh: Edinburgh University Press.

Swinney, D.A. (1979) Lexical access during sentence comprehension: (Re)consideration of context effects. *Journal of Verbal Learning and Verbal Behavior 18*, 545 – 69.

Swinney, D.A. and Hakes, D.T. (1976) Effects of prior context upon lexical access during sentence comprehension. *Journal of Verbal Learning and Verbal Behavior 15*, 681 – 9.

Tabossi, P. and Johnson-Laird, P.N. (1980) Linguistic context and the priming of semantic information. *Quarterly Journal of Experimental Psychology 34A*, 79 – 90.

Taft, M. (1982) An alternative to grapheme-phoneme conversion rules. *Memory and Cognition 10*, 465 – 74.

Tanenhaus, M.K., Leiman, J.M. and Seidenberg, M.S. (1979) Evidence for multiple stages in the processing of ambiguous words in syntactic contexts. *Journal of Verbal Learning and Verbal Behavior 18*, 427 – 40.

Tannenbaum, M.H. and Williams, F. (1968) Generation of active and passive sentence as a function of subject or object focus. *Journal of Verbal Learning and Verbal Behavior 7*, 246 – 50.

Tarski, A. (1931/1956) The concept of truth in formalised languages. In A. Tarski, *Logic, Semantics, Metamathematics.* (R. Woodger, trans.) Oxford: Oxford University Press. (Polish version presented to the Warsaw Scientific Society, 21 March 1931, by J. Lukasiwicz.)

Taylor, I. (1969) Content and structure in sentence production. *Journal of Verbal Learning and Verbal Behavior 8*, 170 – 5.

Thomason, R.H (1974, ed.) *Formal Philosophy: Selected Papers of Richard Montague.* New Haven, CT: Yale University Press.

Thorndyke, P.W. (1976) The role of inferences in discourse comprehension. *Journal of Verbal Learning and Verbal Behavior 15*, 437 – 46.

Thorndyke, P.W. (1977) Cognitive structures in comprehension and memory of narrative discourse. *Cognitive Psychology*, *9*, 77 – 110.

Thorne, J.P., Bratley, P. and Dewar, H. (1968) The syntactic analysis of English by machine. In D. Michie (ed.) *Machine Intelligence 3*. Edinburgh: Edinburgh University Press.

Turing, A.M. (1950) Computing machinery and intelligence. *Mind 59*, 433 – 60.

Tyler, L.K. and Marslen-Wilson, W.D. (1977) The on-line effects of semantic context on syntactic processing. *Journal of Verbal Learning and Verbal Behavior 16*, 683 – 92.

Tyler, L.K. and Marslen-Wilson, W.D. (1982) The resolution of discourse anaphora: Some on-line studies. *Text 2*, 263 – 91.

Valian, V. (1979) The wherefores and therefores of the competence-performance distinction. In W.E. Cooper and E.C.T. Walker (eds) *Sentence Processing: Psycholinguistic Studies Presented to Merrill Garrett*. Hillsdale, NJ: Lawrence Erlbaum.

VanLehn, K., Brown, J.S. and Greeno, J.G. (1984) Competitive argumentation in computational theories of cognition. In W. Kintsch, J.R. Miller and P.G. Polson (eds) *Methods and Tactics in Cognitive Science*. Hillsdale, NJ: Lawrence Erlbaum.

Vendler, Z. (1967) Singular terms. Chapter 2 of Z. Vendler *Linguistics in Philosophy*. Ithaca, NY: Cornell University Press.

Viviani, P. and Terzuolo, C. (1983) The organisation of movement in handwriting and typing. In B.L. Butterworth (ed.) *Language Production vol. 2: Development, Writing and Other Language Processes*. London: Academic Press.

Wanner, E. (1974) *On Remembering, Forgetting and Understanding Sentences: A Study of the Deep Structure Hypothesis*. The Hague: Mouton.

Wanner, E. (1980) The ATN and the sausage machine: Which one is baloney? *Cognition 8*, 209 – 25.

Wanner, E. and Maratsos, M.P. (1978) An ATN approach to comprehension. In M. Halle, J.W. Bresnan and G.A. Miller (eds) *Linguistic Theory and Psychological Reality*. Cambridge, MA: MIT Press.

Watt, W.C. (1970) On two hypotheses concerning psycholinguistics. In J.R. Hayes (ed.) *Cognition and the Development of Language*. New York: Wiley.

Webber, B.L. (1981) Discourse model synthesis: Preliminaries to reference. In A.K. Joshi, B.L. Webber and I.A. Sag (eds) *Elements of Discourse Understanding*. Cambridge: Cambridge University Press.

Weizenbaum, J. (1966) ELIZA – a computer program for the study of natural language communication between man and machine. *Communications of the Association for Computing Machinery 10*, 474 – 80.

Wells, R. (1951) Predicting slips of the tongue. *The Yale Scientific Magazine 26(3)*, 9 – 30. (Reprinted in Fromkin, 1973.)

Wheeler, D.D. (1970) Processes in word recognition. *Cognitive Psychology 1*, 59 – 85.

Wilensky, R (1982) Points: A theory of the structure of stories in memory. In W.G. Lehnert and M.H. Ringle (eds) *Strategies for Natural Language Processing.* Hillsdale, NJ: Lawrence Erlbaum.

Wilson, D. (1975) *Presupposition and Non-Truth Conditional Semantics.* New York: Academic Press.

Wing, A. (1978) Response timing in handwriting. In G.E. Stelmach (ed.) *Information Processing in Motor Control and Learning.* New York: Academic Press.

Winograd, T. (1972) Understanding natural language. *Cognitive Psychology 3*, 1 – 191.

Winograd, T. (1973) A procedural model of language understanding. In R.C. Schank and K.M. Colby (eds) *Computer Models of Thought and Language.* San Francisco, CA: Freeman.

Wittgenstein, L. (1953) *Philosophical Investigations.* (G.E.M. Anscombe, trans.) Oxford: Blackwell.

Woods, W.A. (1970) Transition network grammars for natural language analysis. *Communications of the Association for Computing Machinery 13*, 591 – 606.

Woods, W.A. (1975) What's in a link? Foundations for semantic networks. In D.G. Bobrow and A.M. Collins (eds) *Representation and Understanding: Studies in Cognitive Science.* New York: Academic Press.

Woods, W.A. (1977) Lunar rocks in natural English: Explorations in natural language question-answering. In A. Zampolli (ed.) *Linguistic Structures Processing.* Amsterdam: North-Holland.

Yekovich, F.R., Walker, C.H. and Blackman, H. (1979) The role of presupposed and focal information in integrating sentences. *Journal of Verbal Learning and Verbal Behavior 18*, 535 – 48.

Zadeh, L. (1965) Fuzzy sets. *Information and Control 8*, 338 – 53.

Name Index

Subject Index

access files,
see lexical access, search model of
algorithms, 91, 93, 149, 174, 227, 228
ambiguity, 33, 42, 56, 62–7, 75–7, 79–80, 86, 92, 115–16, 117, 184, 188, 199–201, 202–3, 225
  lexical, 56, 62–7, 115–16, 117, 184, 202, 225
    context-guided access theory, 63, 65
    multiple access theory, 63, 64–5, 66–7
    ordered access theory, 63, 66
  perceptual, 42
  syntactic (structural), 75–7, 79–80, 86, 92, 188, 199–201, 202–3
analogy theory (word recognition), 45, 61–2
anaphora:
  constraints on, 148
  definite noun phrase, 148–52, 157–8, 165, 168–9
  elliptical verb phrases, 147
  identity of reference, 147
  identity of sense, 147
  pronouns, 77, 90, 98, 105, 147–8, 173
    relative, 77, 90
  resolution of, 147–56, 157–8, 165,

168–9, 170–1, 174–5
  use of distance from antecedent in, 152
  use of given/new distinction in, 152
  use of parallel function in, 151
  use of syntactic information in, 105, 147–8
  use of verb semantics in, 151–2
  use of world knowledge in, 105, 148, 150, 157–8, 165, 168–9
  see also referential continuity and models, mental
aphasia, 207
  Broca's, 207
  Wernicke's, 207
argument overlap, 174–5
artificial intelligence (AI), 1, 4, 10, 11–15, 27, 34, 87–93, 104, 116, 126, 130, 134, 136, 141–5, 155, 156, 158, 165–7, 171, 177, 178–9, 195–7, 211–3, 223–8 *passim*
  as an applied science, 12–13, 223
Aspects of the Theory of Syntax (Noam Chomsky), 30, 33, 34, 117, 184
attention, 10, 23, 26, 55–6, 65, 225
  selective, 65
  two-process theory of, 55–6, 225
augmented transition networks (ATNs),